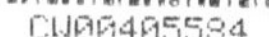

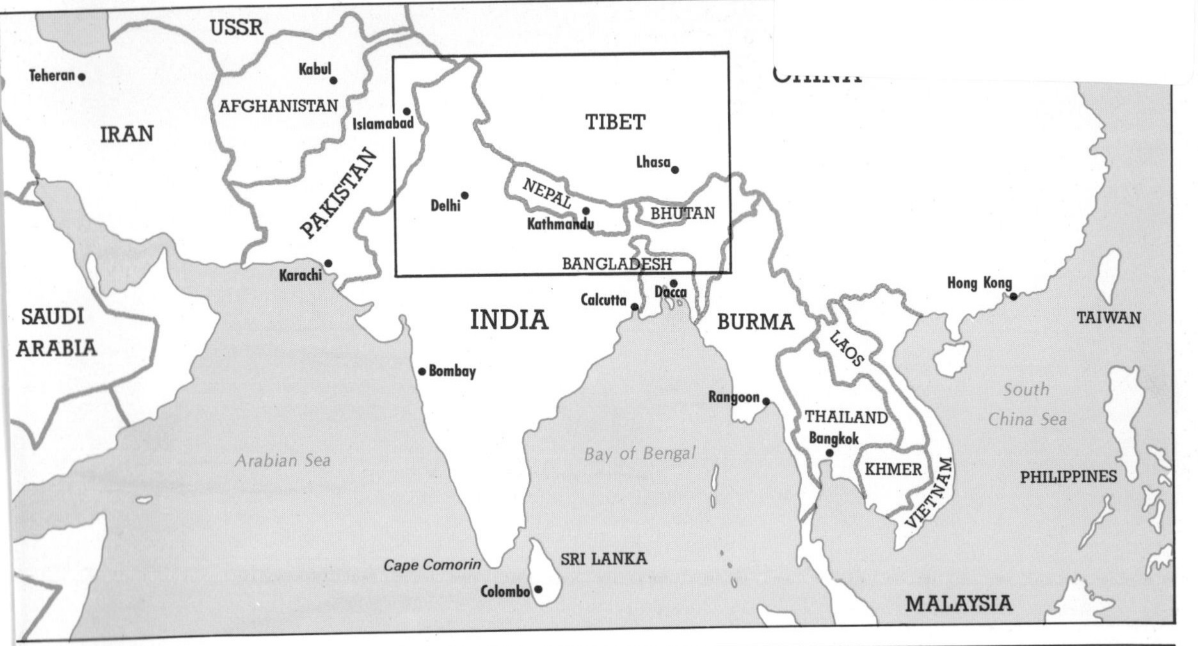
USSR
Teheran
Kabul
AFGHANISTAN
Islamabad
IRAN
PAKISTAN
TIBET
Lhasa
NEPAL
Delhi
Kathmandu
BHUTAN
BANGLADESH
Karachi
Hong Kong
SAUDI ARABIA
INDIA
Calcutta
Dacca
BURMA
LAOS
TAIWAN
Bombay
South China Sea
Rangoon
THAILAND
Bangkok
Arabian Sea
Bay of Bengal
KHMER
VIETNAM
PHILIPPINES
Cape Comorin
SRI LANKA
Colombo
MALAYSIA

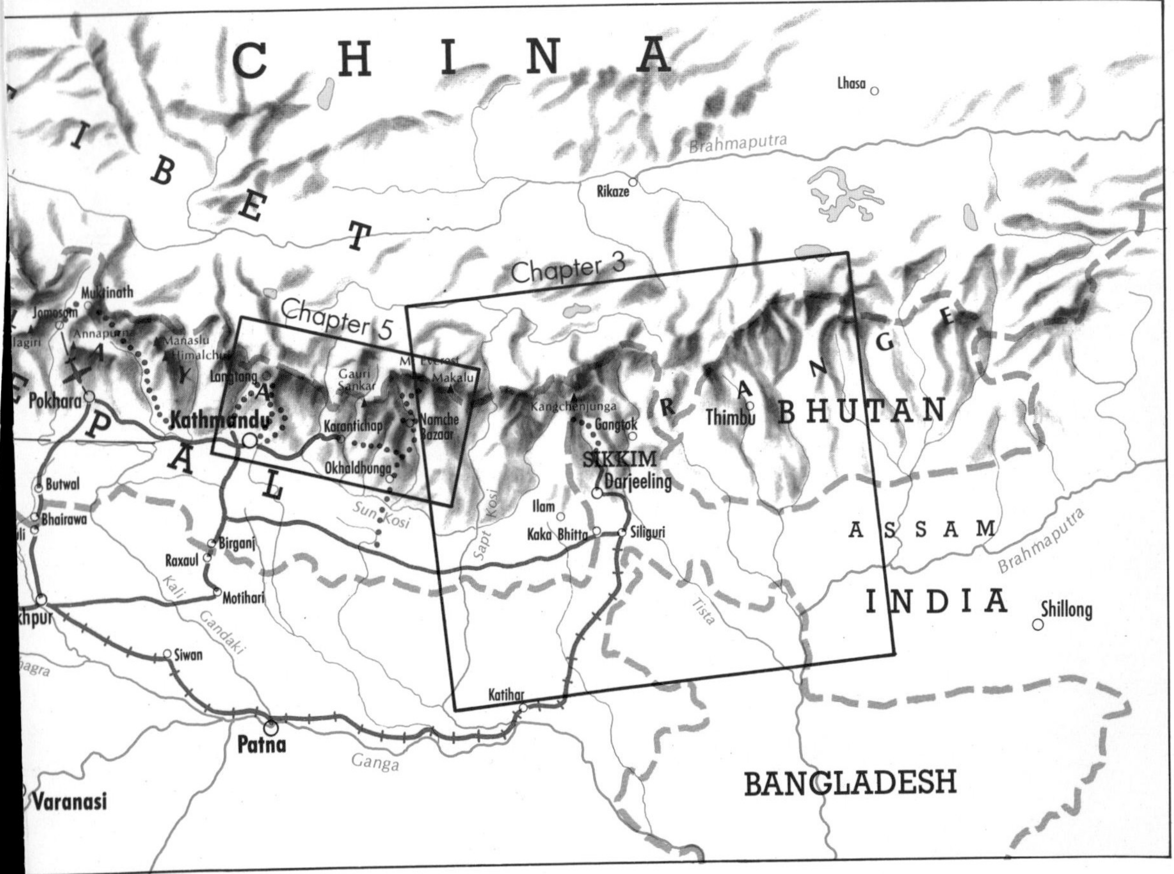
CHINA
Lhasa
TIBET
Brahmaputra
Rikaze
Chapter 3
Chapter 5
Muktinath
Jomosom
Annapurna
Manaslu
Himalchuli
Langtang
Gauri Sankar
Makalu
Pokhara
Kathmandu
Karantichap
Namche Bazaar
Okhaldhunga
Kangchenjunga
Gangtok
Thimbu
BHUTAN
RANGE
SIKKIM
Darjeeling
Butwal
Bhairawa
Sun Kosi
Sapt Kosi
Ilam
Kaka Bhitta
Siliguri
ASSAM
Brahmaputra
Birganj
Raxaul
Kali Gandaki
Motihari
Tista
INDIA
Shillong
Siwan
Katihar
Patna
Ganga
BANGLADESH
Varanasi

Himalaya

TREKKING FROM SIKKIM TO PAKISTAN

ANN MITCALFE and DOUG WILSON

HODDER AND STOUGHTON
AUCKLAND LONDON SYDNEY TORONTO

To Barbara and Prue

First published in 1987.
ISBN 0 340 401176

Typesetting by Acorn Graphics Ltd, Auckland.
Printed and bound in Hong Kong for Hodder and Stoughton Ltd, 44-46 View Road, Glenfield, Auckland, New Zealand.

Contents

Foreword

Our 265-day, 5000-kilometre trek from Kangchenjunga to K2 was the most painful journey I have undertaken. Perhaps true, however, to the law of input for output it was one of my best learning experiences and for much of this I am thankful to Doug and Ann.

When planning the journey I had pondered long over who might be prepared to spend a year describing a loopy line across the Indian sub-continent carrying the gear that the main traverse party would need for resupplies. The group needed to be people with tough bottoms for travelling endless miles on Asian public transport; they needed the legs, lungs and constitutions of yaks for trekking into the resupply points; they needed to be able to negotiate the tricky ways of Asian bureaucracy, but perhaps above all they needed patience to handle the eccentric ways of Pete and me. When Corrina suggested Doug and Ann were ideal for the job I was sure they were the ones.

Doug and Ann have written a wonderfully descriptive account of travelling in Asia, through all the seasons and from cramped bus seat to storm-swept mountain slopes including the joys and the horrors of the Indian sub-continent from colourful bazaar to pristine wilderness. I have enjoyed immensely reliving my favourite places and people through their narrative.

Graeme Dingle
Waihi Village

Doug recently assured me that the single most important part of his education and training for a life in the legal profession was that most complex of journeys, the Himalayan Traverse. May I commend the story, if not the adventure, to all students of quixotic endeavour and thank Ann Louise and Doug for the fun we had during it.

Peter Hillary
Melbourne

I was 17 when I had that first trip to the Himalaya with Doug and Ann Louise. I didn't have many life experiences to make comparisons to, so 10 months in Asia probably wasn't the culture shock it should have been.

One of my vivid memories of that time epitomises India for me. We were walking beside the Yumna River near the Taj Mahal. About 200 metres before we got to the entrance of that incredible structure we saw something in the river being ravaged by a vulture. On closer inspection we found it was the body of some poor soul whose family obviously couldn't afford the wood to burn him in the traditional Hindu way. Such extreme examples of wealth and poverty together will never cease to amaze me.

I've been back to the Himalaya regularly since that time and I'm not sure why; whatever the reasons this region has been a major accelerant in my personal growth. So if you ever want to feel confused, enlightened, depressed, amused, inspired and horrified all in one day (sometimes at once!) then the Himalaya is a definite must for you.

Corrina Dingle
Waihi Village

Prologue

In 1981 we had the good fortune to spend nearly a year in the Himalaya. It was truly a year without winter for us. When we left for the Himalaya in January 1981, it was past mid-summer at home, and the northern hemisphere spring was approaching. On the completion of our journeying, we returned to New Zealand in November, to the start of a southern hemisphere summer.

Our journey was the result of a plan by two New Zealand mountaineers — Graeme Dingle and Peter Hillary — to traverse the entire 5000-kilometre Himalayan mountain chain. They planned to trek along the dividing line between the foothills and the mountains, travelling as close to the peaks as possible. The traverse route would start at Dibrugarh on the Brahmaputra River in northeastern India near Burma, then run westward across Assam, through Bhutan, Sikkim, Nepal and India and northward into Pakistan to the Indus River, ending where the Indus turns suddenly south along the eastern border of Afghanistan.

A significant feature of their plan was the westward direction of the journey. In May or June each year the tropical monsoon brings heavy summer rains that sweep up from the Bay of Bengal in the east of India, piling high clouds, rain and snow on the southern slopes of the Himalayan foothills, rendering travel difficult and occasionally impossible. By starting in the east, early in the year, it was hoped that the proposed expedition would have travelled far enough westward by May to have escaped the worst effects of the monsoon.

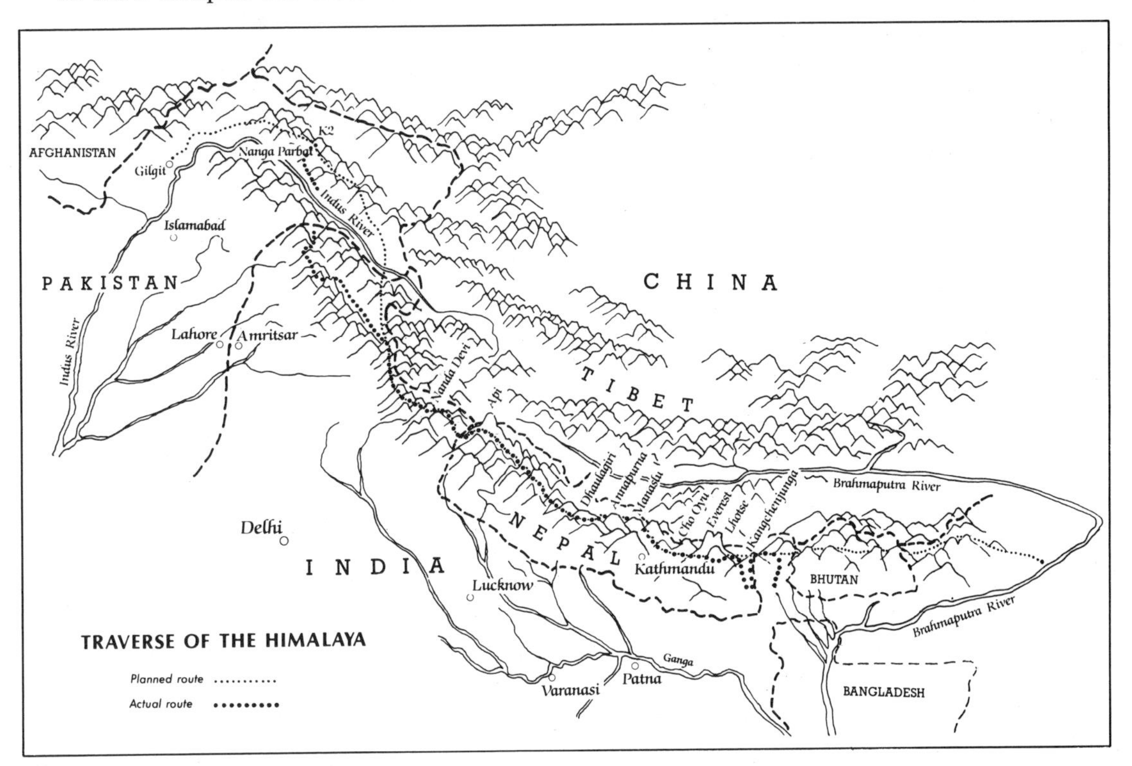

The expedition leaders chose the route. Their next task was to choose some team members. Ding and Pete had planned to carry out the expedition with the aid of a 'support' team. This second team would operate as a mobile base camp, meeting the traverse party at convenient intervals. They would carry spare equipment, food and medical supplies, as well as provide a link between the traverse team and the media, sending out news of their progress. They chose three members for their support team: Corrina Gage, Ann Mitcalfe and Doug Wilson.

Ann and I were living at Mount Ruapehu, in the central North Island, where I was a National Park Ranger and Ann earned a living designing mountain clothing. Corrina had grown up in Turangi, a town near Mount Ruapehu, and been a student at the Outdoor Pursuits Centre, founded by Graeme Dingle. With Corrina and Graeme, Ann and I had shared many recreational activities — climbing, skiing, hiking and kayaking — so we had a good background of experience together. We didn't know Pete so well since he had only recently come to work as a ski instructor on the mountain, but we hoped to spend some time with him before leaving New Zealand.

With the personnel selected, all five of us got involved as the work of detailed planning gathered momentum. Himalayan expeditions are seldom simple affairs. All of those countries fortunate enough to have major Himalayan peaks within their borders regulate the access to their mountains. Considerations of safety, military and commercial expedience and social stability are the reasons for this. It can be difficult and even dangerous at high altitude to have separate groups attempting one route at the same time, so each country has a permit system; you apply for a permit to climb a route on the peak of your choice and a peak fee is payable on booking. For the highest mountains the fees can exceed US$10,000. There may also be a long wait — routes on Mount Everest or Sagarmatha (8848 metres), the world's highest mountain, are often 'booked up' six or more years in advance. Safety is marginally increased by this system and substantial revenue gathered.

The military concerns arise from the proximity of the high peaks to national borders. In India, especially, security is a very real concern of the Government. A cordon, known as the Inner-line, has been drawn at a distance of some 40 kilometres from the Indian border with China. Apart from local residents, both Indian nationals and foreigners need special permission to cross this line.

Further reasons for regulating access to the peaks are the social problems that can occur through dislocation to local farming and industry if a wealthy expedition lures away large numbers of workers as porters for a march into a base camp. Crucial planting or harvesting labour is not then available. The local food supplies are also affected by the influx of extra mouths to feed, whether of climbers, trekkers or porters. Cash is paid for food supplies bought from the hill people, but in lean seasons in these remote areas cash does not go far to fill empty stomachs. The influx of visitors creates a new cash crop also: the conversion of timbered hillsides into firewood for cooking, and for the camp-fire central to much of camp-life, particularly for the porters. Where the timber stood, erosion often takes its place. In some areas of the Himalaya, the number of large expeditions is limited by the permit system specifically to avoid these problems.

Approximately two-fifths of our planned expedition route traversed Indian soil. The Indian Himalaya extend about as far as the Nepal Himalaya and, though less well known, they are no less spectacular. Much of the most interesting mountaineering terrain on our journey, however, lay within the restricted Inner-line and for this portion we needed approval from the Indian Mountaineering Foundation (IMF). Accordingly, much thought was given to organising the expedition in a way which would ensure this approval was obtained. From experience on their earlier expeditions, Ding and Pete knew that such Inner-line permission was more readily granted to combined expeditions, those that include both foreigners and Indian nationals. The solution which recommended itself was to apply to the IMF for their blessing on a joint Indo-New Zealand traverse expedition; this meant that Indian team members would be selected by the IMF to join us five New Zealanders.

By drawing on the extensive personal contacts which Ding and Pete had within the IMF this was fairly easily arranged: the 'Joint Indo-New Zealand Traverse of the Himalaya Expedition 1981' was officially approved and we were invited to apply for the necessary Inner-line permits. The IMF duly forwarded these on our behalf to the Indian Ministry of Defence for their endorsement.

There was an undesirable, but unavoidable, side-effect to making this official approach, however. News of our proposed expedition inevitably leaked out. In mountaineering (as in most other fields) considerable importance is attached to being the first to do something and Ding and Pete wanted to be the first to undertake this continuous traverse. Although virtually every part of it had been explored by others before them, the length of the complete journey added a factor of commitment that made the traverse an objective more significant than the sum of its parts.

The acclaim of being first was naturally attractive to others as well. It was hoped that making our expedition a joint Indo-New Zealand affair might induce the IMF to deny to other parties the permits that they in turn would have to obtain from the Indian Defence Ministry before being allowed to set off after us. Ding and Pete knew that an American mountaineer, Arlene Blum, had plans for a traverse, with an English mountaineer, Hugh Swift. The name of Reinhold Messner, the world-renowned Austrian mountaineer, was also mentioned — was it true that he too was interested? Time was precious and the start of our expedition could not be long delayed.

Through the last months of 1980 we made our final arrangements: we stockpiled equipment, much of it donated by manufacturers; we raised funds — the initial portion from amongst ourselves, then a sizeable proportion by way of an advance from the publisher, Hodder and Stoughton Ltd, on Ding's and Pete's eventual traverse story. A New Zealand outdoor equipment manufacturer, Hallmark International, agreed to underwrite the expedition and provided the rest of the necessary cash. There were publicity duties — press conferences, interviews and television appearances. These were perceived as a necessary part of the expedition's promotion, sometimes to convince sponsors that they would receive exposure for their involvement, sometimes to convince them that there would be an interested market for our book or for a product that was being tested — and sometimes, because increased exposure is one of the goals of expedition participants, irrespective of their background. Yet this last factor is particularly important to the full-time adventurer, who mounts new expeditions on the strength of those that have gone before. Ding and Pete were both in this position; they had future plans to attempt three major Himalayan peaks — Lhotse (8501 metres), Nuptse (7879 metres) and Makalu (8470 metres) — before attempting Mount Everest for which they had a confirmed booking in 1984. A successful traverse would make organisation of these later climbs easier.

In line with international trends in expedition organisation, our expedition had a contract. It took some time to agree its terms and the protracted negotiations showed us new sides of the other members' characters. There were disagreements over how we should fund the trip; whether we should ally ourselves to only one major sponsor; whether we could operate effectively with Ding and Pete as joint leaders; and how we should control the expedition's expenditure. Looking back now at our diaries, it surprises me how clearly I foresaw the implications for the future of our expedition in those early discussions. If you have read the expedition story which Ding and Pete wrote *(First Across the Roof of the World,* published in 1982) you will know that the expedition was marked by fiery clashes of will between them. Our expedition contract, both in the course of its negotiation and in its final terms, held the seeds of much that was to come. But it is not our intention to retell those clashes here — what you will read instead is our story.

Ann and I have described our own experiences of travelling for the first time in the Himalaya. We did a considerable amount of trekking in Sikkim, Nepal and India and in between travelled by trains and local buses, getting into position for resupply and rendezvous points. There were delightful and sometimes frustrating interludes in Delhi, Kathmandu and Kashmir, where we applied for permits, hassled for stores, waited and explored. We went mountain-climbing, just the two of us, near Manali in the Lahoul region of northern India. In Pakistan we trekked (with the rest of the expedition) up the Baltoro glacier to Concordia, at the foot of K2 (8611 metres), the second highest mountain on earth, where the expedition completed its objective.

The opportunity to tell our story in a single book, jointly written, has been both a challenge and (ultimately) a delight. For the sake of the reader, however, we felt it necessary to tell the story through a single narrator and ultimately we settled on Doug as the narrator although the story is one which we both experienced and both wrote. Each chapter moreover is preceded by a passage placing our narrative in the context of the traverse expedition's progress.

Ding and Pete set a departure date of 14 January 1981. As this date approached, less personal causes for concern about the success of our expedition arose. From friends in Nepal Ding learned, in late December 1980, of the existence of something called the 'Trans-Himalaya Expedition', and it wasn't us. This 'Trans-Himalaya Expedition' had apparently already embarked on a traverse similar to ours, beginning on 20 December 1980, and its members were almost exclusively Indian Army personnel. This last fact was particularly sinister. The joint expedition approach we had adopted with the IMF was supposed to confer on us some protection against competition from other foreigners. What we had not foreseen, however, was that it could not protect us against an entirely domestic Indian expedition.

Then early in the new year we received two enigmatic telegrams from the IMF, suggesting we postpone our trip and advising that the IMF was encountering 'difficulties' in obtaining the necessary permits from the Indian Defence Ministry. We did postpone our departure by one week but then decided we had too much to lose if we delayed further. We departed for India on 21 January with doubts about how our cooperative venture with the IMF could succeed. But for all those doubts there was no question that we were tremendously excited about the new experiences which lay ahead.

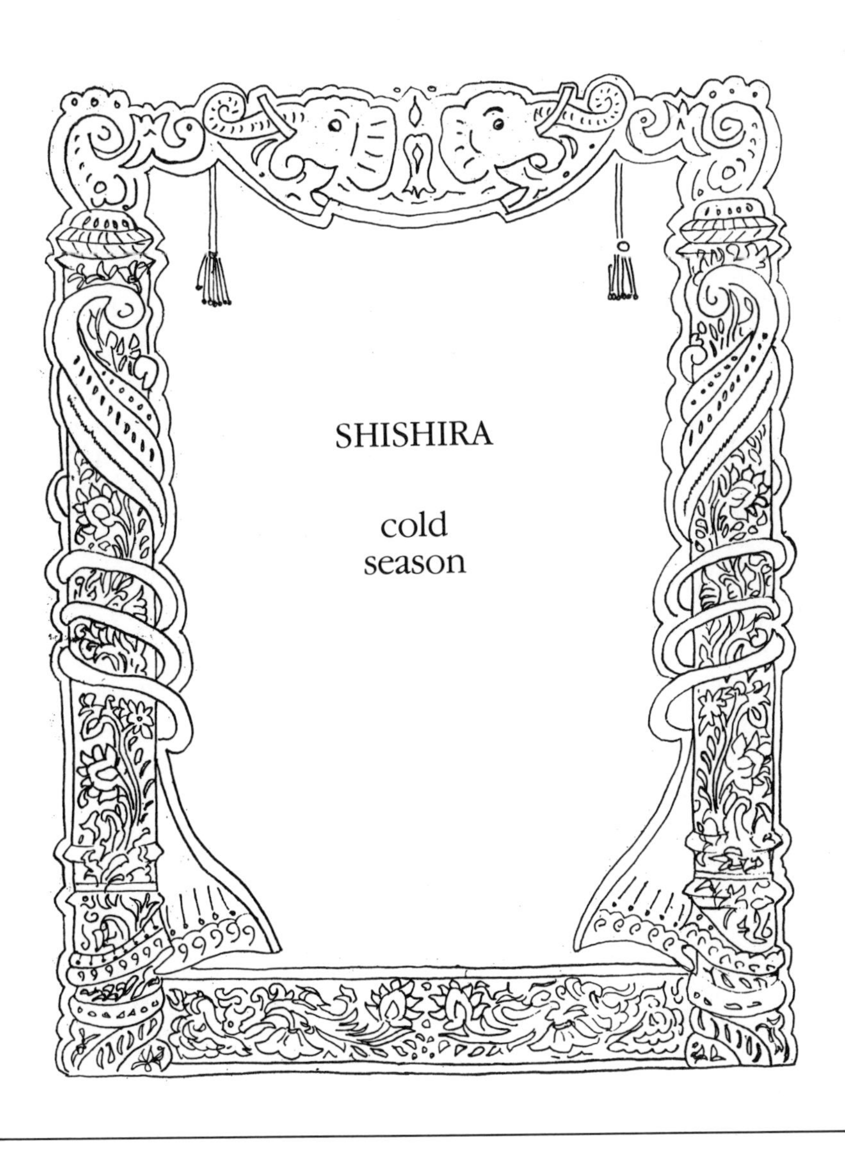

SHISHIRA

cold
season

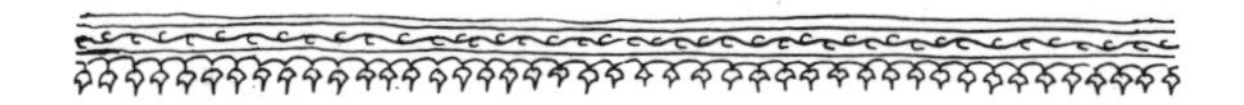

We arrived in New Delhi on 24 January. We did not leave from there for nearly three weeks. We were kept waiting by the Indian Mountaineering Federation and at some points our frustrations with the IMF came close to explosion point.

We had to wait while we tried to find out if our Inner-line permits would be issued and whether our Indian fellow team members were actually going to be produced. We had heard, not long after our arrival, that the first two of the members nominated to join us, two of India's most experienced mountaineers, Colonel Balwant Sandhu and Major Prem Chand, had had to withdraw from our expedition, for reasons that were never made clear to us. Then, in a series of meetings, we were informed that we would not be able to start our journey at the Brahmaputra River nor trek through Assam as originally planned. Political unrest in the state of Assam was given as the reason for the change, our protection being the IMF's concern. Equally, we were told we would not be granted permission to leave India in order to enter Bhutan. Given that we had yet to receive a positive response to our visa applications from Bhutanese officials, our traverse of that country did not look very hopeful either. The upshot of all these meetings in New Delhi was that both Assam and Bhutan were no longer approved as part of our route. We could feel the traverse being whittled away and it was making us all rather unhappy.

The arrival of our first Indian team member, Shiv Prasad Chamoli, after two weeks of this waiting around, did a lot to relieve the tension. It seemed to hold out promise that the IMF were in fact going to come through with some of the support they had earlier promised. Then, just a couple of days later, we were told that permission had been granted for our entry to Sikkim, some progress at least. It may just have been that Sikkim permits could be granted by the IMF, whereas Assam permits were the domain of the Defence Ministry, but no one would tell us. It was probably this lack of frankness that irritated us the most — we could have put up with any amount of bad news if it had been given to us directly. But everyone at the IMF kept pretending that there was no problem, a position which became increasingly untenable as the rest of our necessary permits and Indian team members failed to materialise.

1. Delhi

Our plane arrives in New Delhi at two in the morning. It is January, crisp and cold. We are waved through Customs and in a few minutes find ourselves outside in the street. Low-powered yellow streetlamps cast a wan glow on a softly murmuring chaos. Our breath rises in wispy clouds as we negotiate for a taxi. I am surprised as the cold brings home the reality of northern India at the end of winter: expecting heat, noise, short dark people, we find instead the tall northerners, draped in khaki ex-army greatcoats, their turbans towering above us.

We drive away from the airport with our huge pile of luggage tied improbably on the roof, the cab in darkness. For the first few minutes we chug slowly past

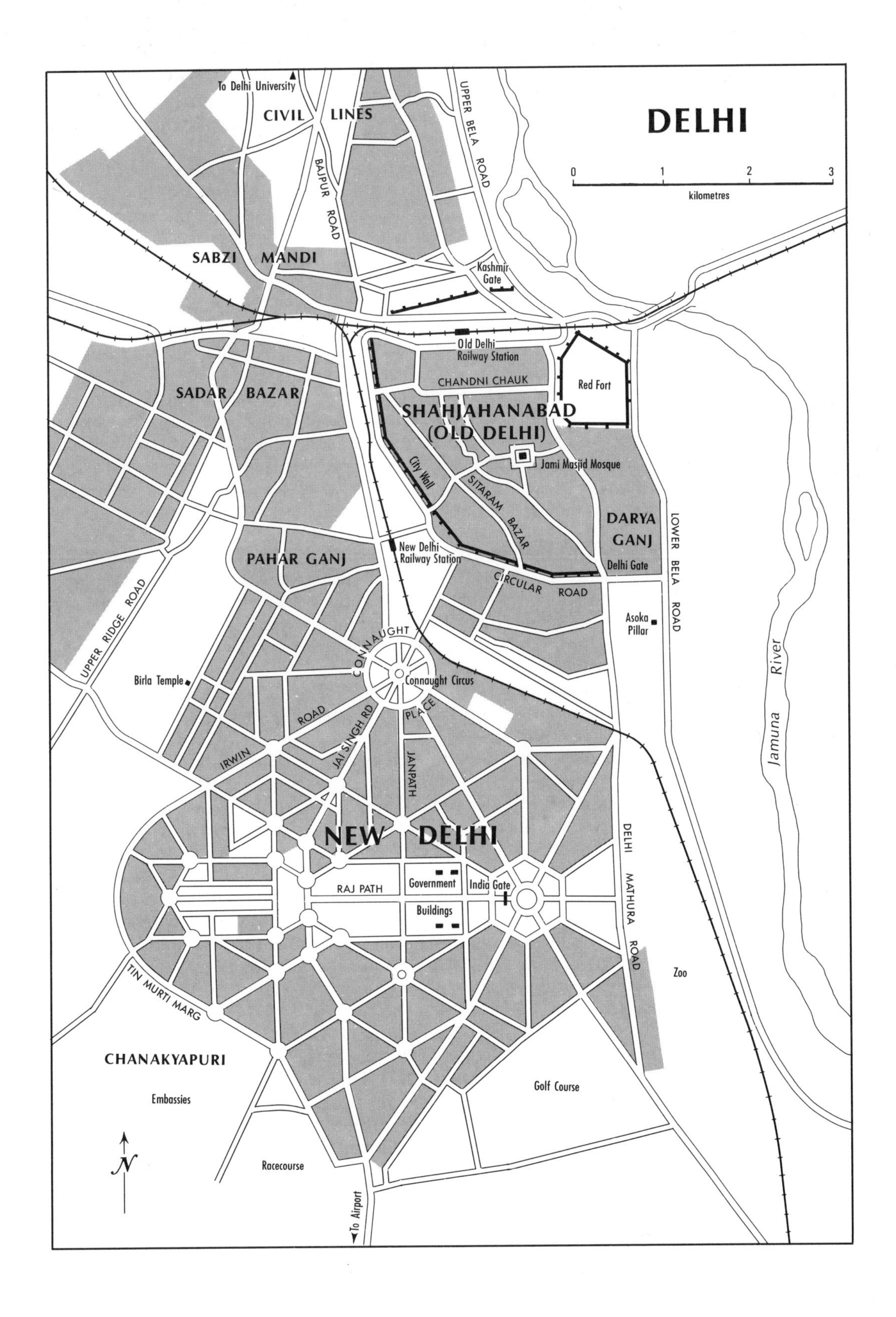
DELHI
0
1
2
3
kilometres
To Delhi University
CIVIL LINES
UPPER BELA ROAD
BAJPUR ROAD
SABZI MANDI
Kashmir Gate
Old Delhi Railway Station
CHANDNI CHAUK
Red Fort
SADAR BAZAR
SHAHJAHANABAD (OLD DELHI)
City Wall
SITARAM BAZAR
Jami Masjid Mosque
DARYA GANJ
LOWER BELA ROAD
New Delhi Railway Station
PAHAR GANJ
Delhi Gate
CIRCULAR ROAD
Asoka Pillar
UPPER RIDGE ROAD
CONNAUGHT PLACE
Connaught Circus
Birla Temple
IRWIN ROAD
JAI SINGH RD
JANPATH
Jamuna River
NEW DELHI
DELHI MATHURA ROAD
RAJ PATH
Government Buildings
India Gate
TIN MURTI MARG
Zoo
CHANAKYAPURI
Embassies
Golf Course
N
Racecourse
To Airport

a row of hundreds of taxis, their drivers asleep on the seats. In the absence of headlights, we navigate by the streetlamps, cruising through a dusty, grey murk. The streets seem deserted until we pass three camels, gliding with exquisitely fluid movements through the night.

Although we arrive at three in the morning the hotel is a blaze of light. Ding books us rooms while Pete, Corrina, Ann and I bundle the luggage, kitbags and rucksacks, from the roof of our taxi into the foyer. A smartly uniformed porter hastens across to stack the heap less obtrusively beside the desk for us, mirroring the upraised eyebrows of the young desk-clerk as the mound collapses, 27 bags thudding across the floor.

Insulated by the fairly familiar trappings of a hotel foyer and the darkness outside, I receive no sense of foreignness from our surroundings. I sniff cautiously, with pungent descriptions of the smells of India in mind. All I can detect is a faint tinge of creosote from the street.

The restaurant is open and we go there for a snack. Pete calls with an authoritative air for *pakora* and *chai.* The tea is strong and dark and is served with boiling milk. The custom is to add much of the rough, granular sugar to the *chai.* The *pakoras* are delicious — sticks of curdy cheese or thinly sliced tomato and capsicum, dipped in batter with a hint of chillies and deep-fried. Below the restaurant, in the floodlit central courtyard, an awning has been stretched to form a spacious arcade, and there seems to be a party in progress. Strings of coloured lanterns and patchwork backdrops of fresh flowers, each bloom interwoven with the next in intricate geometric patterns, dazzle above the heads of a cheerful crowd. Five musicians with tiny brass finger-cymbals, drums and a piano accordion play valiantly to swell the noise of the crowd. Ann asks the waiter what is happening.

'It is a wedding, memsahib,' he explains. 'We are very busy with weddings at this time, every night.'

'Why at this particular time?'

'Oh, this is an auspicious time of year for marriage, memsahib. All of the astrologers are agreed on that.'

We find our way up to our room and fall asleep to the slap and flutter of *tabla* drums.

I wake to the sound of more rhythmic slapping. It is different now, not melodic but morose, a slap-slap noise on concrete. I lie in bed, reorientating myself, staring puzzled for a moment at the cracked plaster ceiling, at the large wide-bladed fan hanging silent and still. It all comes back — India!

I pull on my jeans and jacket, dressing quickly in the cold. The side door opens out on to a narrow balcony. I look down to the rear of our hotel where a huge laundry operates. Rows of squatting men and women pound sheets and clothing in shallow concrete troughs of cold water. Washing is hung all about to dry: on fences, on hedges, and on the net of the hotel tennis court. Grey clothes, grey sheets, all under a strange grey sky.

From our balcony I look out across the roofs of the city. They run on and on in a jumble until the dense grey dust of the sky comes down, much closer than I would have expected the horizon. Here and there the flat roof-lines are pierced by the gilded domes of tall mosques. One stands close by and there is a sudden polite amplified 'cough, cough' as someone diffidently clears his throat before a microphone. Birds take alarm in a lofty plane tree — sparrows and crows climb slowly, protesting, into the sky. The loudspeaker crackles again and then comes the whining singsong call for the Muslim faithful to pray.

They say it begins: 'God is most great. I bear witness that there is no god but God. I bear witness that Muhammad is the apostle of God.' The morning call ends:

'... and prayer is better than sleep.'

Dawn is short-lived in Delhi. Each morning the sun rises as an inflamed red globe, hanging immense and close, screened behind a grey pall of dust and smoke. These winter skies are the clearest of any season but to us, from the less populated southern hemisphere, the air seems dreadfully smog-laden and it hurts my throat to breathe. Ding and I both develop bad throat infections during our stay in New Delhi, and the others complain of increased mucus from the irritation of the smog.

On the dresser in our room stands a small card, 'The House Astrologer operates from the Health Club and Sauna'. Someone pushes a newspaper under our door, the English-language *Times of India.* Ann and I sprawl out across the bed and leaf through the news. A riot of blind people here in New Delhi has blocked the railway station ... in Kashmir two young girls have been rescued by their mother, at the last moment, from marriage to 'old Arabs' ... a report of police beating striking workers in the south ... the anniversary of the Indo-Soviet friendship treaty ... the cricket ... several pages of advertisements in which proud parents seek suitable marriage partners for their children. Corrina knocks on the door — the others are ready for breakfast and then we shall go into the city.

New Delhi, the planned part of the city in which our hotel is situated, was created by the British as their imperial capital. In 1911 King-Emperor George V decreed that the design of this new city must complement the beauty of the ancient and vibrant city already present, which had been the Mogul capital of India for seven centuries. Twenty years later New Delhi was completed, a spacious airy city of broad tree-lined streets and buildings of tall marble. The centre of New Delhi is laid out in concentric circles of tarsealed streets, intersected by radial roads. These circular thoroughfare lie on an axis road that leads to the Jami Masjid mosque, an impressive feature of the older part of Delhi. This mosque is the largest in India and was built by the Mogul emperor Shah Jahan in the 17th century. The great majority of Delhi's population at that time was Muslim. Urdu was the principal language. Then, at the partition of India upon independence from Britain in 1947, New and Old Delhi were retained in predominantly Hindu India, separated from the new Muslim republic of Pakistan.

The innermost of the ring-roads in the new city are called Connaught Circus and Connaught Place. In their very centre lies an expanse of parched lawn; a massive modern sculpture in pale concrete; and a garden, alive with small striped squirrels, their long tails flying as they scamper amidst a tangle of wind-blown paper.

Ann and I walk through the garden, trying to get our bearings from a rough street map, our footsteps dogged by a disturbing cloud of begging children. They reach small hands up to us and repeat over and over the sometimes magic words, 'Oh sahib, oh memsahib'. On the surface such pathos fails to move us: afraid of revealing ourselves as rank newcomers to India, we pretend a blase indifference. Inwardly I am appalled by their apparent poverty. We hurry away through the rings of streets, small groups of beggars eddying in our wake.

Later on during our time in Delhi, we return to Connaught Circus on a Sunday and see a very different scene near the inner garden. Small groups of children herd goats under the tall shade trees. High up amongst the branches older children break off clumps of foliage and drop them to the ground. Those households that can afford to, keep goats, and each day the children lead them in search of fodder. During the week policemen chase them out of the central city area, but on a Sunday they are free to scavenge what they can.

Two groups of gardeners are working in the park nearby. One group spreads elephant manure over the parched lawn, breaking down the lumps with sticks. The other group leads a bullock, which tows their large reel motor-mower back and forth across the grass, the blades turning with a slow chatter.

In the large modern buildings of the new city we conduct such business as we have — banking, travel, post. Everything is more difficult than we expected and the days begin to merge, one into the next. We have difficulty adjusting to the new rules. At first we arrive in the central business district too early, nothing is open. Then we go to a small restaurant for lunch and return to find an office closed for the day at two or three pm. It takes time to adjust to this new pace of life.

As we wait we browse in the bookshops on the Janpath, where the tourists shop, trailed by swarthy men selling sinuous carved wooden snakes, peacock fans, brass knives. We move from stall to stall inspecting cheap clothes and leather goods. With time on our hands and a year over which to stretch our money, we seldom buy, but compare prices instead and turn down bargains — 'special price', 'morning price', 'evening price', 'no sale today price'. Few shopkeepers have fixed prices for their goods. Prices depend on many factors, not the least of which is the rapport that springs up, or does not, between the seller and the buyer. Morning price is often the cheapest. If the first customer of the day does not buy, it is said that bad luck may follow for the merchant. The next cheapest is no sale today price.

We are approached in the business district by fortune-tellers and young men selling cheap airline tickets to Bombay and Bangkok. Men come up to us in even the cheapest roadside cafes and ask if we have anything to sell. Whisky, cigarettes and calculators are much in demand. We have none.

Each day in the rush hour billowing crowds of workers, predominantly men, emerge from tall office blocks to squeeze aboard the city's ramshackle buses. I watch as one such bus drives slowly round a corner, so heavily laden with people that one side of the tilted bodywork scrapes the ground. Rather than wait at the bus stop and fight to enter, many commuters wait a block up the road to try to board the bus at a run as it approaches the stop. One man misjudges his attempt and falls, rolling over and over to the gutter. He picks himself up and limps along the street without assistance. By the time he reaches the bus stop, the bus is more than full and drawing away from the kerb.

Most of the cars in the street are taxis, painted yellow and black; private cars are the privilege of only a wealthy few. There are only two models of car to be seen, based on a 1957 or 1958 Morris Oxford and a smaller elderly Fiat. India is a socialist state with a policy of self-sufficiency. Imports are restricted and India makes these two models as her own cars under the names 'Ambassador' and 'Padmine'. Since there are only these two models, parts are readily available throughout the country.

'Be Indian — Buy Indian' slogans from the self-sufficiency campaign are pasted up on hoardings. More colourful are the posters advertising movies. The format differs slightly for each one but the central figures are always the same: a well-fed but stressed-looking young Indian gentleman; a patient, loving mother-figure somewhere in the background; and, to the fore, a young fair-skinned Indian damsel in distress. Melodrama is the keynote. The movie theatre in Connaught Place has queues outside it whenever we pass. There are showings four times a day, the last near midnight. Each movie is approximately three hours long and employs scores of extras for song-and-dance routines and the virtually obligatory fight scenes. The Indian film industry, based in Bombay, is larger even than that of Hollywood.

When we realised that we might be in Delhi quite a long time we moved out of our original hotel to a cheaper hostel, and the route from that hostel to the Embassy area of New Delhi, in Chanakyapuri, takes us along the Raj Path (or King's Way), a huge street designed for state parades. One afternoon I am travelling in a motor rickshaw to the New Zealand High Commission to check for our mail when a young

The rising sun over Delhi is partially obscured by a dense haze of dust and smoke above the city roofs.

Ding (left), Pete and Chewang Tashi completed the Sikkim, Nepal and India sections of the traverse.

Left: Shiv Prasad Chamoli (SP), the first of our Indian team members to join the expedition. (Peter Hillary)

Right: Corrina at Jomosom village in central Nepal.

A stone carving by the trail from Busti village on the Tamba Kosi in eastern Nepal.

Bamboo foliage, Sikkim.

The trail down from Trakshindu La to Manidingma village in east Nepal passes through groves of heavenly scented daphne bushes.

A mani stone from the cairn marking the top of Thorong La (5416m) in central Nepal.

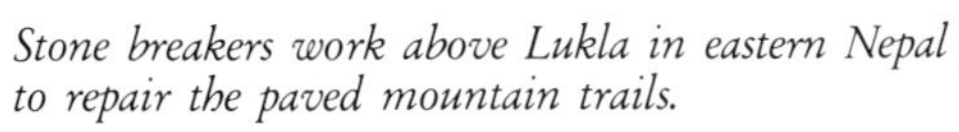

Stone breakers work above Lukla in eastern Nepal to repair the paved mountain trails.

Child in a house doorway at Mani bhanjyang in the Helambu region of Nepal.

A painted Buddha at Bagabandewa stupa in Kathmandu.

A Sikkimese boy herds his family buffaloes to graze.

man leaps out into the road ahead and flags down my driver. The youth pushes his way in through the open side of the rickshaw, crowding me into a corner. He has a notebook in his hand.

'Good morning, sir, good morning. I am a student, collecting for orphans.' He reaches in his pocket and extracts a small paper flag of India — green, orange and white, with the spokes of Ashok's wheel in the centre. This he pins with a flourish to my shirt pocket. 'Now, sir,' he says, 'how much are you giving?'

The notebook is opened and thrust in front of my eyes. The page is lined and divided into three columns headed 'name', 'nationality', and 'amount'. All the entries are in pencil and a cynic might have thought that they were all in the same handwriting. Of course, since such a diverse range of nationalities is recorded, that assumption could not possibly be correct. The amounts listed are generally high, hundreds of rupees, and the last entry records that one Svenson of Norway has donated Rs 280 to the orphans. Good on him, I think, but I decline to follow his example.

'Where is your office,' I ask, 'the office of this charity?'

'No, no office,' he replies, shaking his head up and down to emphasise the 'no'. The familiar yes and no shakes of the head are reversed in India; they shake from side to side for yes, up and down for no. It is very disconcerting at first. Now the young man is joined by an older chap of about my own age.

'Sir, I am a teacher,' he says, from over the youth's shoulder. 'This boy is one of my students. He is just doing his duty, collecting for poor orphans. Have no fear, sir, have no fear, all is above-board, sir.'

'Do you give receipts?' I ask.

'No, no receipt,' he says, growing more truculent in tone, 'and no office going to — you are giving here, sir.'

'No, I am not giving here,' I reply, shutting the notebook and returning it. I reach forward and tap my driver on the shoulder. 'Chalo,' I tell him, which means move on.

With a look that speaks volumes about his contempt for my callousness towards the plight of poor orphans, the young man reaches over and retrieves the flag of India and his pin. They step back, faces full of injured innocence; the driver guns the motor and we are off.

As our official chores for the expedition are completed, our interest in the central business district diminishes and we have more time to explore. Ann and I venture further afield on foot, making our way into the streets of a different Delhi. Down by the Old Delhi railway station, Chandni Chauk Bazaar sprawls in ripe organic confusion, defying organisation and town planning. The shops and stalls of the market are jammed together, higgledy-piggledy, below two and three floors of shuttered living quarters that jut out precariously over the cobbled street and its thronging crowds.

There are few tourist goods on sale here. Leather sandals, plastic shoes, engineering tools, brass and copper wares, kerosene stoves, bolts of silk and cotton, clothes, and cane chairs and tables festoon the narrow shops. Merchandise spills out from the store fronts, is piled on boxes in the street or hung on racks suspended from the protruding floor above. Shopkeepers sit erect on low cane stools, flicking impassively at goods and flies alike with grubby dusters or light sea-grass fans. They keep their money tucked away in the folds of their dhoti or deep in voluminous *kurta* pockets.

The already narrow lanes are further choked by portable stalls consisting simply of a rectangular tray, two metres by one metre, mounted between four bicycle wheels. Parked in rough rows on both sides of the street, in amongst the shop displays, they too are heaped high with produce, vegetables and fruit or neat arrays of household oddments — combs, mirrors, hairpins, padlocks, spoons, cups and plates.

This seems more like the India we have read of. There is a pungent odour of small dried fish mingling with the two stronger smells I grow to associate with urban India — unburnt motor fuel and urine. Occasionally a car intrudes, nosing slowly through the crush. Beep-beep! Beep-beep! More common are Vespa motor-scooters, darting through the gaps, piloted by earnest middle-aged men with their plump sari-clad wives seated side-saddle on the rear. There are bicycles and bicycle rickshaws and the urgent ringing of bicycle bells, and Delhi's famous black and yellow three-wheeler taxi-cabs powered by ancient side-valve Harley Davidson and BSA motorcycle engines. Bullock carts, with their tall wooden wheels, creak and sway through the streets, the hollow-flanked bullocks protesting as the drivers urge them on, 'Tckchaa, tckchaa'. Gaunt white cows, their hindquarters spattered with dung, wander at will through the market, poking and snatching at vegetables and fruit. Some stallkeepers try to shoo them away; most do not.

At a major intersection on the outskirts of the market, two women squat, washing clothes in a shallow puddle on the corner. They have their backs to the traffic, calmly pounding cloth in the muddy water. Truck drivers sound their horns loudly but take care to leave room for the women. A taxi stops and the driver gets out. He moves over to a wall and urinates against it. There are several thousand people within sight but no one seems to notice.

Every hundred metres or so, we pass eating-houses with massive aluminium *dekshis* of rice, and bubbling curries of lentils and vegetables on the hob. Potatoes, peas, cabbage and cauliflower take on varying hues of orange in fierce curry sauces laced with chillies and spices. Waist-high cylindrical clay ovens glow and roar from the heat of fine charcoal heaped in their bases. Kitchen boys labour at a pair of bellows, showering clouds of sparks over the diners. A perspiring cook slaps thin unleavened dough for *chapatis* into a narrow hole at the top of the oven, and the dough clings momentarily to the curved interior. Then each *chapati* is flicked dextrously off and out into the open, puffed with air, and blisteringly hot, ready to eat — two cost one rupee.

At night in the Bazaar there are no streetlamps and each shop is illuminated instead by smoky yellow kerosene lanterns, hissing and spluttering in the evening breeze. Most shops have transistors also, wailing out the intricate and popular Indian songs and movie-scores, at full volume. People press close, without jostling, as we wander. Pete remembers a stall where we can get freshly squeezed orange juice in thick glass mugs for just a few *paisa.* Ann is too wary of stomach infections, the legendary 'Delhi belly', to indulge with us. She follows the guidebook advice: never drink the water, stick to boiled tea; eat only hot, cooked food, or fruits with a skin that you can peel.

Pete and I look longingly at the glass-fronted display in a sweet shop, all tinselled and mirrored — pyramids of dripping honey cakes, coconut ices and twisted *jelebis* which are deep-fried clumps of sweetened condensed milk. The displayed *jelebis* are cold. We watch as the cook squeezes more condensed milk out of a tube into a pan of boiling fat. The milk fries solid in an instant, and the cook's boy weighs out the two hot finger-sticky *jelebis* on to a piece of paper for Pete and me.

While buying fruit, Ann and I experiment with our new Hindi phrase book. We watch the local women buying from a stall holder and try to assess the price they pay. Then, 'Kitina paisa? (How many pennies?)' I ask. The fruitseller laughs.

'Nahin, kitina rupya? (No, no how many rupees?)' he corrects. Then he adds, 'Tin rupya ek Kg . (Three rupees for one kilogram.)'

I feign amazement. Not 'tin rupya', surely not.

'Bahut manga hai, kuch kam kijiye, (Too expensive for these bananas,)' Ann declares. Now the passers-by laugh: Ann is right and we carry away our bananas at the local price.

Ann is working hard at learning Hindi, making the most of these days that we wait in Delhi. Most people we have met here have spoken enough English for us to scrape by without Hindi, but this will not be the case once we are trekking.

Our development in Hindi is interesting. I am shy and reserved and generally make slow going of it, acquiring a few stock phrases but hesitant to stretch them. Ann is more outgoing, eager to learn. She will launch boldly into something, finding that if she does make mistakes the Hindi speakers will just chuckle kindly and correct her. Unembarrassed by these mistakes, she smoothes the way for bargains and friendly exchanges that further build up her experience. By the end of a fortnight, she is far ahead of the rest of us.

On the vacant lot next door to our hostel lives a small company of *harijans* (untouchables). There is seldom anyone to be seen there during the day, but their presence is indicated in the early morning and late evening by the glow and flicker of small cooking fires. Their home is a tiny collection of lean-to shelters built in a square round a courtyard against the hostel side wall. Entry to their courtyard is by a narrow gap between the lean-tos. There are no windows and the roof is just oddments of canvas and cardboard with an infrequent patch of scrap iron. The roof is so low I could not stand upright inside. It must yet be an improvement on living in the street.

Untouchability has been banned by law, but the law is much in advance of the feelings of many Hindus. The caste system is not so obvious in the major streets, but it begins to intrude in the markets. Near Chandni Chauk we saw a stallkeeper refusing to sell to an untouchable. The customer stood in the street, holding his money out, but his quiet request was drowned out by the bullying and shouts of the stallkeeper who eventually drove him away. Others will sell to them and take their money, but drop the change into the dirt from where the untouchable must scrabble to retrieve it.

Turning homeward one night from the old city we need to walk carefully around bands of street people. Whole families squat crosslegged in a small circle on the footpath, a fire of twigs glowing in the centre. A *bidi* cigarette is passed around one circle while a woman nurses a metal dish on the tiny blaze, warming *chapatis* one by one against the embers and then stacking them close to the flames. All eyes are cast inward upon the fire, oblivious of the flow of the crowd around them. Other family groups, their scanty meal consumed, wrap the ends of their thin cotton dhotis over their faces and lie down to sleep. We step with care over the outstretched feet of the sleepers and watch out lest we edge too far sideways into the heavy traffic.

On our floor of the hostel two guards sit. Apparently always on duty, one squats against the wall while the other lounges in a broken cane chair, surrounded by room-service trays laden with teapots and cups. They salute us languidly but with great sincerity as we pass, 'Goodnight, sahib, goodnight, memsahib.'

'Goodnight.'

In the second week of February we finally left New Delhi in two groups. Ding went up to Kathmandu with Corrina and Ann to establish a dump of equipment which we would need in Nepal. They were to leave it in Kathmandu, arrange for our Nepal trekking permits, and make their way to Darjeeling where they would meet up with Pete and me and the first of our Indian team members, Shiv Prasad Chamoli.

SP (as we came to call him) worked for one of India's many paramilitary forces, the Indo-Tibetan Border Police, and held a rank roughly equivalent to that of major. He was a solid-looking man in his late thirties. The first we knew of him was when he walked into our equipment room at the IMF, looking somewhat out of place in his dark suit and tie, and introduced himself to our scruffier-looking mountaineering group as Mr Chamoli. Ding took him outside straightaway to the back of the IMF where we had established an 'artificial' climbing route by hammering pitons into the mortar between the stones of the back wall of the Institute. SP struggled gamely up the route, feeling with some justification that he was on trial. He was.

SP's coming on the scene galvanised us into action. The IMF wanted us to wait for the other two Indian members to make our team complete but Ding and Pete were ready to start and felt that one Indian member was enough for the time being, the others could always join us later. 'If they don't, too bad,' was the unspoken message to the IMF. Too much energy had already been wasted.

It was time we were all out of Delhi; the strain was telling and we were getting scratchy with each other. There was a limit to how much we could offset the uncertainty by diving into Old Delhi to go sightseeing. Ding, Corrina and Ann left for Kathmandu. I hoped that the time those three had together would ease some of the tensions that were arising in our group. Ding and Pete had both become irritated by Ann's competence in Delhi. Although both of them had spent a lot of time in India and Nepal, neither of them spoke much of any of the languages. Ann had applied herself to learning Hindi at a rate that left me for dead. Within a matter of days her increasing grasp of the language gave her the opportunity to act as the group's interpreter, forcing the others to take something of a back seat on occasion. It was not a position they found comfortable.

And then there was the problem of getting to know Pete better. We hadn't known him well in New Zealand, just met him at a few social gatherings and skied with him a couple of times. We had tried to spend more time with him after joining the expedition, usually fairly amiably, but I could tell that he wasn't prepared to relax with us yet. When delays in Delhi became intolerable we took a side trip to Agra as a group to see the Taj Mahal; even that sight failed to improve matters. Pete was obviously unhappy with the 'happy families' atmosphere between Ann and me and between the other couple, Ding and Corrina. It was decided that I should remain in Delhi with Pete while the other three went on to Kathmandu. This way, it was hoped, Pete and I would build up more common experiences that might make him feel a little less 'on his own' in the expedition.

Pete and I stayed a few more days in New Delhi with SP, at the IMF headquarters, just long enough to extract the written permit for our entry to Sikkim. Then we took a train to Siliguri, from where we would catch a bus to Darjeeling, departure point for our trek through Sikkim and the place where we were to rendezvous with Ann, Ding and Corrina who would come over by bus from Kathmandu.

In the chapter that follows we have written as if Ann were with me on the train although she was, in fact, in Kathmandu. As we did share other train journeys and some of the incidents described here, please bear with us — there were train journeys in India where all this did happen to us, somewhere on the way to the hills.

2. Tinsukia Mail — The Train Journey to the Hills

The Tinsukia Mail is to leave Old Delhi station at 10.30 pm. We arrive with time to spare, our taxi rattling to a halt in the crowded forecourt. An army of porters descends on us to argue over the right to carry our luggage; every one of them wears a badge identifying him as an official, authorised station porter. Each of the victors of the fray takes several kitbags, 40 kg each at least, adjusts his turban and balances them on his head. Then, with one hand raised to safeguard the baggage, they turn and slip into the streaming crowd. We hurry after them, trusting that their quick glance at our tickets will get us to the right train.

We follow our bobbing loads through tall vaulted foyers echoing with the hubbub of voices. Around the feet of imposing marble columns sleep groups of travellers, their cardboard suitcases and canvas bedrolls wedged in behind them. One man sleeps alone, in a crouching position, out in the middle of the concourse. He has two small cases arranged in a 'V' in front of him; the crowd parts like water at the bow of his little ship, surges past, and joins behind.

Through the wide double doors we go, out under the stars again, along Platform One. The station stretches away as far as the eye can see — platform after platform, train after train, wreathed in steam and smoke. We wind our way in and out between stalls and baggage trolleys, following our porters up a wide, wooden staircase to an overhead walkway. Line after line of wide-gauge track pass underneath us until, at last, we descend on to Platform Twenty. The porters pad steadily along beside the train standing at the platform and stop in a group. One porter points to a list of names outside a carriage. I run my eye down it — there it is, 'Mr Douglas'. I nod agreement and loading begins.

A fellow passenger steps carefully past us and, smiling, raises his hands and places them together, palm to palm, finger to finger. 'Namaskar,' he says. SP returns the gesture.

'Namaskar,' he replies, then turns to me. 'I am forgetting my manners, Douglas. I should be showing you these things. Namaskar is a greeting and it is polite to return it. You do it so,' SP repeats it and watches as I try. 'Yes, that is right. The hands should be in front of the chest, at that level to greet equals. If you were greeting a holy man or guru you might place the hands together at the forehead.'

'What is namaste, then,' I ask, 'because I've heard people using that too.'

'Namaste is also correct, but it is less formal. It is the more casual way of making the same greeting.'

From our seat we look out and watch the stallkeepers at work on the platform. Near us there is a bookseller, his stall packed with brightly coloured books all in Hindi script. He has many of the popular 'Filmi' magazines filled with photos and gossip about the lives of Indian movie stars. Beyond him is a glass-sided tobacco stall. There are snuff, chewing tobacco, and many different grades of cigarette for sale — 'Sportsman', 'Luckys', some very cheap packets, as well as cigarettes sold singly. Cheapest of all are the local hand-rolled *bidis,* tobacco-stuffed leaves, fat at one end, narrow and twisted at the other, packed in conical packages tied with a thread. At the edge of the stall a thick hemp cord hangs, smouldering slightly at the bottom. A customer takes the wick, knocks off the ash and blows the burning ember into a glowing coal. He cups his hands around it and puffs furiously to light his *bidi.*

Activity on the platform grows more and more urgent. Guards and policemen bustle past and there are shouts and whistles. A transvestite beggar comes along the platform and seeing us begins gruffly to demand money; he bangs on the bars and shouts, 'Hey, baksheesh, baksheesh.' We ignore him, but he does not go away; we do. A jolt comes, then another, then a protesting creak and squeal of metal as the train begins to move. The platform slides past us, jumbled high with sacks and padlocked tin-trunks, with groups of waiting travellers perched upon them. We steam away more quickly, swaying clickety-click, clickety-click over a forest of switches, an extensive lattice-work of metal.

We pass through grey industrial suburbs for a long time before the city area of Delhi fades behind us. In the yellow glow of the carriage lamps we take stock of our surroundings. On Pete's recommendation I booked us a second class sleeper with three tiers of sleeping berths on either side of the compartment. During the day we sit on the lowest tiers of berths which seat three people each; at night the backrests lift up to become the second tier of sleeping berths, and benches come out from the wall, just below the ceiling, for the third tier of sleeping berths. The passenger aisle runs down one side of the carriage past the sleeping compartments.

This is a quite adequate and comfortable means of travel. Mahatma Gandhi is said to have always travelled third class, but third class has been abolished. Perhaps the Government has no wish for more Gandhis. Instead there are now three grades of second class, partly subsidised by the charges for first class accommodation. First class is much more expensive than the best second class but in winter not much more comfortable.

Every window in our carriage can be secured in four different ways. First, there are bars of stout iron on the outside, placed so that only an arm can reach between them. Then there are three sliding shutters: the outer one of thin steel which can be locked in place, the middle one of glass, and the interior one of insect mesh. This added security can sometimes be important. There are *dacoits* or bandits in India still, and in the newspapers in Delhi we read frequent accounts of their exploits. An entire train was recently held up and robbed not far from Calcutta. There were so many bandits that they used buses to make their escape. When something like that happens, each carriage is on its own in the attempt to barricade itself off from the attackers. The main benefit of paying for a first class compartment is that the locks on the doors usually work as well as those on the windows.

The door locks on our second class carriage look decidedly shaky but we at least have a guard who is armed. His presence is meant to protect us against another class of bandits who book tickets and get aboard the train disguised as honest passengers. The guard has an old British Army Lee Enfield rifle secured by a chain to his waist. The purpose of the chain is not clear — perhaps it is to prevent his selling the rifle to the *dacoits,* perhaps merely because he spends so much of his time asleep.

Our rucksacks and kitbags are on the floor beneath us, carefully tied together so that no one can slip one out while we sleep. Apart from that there seems to be little we can do to prevent trouble occurring. We get out our sleeping bags, adjust the benches and lie down. I find it hard to sleep. Rock and sway, clatter and rattle we go, thack-thack, thack-thack. A train passes, bound south-west with a rush and a roar. Our carriage lights dim and, one by one, go off. Now and then comes the flare of a match and the glow of a cigarette where another sleepless traveller waits out the darkness.

I am too excited to sleep. My relief at leaving Delhi merges with increasing delight at the prospect of getting into the mountains. Ahead of us is Darjeeling, of which I have read so much, and then Sikkim, about which my ignorance is immense. Still, we have a map, and no doubt anything of importance in those hills will be revealed as we pass. Eventually peace does come and I sleep soundly on my narrow bench, my jacket folded underneath my head.

Morning arrives with the stir and rustle of people waking in other sleeping compartments. I reach out from my sleeping bag to lift the shutters and bright sunlight comes streaming in. I turn on my side and lie propped up on one elbow watching the country pass by. The railtracks cut through farmland, waving tall and green with maize and sugarcane, then stretching flat and wet with rice paddy. Barefoot workers are wading in the paddy, bending to pull weeds in the reflected silver of the sky.

Waterfowl are wading also. There are pale grey herons and green-brown ducks with splashes of gold across their wings. Wrybills and a sandpiper prospect in a shallow stream bed. A young boy urges on a buffalo yoked to a waterwheel, the buffalo marking out its small circle with measured tread. As the wheel turns, wooden buckets rise, dump their water in the irrigation ditches, drop and rise again.

A dusty road runs alongside the railway for a time. A Hindu temple sits just across the road: an enclosing wall of white-washed mud, a tree-shaded courtyard and a small raised building in the centre. On the white-washed wall is daubed a crude swastika — a symbol of good omen, of creation, for Hindus and Buddhists alike.

Across the compartment from me SP rises and carefully folds his sleeping bag. Then, cross-legged, he sits to do his *puja* or prayers. I watch as he prepares himself quietly and methodically. He cleans his face and hands, gargles to clear his throat, then props up on the seat before him a pair of framed photographs. One is in black and white, indistinct. The second is a portrait in bright garish colour of a plump Indian male in his early thirties, sporting an immense bush of curly hair. Between the pictures he stands several sticks of incense, taking his time over securing each one. He bends forward shielding a match against the draught to light them and then, eyes closed, rocks slowly and mutters his prayers.

The light grey haze of incense smoke drifts up through the carriage, sweet and acrid. Far off stewards are calling, relaying orders for breakfast from the first class carriages. Nearby there are snatches of conversation and a clatter of tiffin-pans, as others begin to breakfast on food carried with them. SP prays on undisturbed.

I close my eyes and roll over, dozing until the train stops at the next station when I shuffle out of my sleeping bag in the hope of breakfast. Hawkers move briskly up and down the platform. 'Garam chai, garam chai, garam chai, (Hot tea, hot tea, hot tea),' comes the sing-song call. We signal through the window to the *chai wala* who serves us tea, ready mixed and hot, from a fat enamel kettle.

We need not worry about infection from dirty glasses — the tea is poured straight into *chattis,* newly-fired earthenware tea bowls. When the tea is finished, the unglazed cups are not returned. Following the lead of our neighbours we simply drop the bowls through the bars on to the ground and there is a soft crack as they break. I rationalise the apparent waste to myself, thinking of the employment assured at the local kilns. The practice is certainly hygienic and it solves the caste difficulties which devout Hindus might otherwise face while travelling. If the cup has been used previously, a person of high caste would be polluted by touching it and would have to undergo ritual cleansing.

After *chai* we buy fresh hot *samosa,* small pyramid-shaped pastries filled with rice and vegetables. They are fried in a wok on the platform, over a bed of hot glowing charcoal. There are hands of the bananas known as 'ladies' fingers' for sale too. I find the correct change for the banana seller with some urgency, as the train begins to move off before we are finished. I hand him the money as he trots along at the window.

Later that morning a prosperous-looking Indian gentleman in a sobre grey suit and tie comes over to our seat, introducing himself as Mr Mathura. He asks if we mind if he passes some time with us.

'Not at all,' we reply. I put aside my book and make room for him on our bench.

'What is your opinion of my country?' he begins and is disappointed when we protest that we have hardly been three weeks in India. 'But surely you have some opinion?'

'It's so big, so vast. I didn't realise that there were so many different peoples, so many languages,' ventures Ann. 'So far we've hardly been out of Delhi and I haven't even made up my mind about that yet,' she finishes with a grin.

'Ah ... you are interested then in my country?' We agree. 'I must tell you then of one thing that concerns me. The great problems of India, they stem from too many children. It is simple. Birth control is the answer and it is a blessing that many more people are understanding this than did so previously. But ...' with his voice lowered in confidence, Mr Mathura looks around him at some of the other second class passengers, 'many of the village people, they still do not understand this.'

I remember having read critical news reports back home about strong protests in parts of rural India against an ill-administered birth control campaign. It was said that sterilisations were forcibly administered, under the guise of other operations, and bribes and inducements such as transistor radios and watches were offered to enable medical personnel to meet their local 'birth control quota'. Hesitantly I mention it and Mr Mathura commiserates with us instantly on what he calls the 'villainy of some of my countrymen'. He has an air of honest earnestness.

'This is what politics can be like,' he says, 'interfering in a person's life, resorting to force or bribery.' He shrugs his shoulders as if to clear away a burden and smiles again. 'In any case it is hard to blame the village people for clinging to the old traditions — children are wealth to them, insurance against a destitute old age. If the children do not look after the old people, they will starve. There is no pension for them as there is in other countries.' His hands gesture eloquently to encompass his sober yet expensive attire. 'For myself, I am happy. I have lived a good life. My wife and I have one child, a son, who is a source of great pride. Perhaps we will have one more child, perhaps not. Children are a blessing from God,' he says, and then adds with wry humour, 'but, of course, if man is not making the effort, God is not blessing.'

His own experience is wide. He qualified as an engineer and works as Process Controller for a multi-national oil company, spending quite a bit of time in the United States.

'You would be unusual, though?' Ann suggests.

'Oh no, this is very common for our graduates now. All the young men and women want to travel, to have more than just a glimpse of the western world. Yet myself, I am content now with being at home, life is not irksome.'

He describes the Indian extended family to us. He, his wife and son, his older brother and sister-in-law and their two children, all live in the same large house with his elderly parents. 'In that house my father's word is law,' says Mr Mathura, a little amused when I ask if he finds this restrictive, especially after living in America. It seems that the authority of his father is exercised with a considerable amount of restraint.

'My father is a very pious man. He neither drinks nor smokes, nor does he eat meat. Myself, I do all of these things, but never at home. One day, a very holy man came to our house and told my father that I was doing so. The holy man did not say that it was not good for me, but did say that he thought that it was not good for the family. My father came to me and asked if this was true. I replied, "Father, I never want to hurt you — the truth might cause you pain. Do you still wish me to answer?" "Ah, you are a good boy, my son," my father told me and went away again.'

Of the English, Mr Mathura is cautiously approving. 'They had their faults,' he tells us, 'but they brought us together. You know, even now we have no official national language, for Hindi is only common in the north. Elsewhere there may be a different language in every state, so the only one that is truly national is English. In the south they do not speak Hindi and many of them will not learn it. When I meet a Tamil man we speak in English.'

Mr Mathura leaves the train at the next halt, buying a small bunch of bananas from a hawker on the platform to hand to Ann through the bars of our window. We part with a smile and a wave.

The shadow of the train moves slowly from one side of the tracks to the other, growing longer with the passing of the day. The character of the country changes, becoming dustier, more open. There are no waterwheels now, instead there are occasional wells with a single wooden bucket hanging from a counter-weighted pole. The water-table must be very low because the buckets hang on a rope about five metres long. A cloud of insects hovers over each well and small birds swoop over the wells, feeding on the clouds of insects. Lines of bricks are stacked beside a sprawling kiln, the same rich orange ochre as the *chai* bowls that we drink from at each station.

During the night someone has stepped heavily on one of our rucksacks and a seam has parted. I remove it from the web of ties, unpack it and examine the stitching.

'What do you think?' asks Pete.

'No problem,' I reply. 'I can do it with the "speedy stitcher".' I pull out the small nylon stuff-bag which contains my repair kit, select the heavier of the needles and assemble the stitcher. SP watches closely. When it is ready I take the rucksack and make the first needle hole, draw through the free end of the thread, make a second hole and draw the loop through tightly.

'But this is fantastic,' says SP. 'This is just like a sewing machine.'

'The same principle,' I agree, clenching the thread between my teeth, 'but not so fast.'

'Of course not, but with that thick needle and the round bulb in your hand you could be sewing very thick material?' I nod. 'Yes, I've sewn boots with this.'

'But where are you learning these tricks?' he asks.

'A friend showed me the first time, then I just taught myself. I always take it when I go into the mountains. You never know when something might break and an ordinary needle and thread isn't strong enough for many repairs.'

'But I cannot even use a small needle and thread,' SP says. 'My servants do these things at home or we go to a tailor. When I'm on service I have a batman and that is his job.'

'Well, I have no servants, SP, so I learned to do many things for myself.'

'No servants!' repeats SP, obviously thinking over what this situation could be like. 'But you must be wealthy chaps. Here you are travelling in foreign parts, taking a year off your employment — surely you must be wealthy? Why,' he exclaims in sudden inspiration, 'you were telling me that you had a motor car. In India only very wealthy people can afford a motor car and even if you are having the money you need influence to get on the list.'

'At home, SP, it just isn't that way at all. Many people have cars and very few people have servants. Besides,' I add, somewhat irrelevantly, 'mine is a very old car and I fix it myself sometimes, because I can't afford a mechanic.'

'But who is doing all the things around the house? The washing, the cooking, the cleaning and so forth?' Ann grins at this.

'We do, SP,' I tell him. 'I'm pretty good with an iron too.' He shakes his head in amazement and I add, 'It's all to do with economics, SP, I think.'

'I am having a degree in economics,' he replies, 'but it is still too much for me.'

The train stops often now, picking up college pupils in one town to drop them home in the next. Ann and I take turns to snatch quick walks on the platform, stretching our legs. During her turn Ann buys some oranges and delicious *puris,* a pale deep-fried bread that looks like flattened airy dumplings. We eat in the carriage rather than leave our pile of bags unattended.

A road follows the railway again. It is filled with workers, mainly women and boys, carrying sickles or short mattocks, returning home from the fields as dusk settles down over the land. A family rides along a track in a wooden-wheeled bullock-cart, a man and a woman seated at the front and a very young child perched on a massive load of straw behind them. In small thatched huts, cooking fires are lit and everywhere there rise narrow pillars of smoke. The darkness grows until only cosy firelight outlines the figures of people in doorways.

At one stop hawkers board the train and ride to the next station, moving through the carriages selling at their leisure. Two of them come through ours, dextrously holding their bamboo trays aloft as they pick their way amongst the baggage. The first has stocks of plastic-wrapped candy bars, assorted nuts and spices, lime paste and chewing tobacco. Stopped by a passenger nearby, he quickly mixes the requested spices and paste, folds them in a small, flat betel leaf, and hands the neatly parcelled chewing mixture, called *pan,* to his customer. He sells betel-nut also, to others who prefer the nut's soothing scarlet juices. Betel-nut chewers are easily identified by their red-stained gums and dark, worn teeth; the streets and paths in Delhi were splashed with the vivid spittle of betel-nut chewers. Restaurants had signs forbidding spitting or else identifying the location of the spittoon.

The other hawker has the brightly coloured ingredients for the *tikka* dot. He puts sandalwood oil on his finger and then vermilion powders. Devout Hindus in the carriage raise their forehead for him to apply their *tikka* and hand him a few *paisa* in return.

We rest for some time at the next station, jolted as the train inches slowly into the correct position under a tall water tower. A respite from the constant blasts of coal dust and sooty air from the engine is more than welcome after nearly 24 hours of travel. Five of the station's elderly stallkeepers have put away their goods for the night and their small trolleys are covered with a patched, old oil cloth. They squat in a close semi-circle on the platform, elbows on knees, ignoring the presence of the train as one of them packs a *chillum,* a small clay pipe-bowl, with marijuana. He cups his hands at the base and sucks furiously, while his neighbour holds a flame to the top. When it glows properly, he passes it to his right. Slowly the pipe progresses around the circle and a cloud of acrid smoke eddies across the platform.

Late in the night the train pauses briefly at a small country station. I sit up in my sleeping bag on the bench and look out. It is cool now and stars are bright in the sky. A table is drawn up against the wall of a ramshackle station office where a kerosene lantern provides the only light. Three soldiers sit at the table, one wearing an officer's cap.

On the platform other soldiers are standing, talking softly and smoking in the darkness, their kitbags strewn over the concrete. They hold their rifles in a languid grip, an attitude already familiar to me from the soldiers we saw in Delhi. I keep expecting to see a soldier with his little finger down the muzzle, dragging the weapon behind him, like a child.

We glide away again. The light and the soldiers fade behind us, like something in a dream. I stay sitting up and stare out into the night. The darkness grows dense enough to touch and I realise, with a start, that the stars no longer come down flat to the edge of the plains. Far to the north, black against the myriad pin-pricks of light, is a line of hills.

VASANTA
spring

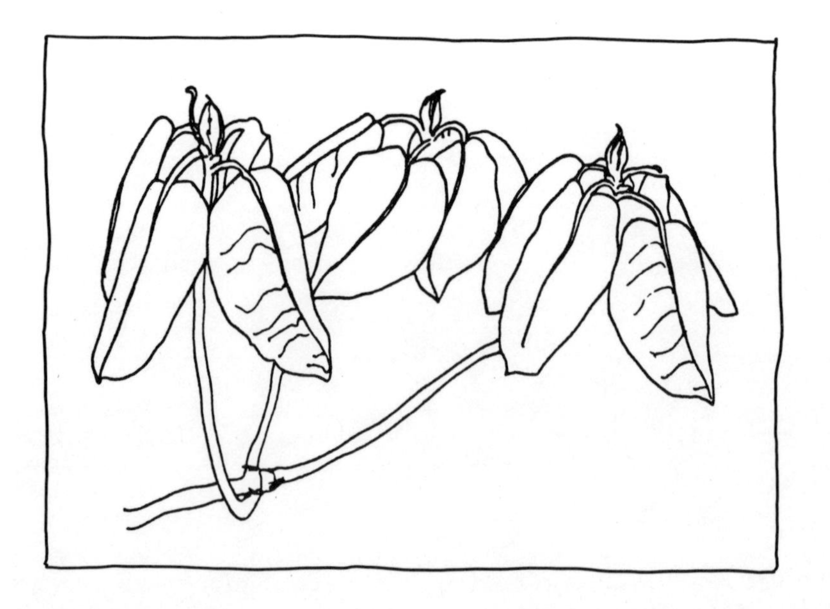

Pete, SP and I arrived in Darjeeling on 13 February. We were provided with a base at the charming Himalayan Mountaineering Institute (HMI), nestled among tall trees on the brow of one of Darjeeling's sprawling ridges. The three of us busied ourselves with food purchases while we waited for Ding, Corrina and Ann to arrive. Each day we would wander into the markets, winding up and down steep streets that were often wreathed in cloud.

In Darjeeling we were frustrated by yet more hindrances to the official progress of our expedition. The Sikkim permit which had been handed to us in New Delhi (and for which we had waited nearly three weeks) was pronounced defective by the local authorities. 'Delhi is a long way away,' we were told. 'What do they know down there?' The principal of HMI, Group Captain Chowdhury, stepped in on our behalf and solved the problem, making certain amendments to the permit under his 'delegated' authority.

The Group Captain was helpful in another way as well. We were to be assigned our second Indian member from amongst the instructors at HMI, but the instructor assigned had to withdraw only a day after joining us, for family reasons. Where would we get a replacement at this late stage? The Group Captain solved this problem. He introduced us to another of his instructors, Chewang Tashi. On little more than 24 hours' notice, this instructor rearranged his affairs so as to be able to leave with us on a journey that proved in the end to require eleven months of 1981.

Tashi immediately impressed us. He was a compact hill man, born in Kathmandu a little more than 40 years ago, quiet and exuding an air of dependability. He spoke good English, Hindi, Nepali and Tibetan plus a smattering of numerous dialects. Some of these languages he had picked up during service in SP's force, the Indo-Tibetan Police Force, working mainly as an interpreter with Tibetan refugees. During that time he had gone as a high altitude porter to many of the difficult peaks in India, among them Nanda Devi (7816 metres), and on the first ascent of Changabang (6864 metres). Later he had been invited to join the Indian Government's Himalayan Mountaineering Institute in Darjeeling as an instructor.

Taking our cue from his nuggety physical appearance, we invited Tashi to travel with the traverse team, asking SP if he would like to join the support party. It was too soon to tell at that early meeting, but before more than two of our traverse stages were completed, it became clear that in Tashi the traverse team had obtained the rock upon which much of their success was founded.

Ding arrived in Darjeeling on 15 February, without Ann and Corrina. He took me aside and told me that they had decided not to come to Sikkim, to wait instead in Kathmandu. I couldn't understand this, knowing how keen Ann was to start the trekking — particularly in such a rarely visited place as Sikkim. However, my puzzlement could not be relieved by any communication with Ann or Corrina, so there was nothing for it but to accept that something must have happened and wait to see them in Nepal.

The plan for this first section of the traverse was to enter Sikkim by road from Darjeeling, completing border formalities at the roadside checkpoint, and then trek up into north-western Sikkim, near Mount Kangchenjunga (8598 metres), to the Ratong La, a pass of 5197 metres, on the border between Sikkim and Nepal. Here the party would separate — Ding, Pete and Tashi crossing into Nepal, and SP and I, the somewhat attenuated support team, returning the way we had come.

We left Darjeeling on 17 February, still with only two Indian members, SP and Tashi. The arrival of the third (and final) member of their team had been promised daily but we were too impatient to wait. The year was slipping away.

The third Indian member for our expedition did in fact arrive, a day or so later, and although we never met him or knew his name, we heard later about his part in the traverse. It seems he was a military man and had received orders to report to Darjeeling for an expedition of ten months' duration. He was shortly to marry but orders are orders, and he duly packed up and set off for Darjeeling, sending a telegram home to the effect that he was going away for a year and could they please postpone the wedding.

HMI outfitted him and provided a driver to take him up into Sikkim and our road end at Yuksam. He is reported to have got out of the vehicle there, put on his rucksack, and grimly faced the hills into which the rest of 'his' expedition had disappeared some days previously.

He stood there for a few long minutes, then turned to the driver, complaining of sudden chest pains — owing to the altitude no doubt — and concluded that it was inadvisable to proceed further. I have a strong mental picture of him, standing there at the road end in the weak spring sun, bracing a little against the cold wind, making his decision. Honour satisfied, he returned to Darjeeling and was allowed to withdraw, return home and marry. He sounds like a sensible chap and I am sorry we never met.

3. Darjeeling and Sikkim

At the bus terminal in Darjeeling I sit with our luggage until accommodation can be found. I watch as the young porters gamble while they wait for work. They draw a square in the dirt and each one places a small twist of paper inside it. Then they stand back at a mark and throw a rupee coin to try and knock their papers out of the square. They push and jostle good-humouredly, shouting applause or jeering at a poor throw.

Above me rises Darjeeling township, rank upon rank of houses built in steep-gabled English style. It is one of the most famous of the hill stations of India, developed during the rule of the British Raj as a summer retreat. Each year in May or June the administrators of the Bengal Government and their families would escape here from the heat and dust of Calcutta and the plains; fleeing also from the threat of disease and flooding that accompanies the summer monsoon rains.

Pete discovers that there are rooms for us in the HMI and coolies carry our loads there through streets too narrow and rugged for cars. The Raj and the British have gone from India now and only their houses remain. Although dilapidated, the houses are at least in use. We pass the Anglican Church, tattered and empty, its door ajar: it exercises a strong hold only over the occupants of the cemetery. Inscriptions on the headstones, all leaning and askew, bear pathetic testimony to the ravages of disease amongst the children.

From the window of our room I look north to the mountains at last — a motionless wave of snow, 50 kilometres away, a striking pure white against the blue sky. By midday clouds have risen from the high plateau of Tibet and our

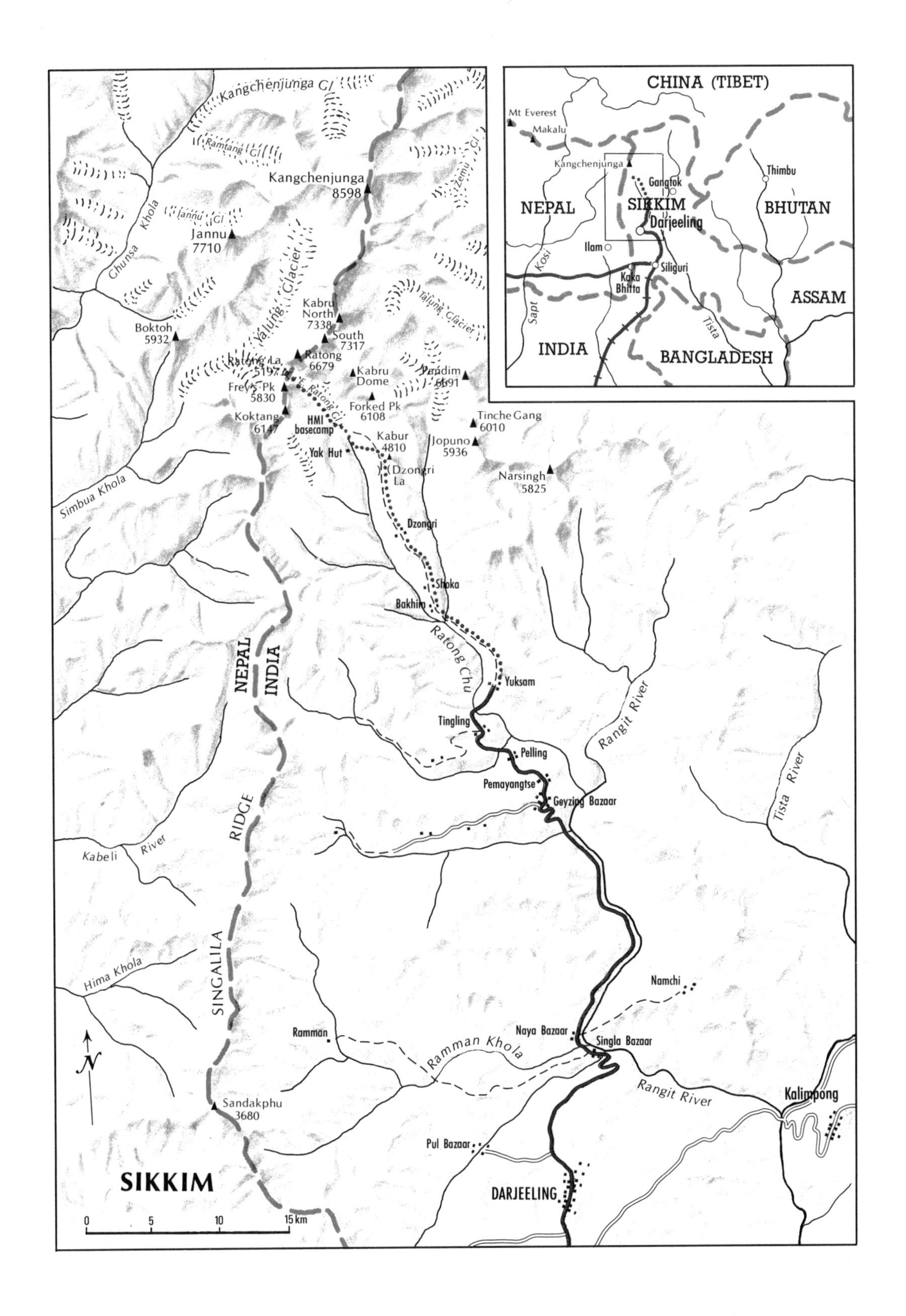

CHINA (TIBET)
Mt Everest
Makalu
Kangchenjunga
Gangtok
Thimbu
NEPAL
SIKKIM
BHUTAN
Darjeeling
Ilam
Siliguri
Kaka Bhitta
Sapt Kosi
Tista
ASSAM
INDIA
BANGLADESH
Kangchenjunga Gl
Ramtang Gl
Zemu Gl
Kangchenjunga 8598
Jannu Gl
Jannu 7710
Chunsa Khola
Yalung Glacier
Talung Glacier
Kabru North 7338
South 7317
Boktoh 5932
Ratong La
Ratong 6679
Kabru Dome
Frey's Pk 5830
Ratong Gl
Forked Pk 6108
Koktang 6147
HMI basecamp
Kabur 4810
Tinche Gang 6010
Jopuno 5936
Yak Hut
Dzongri La
Narsingh 5825
Simbua Khola
Dzongri
Shoka
Bakhim
Ratong Chu
NEPAL
INDIA
Yuksam
Rangit River
Tingling
Pelling
Pemayangtse
Geyzing Bazaar
Tista River
RIDGE
Kabeli River
SINGALILA
Hima Khola
Namchi
Ramman
Naya Bazaar
Singla Bazaar
Ramman Khola
N
Rangit River
Kalimpong
Sandakphu 3680
Pul Bazaar
DARJEELING
SIKKIM
0 5 10 15 km

mountain view is gone.

I lunch with SP and Ding in an open-air restaurant, on the ridge after which Darjeeling was named. The Buddhists called it Dor-je-ling-gang, 'Hill of the Thunderbolt Town', and the ridge is as steep and jagged as the name suggests. One of the few flat areas in Darjeeling, near the restaurant, has been sealed and has a large bookshop that beckons with its sign, 'Browsers Welcome'. From this square we watch families of Indian tourists from Bengal riding hill-ponies along the ridgetop road to the zoo. The plainsmen are distinguished by their wool-lined caps and long earmuffs, bought especially for this trip to the mountains. The pony-boys urge on their ponies from behind, whipping them with sticks, and the group breaks into a canter. The riders' earmuffs flap up and down in unison.

In the zoo there are red pandas, waist high and surprisingly powerful looking, and a caged tiger being teased with stones by a crowd of young boys. The tiger has barely enough room to snarl and the sight makes me suddenly angry. The boys only renew their teasing after sensing my disapproval.

I leave the zoo and walk along the upper edge of the town and out into the tea plantations. I am expecting to see a scene straight out of a Darjeeling Tea advertisement and anticipate the pleasure of walking among damp misty hills covered with glisteningly clean tea bushes and sari-clad maidens plucking 'only the choice top leaves'. But advertising does not reflect real life. Tea bushes are small, dusty and heavily pruned; the air is cool but dry; and it is men who push through the tight rows of growth and they have motor-driven insecticide sprays on their backs. The day is made raucous with the sound of the tiny engines, the air thick with offensive petrol fumes.

Back in the bazaar we buy foodstuffs — biscuits, bread, jam, tinned butter, flour, 'Kangchenjunga' brand tea, sugar and rice. Although it is rationed we manage also to find some kerosene for our stoves. I buy a passport bag, and then another for Ann, appliquéed with brightly coloured Tibetan brocade. My passport and money now hang secure around my neck, hidden beneath my shirt.

Chewang Tashi, our second Indian team member, arrives. As well as being a friendly unassuming chap, he is stocky, strong and resourceful and starts work virtually the minute he arrives. He arranges transport for us in a battered green jeep, whose driver promises that he can take the five of us and our month's supply of equipment and food over the border to the road end in Sikkim.

The jeep comes early one fine morning and Pete and I clamber all over it, tying the rucksacks on the roof. When they seem sufficiently secure we all crowd into the jeep, seven of us including the driver and his boy. From Darjeeling the road has to descend 1300 metres in one dramatic drop of hillside to Singla Bazaar on the banks of the Rangit river. The tiny buildings of the bazaar are visible from just outside Darjeeling but the descent takes more than an hour. Our driver has to reverse several times to negotiate some corners, his boy leaping out to prop stones behind the wheels in place of a hand-brake.

This first hour seems a long one and it sets the pattern for the rest of our day's journey into Sikkim. To travel what appears only a short distance from one town to the next in these green hills means laborious hours spent winding and braking, switchbacking endlessly down precipitous valley walls, only to climb again at a snail's pace, radiator steaming noisily, up the other side.

After crossing the Rangit we stop for the border, entering our passport details in a dog-eared exercise book. Our permit is scrutinised and approved. We climb back into the jeep, tucking our passports away, and enter Sikkim.

Sikkim is a small state, east of Nepal and west of Bhutan. It is roughly rectangular in shape with the long sides on the east and west borders. To the north lies China,

Our Sikkimese porter at his home near Yuksam. His father, ex-Rifleman Gurung, displays on the charpoy beside him the medals he was awarded as a Gurkha soldier in World War II.

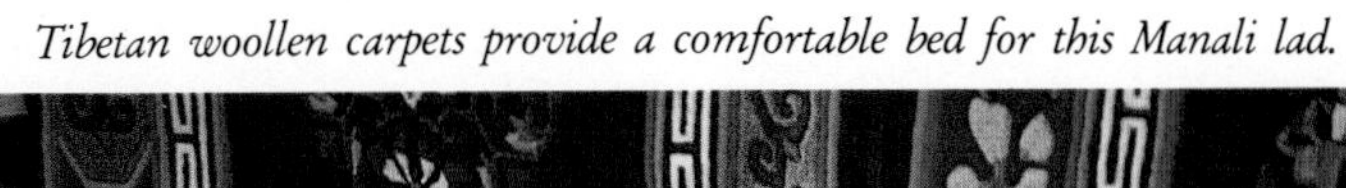

Tibetan woollen carpets provide a comfortable bed for this Manali lad.

A stupa crowned with prayer flags in Bhandar village, eastern Nepal.

Kangchenjunga's south face is framed between Doug (right) and Ding. The vertical prayer flags mark the high point on the ridge below Dzongri village in Sikkim. Our route to the upper Ratong valley lies at the foot of the ridge on the right side of the photo.

Adult Himalayan griffons stand a metre tall. This pair made short work of a calf carcass they alighted upon in the Marsyangdi valley of central Nepal.

A hawker near the Bagmati river, Kathmandu.

Clouds pile up behind the Mingbo face of Ama Dablam (6858m). In the foreground is the Buddhist monastery of Thyangboche in the Khumbu region of Nepal.

This 111-year-old Hindu pilgrim, Akandanan Yoga Abihasi, travelled from Haridwar in northern India to the annual Shivaratri festival at Pashupatinath on the outskirts of Kathmandu.

Corrina and Gerry, a forester from the Australia-Nepal forestry exchange programme, trek south past the haystacks and wheat fields of Sipaghat village in the Indrawati river valley east of Kathmandu.

to the south India. Like others of the buffer states between these two giants, Sikkim's rulers long feared annexation. In 1947, when India gained her independence from the British, Sikkim became an Indian protectorate and from then the future was no longer in doubt: in 1975 Sikkim became officially part of India.

Although it is now only a demarcation line between one Indian state and another, this border is watched more carefully than other state borders and all foreigners who enter Sikkim must obtain those same special permits that we had waited so long for in Delhi.

The hillsides are steeper on this side of the Rangit and the plantations of tea give way to mixed cultivation. Small terraced fields are cut into the slopes. There is wheat growing and maize, occasionally millet and mustard. Most common are plots of tall cardamom, the spice that is Sikkim's main export crop.

Our jeep stops at Geyzing Bazaar and we wait while the driver and his boy borrow blankets. It seems that we will not reach the end of the road until just on dark, so the driver and his boy will sleep there and return tomorrow. No one will drive on these roads at night, a result partly of the poor quality of the electrical components in the vehicles; with inadequate lights, or none, there is too great a risk of accident. Moreover, should the vehicle break down, we might suffer attack from bandits and thieves. Besides, demons and vengeful gods roam abroad by night.

Geyzing Bazaar has been built in a hollow square around two massive trees, the pipal and the banyan, planted so that their leaves and roots will intertwine in a blessed 'marriage' that will protect the bazaar from evil spirits. We eat our lunch on the paved stone platform or *chautara,* a rest stop provided for porters, beneath the spreading branches. The upper stones have been arranged at a perfect height for resting a load without having to lower it to the ground. A chattering, fluttering cloud of sparrows and blue rock-pigeons hop amongst us pecking inquisitively. Next to arrive are a flock of solemn, staring children who gather as we sit stretching our cramped limbs. SP tells the children to move on; they scamper away only to return slowly, step by step. We let them stay; they are too shy even to speak to us.

On three sides we are faced by the open shop fronts of the bazaar. The fourth side, fringed by the road, falls away to a river, 600 metres below. Across from the porter-rest sit three elderly women selling vegetables. Spring onions, potatoes and dried red chillies are neatly laid out on sacking at their feet. One woman holds a small curved sickle, little more than a handspan across, and with it she carefully cuts slivers off her toenails. Her companions talk quietly and occasionally wave at the flies that hover over the pungent onion bulbs.

Beyond Geyzing we stop to look at the Buddhist monastery of Pemayangtse. The capital of Sikkim was here once, before the Kings moved it to Gangtok. The Kings are gone now, and political power has moved again, from Gangtok to New Delhi, but the monastery remains. The walls of the inner courtyard are covered with finely detailed paintings of scenes from the life of Buddha, and are flanked by cloistered walkways which are elaborately carved and painted in deep maroon and gold. Inside I can just make out the shapes of many statues, some gilded, some painted, almost hidden in the gloom of the temple. I recognise a statue of Buddha, sitting cross-legged in an attitude of meditation. Tashi points out a statue of Shiva, a Hindu god who brandishes a trident in one of his four hands, and then another of the lama who built this monastery. Each carved image is blackened by the smoke of thousands of small brass butter lamps.

Many Westerners come here to study and worship. All around in the forest are guesthouses and a bustle of people coming and going, magenta-robed monks and blue-jeaned students.

The last town of any size is Pelling through which we pass without stopping, all of us nodding and dozing as the hills' shadows lengthen. The driver's boy perches on the back of the jeep and plays a mournful tune on a mouth-organ. I am lost in my thoughts, recalling other similar journeys by jeep, cramped, dusty and tedious, with my father in Borneo, bound for a headhunter burial cave, weighed down with the stuff of archaeology.

Just on twilight the road runs out at Yuksam. From here, in the morning, our trek will begin on a paved foot track. The driver's boy is sent for the resthouse *chowkidar* while we ferry our rucksacks from the jeep to the porch. The *chowkidar* arrives, clutching a huge key and an impressive leather-bound visitors' book. The resthouse has been locked for the winter and we are the first trekkers of the season. The furniture is all in storage but we sleep soundly on bare boards.

The next morning we eat a hasty breakfast and repack our rucksacks, eager to be on our way. Then we find that we have to wait for our porter to arrive. I lace my boots, sitting on the step in the sun with SP, and look around at Yuksam. On our right is a stream, deeply cut into the earth. Its sides are choked with tall bamboos, all yellow and green, and squat shrubs. There are small terraced fields: some are planted; others, recently turned with a plough, lie fallow. Southward, terraces rise in gradual steps to a low knoll where a house with upturned eaves crowns the skyline. A half-naked child herds two buffaloes with wide, curving horns.

To a rural family, a buffalo means both health and fortune. This large ungainly beast will plough the family fields; produce dung which enriches the soil, although dung is more often collected and used to fuel the household fire; produce (if the buffalo is a female) rich milk which can be sold for extra income; and, in death, yield buffalo meat which can be eaten and a hide which can be tanned for utensils and footwear.

This young boy will spend more time each day with the buffaloes than he does with his family. He will leave home with the buffaloes early each morning, lead them to work or in search of fodder, coax them over rough ground, bathe and water them in hot weather. Only in the evening will the trio return home, for the beasts to be stabled in security for the night.

To the north, the landscape appears untouched by cultivation. Steep, dark green, forested ridges fall into the deep gorge of the Ratong river, one after another, until, at the far distant head of the valley, they rise to the summit of Koktang (6147 metres), gleaming snow-white in the sun.

Our route lies up this valley of the Ratong, but near its head the gorge is too deep to follow and the track cuts north up a ridge to a village called Dzongri. From there we must cross the Dzongri La, a pass of 4600 metres, back into the upper valley of the Ratong glacier.

Rivising, our porter, comes. After Tashi explains our destination to him, Rivising tests the load, lifting it from one side and then the other to see if we are trying to cheat him by overloading. He pronounces it satisfactory. Then, since we will be away from settled areas for probably five of the next ten days, he sends the driver's boy to his home to fetch a blanket which he slips on to the top of his load.

We set foot on the trail at last. The small terraced fields of Yuksam soon end and we push on into forest. Through stands of oak and rhododendron the track rises steadily, gently, broad and stonepaved.

'You will find this everywhere in the Himalaya,' says Tashi, when I comment on the quality of the track. 'Where there are people and no motor roads there will be good tracks. Each village has to maintain the track near it, sometimes halfway to the next village. There is often one family responsible for the work — the village people support that family's farming while they work on the track. People have to travel and trade must go on.'

We wind in and out of small gullies and cross swift streams, clear and cold. After my restraint on the populated plains, I give way to temptation, stopping often in the leafy shade to drink the chill water. There seems no possibility of polluted water here. Birds call in the forest — finches and a yellow-bellied warbler. At one point the track is thick with acorns, great lumpy bulbs with three in each clump, and prickly chestnut seed cases. It feels marvellous to be walking again, to have left behind the cramped days on buses and trains. The air is cleaner, feels softer, and I revel in the change of surroundings, as we all do, glad of the exercise at last.

Around midday Tashi takes a small, faint trail between the trees. He leads us a short distance into a raw new clearing with three matting huts. An old woman comes out of one hut to greet us. Tashi addresses her with respect as *didi* or elder sister. She offers to cook our rice for us and invites us inside the largest shelter. The hut is low roofed, about four metres long and not quite two metres wide, with the hearth midway along one wall. There is no chimney and the smoke finds its own way out through chinks in the woven matting.

We sit on what must be the sleeping platform, marked off from the rest of the floor by a line of low stones. Underneath us the earth has been covered with a thick layer of fresh leaves and aromatic branches. A low shelf of levelled wood has been wedged above the fireplace to hold several battered tins. The only other item of furniture is a small locked tin trunk, its hasp closed with a cheap Chinese padlock.

Tashi explains that the inhabitants are from a higher village, Shoka, which we will reach in another two days. Each year the villagers migrate here to avoid spending the winter at over 3600 metres; for six months of the year their yaks and cattle are grazed in this forest. We saw buffaloes near the track about half an hour back, tearing at the vegetation, and heard others far off, their brass neckbells sounding out through the trees.

Our billy balances over the fire, propped up on three up-ended stones, with embers piled high between them. The old woman offers us a few radishes, the only food that they have to spare, and she boils them with our rice. Eyes wrinkling from the smoke, she talks with Tashi, sometimes laughing and joking, sometimes more serious, as he passes on news of the world outside. Tashi is well known in these hills through his many treks and courses run from the Institute. In time we discover that he has the happy gift of making friends wherever he goes.

The old woman offers to make tea for us as well, and apologetically shows Tashi their remaining supply of sugar, a meagre handful in the bottom of one of the tins above the fireplace. It is nearly the end of winter and their food stocks are low. Pete digs into his pack for our own supply.

I take my bowl outside into the fresh air and the others follow. From the next hut a younger woman and three children watch us. A boy and a girl, the elder probably five years old, peek out at us from behind their mother's skirts and their older brother, maybe nine or ten, comes closer. He cautiously runs his hand over the nylon of our rucksacks and gently fingers the teeth of an ice axe. He wears rough, brown, homespun, knee-length trousers and a cotton shirt. His Tibetan boots with scarlet uppers are not the thin, leather-soled items that are on sale in Darjeeling for tourists like ourselves: these are working boots with thick hide soles, turned up all around for over two centimetres.

I eat my rice and radish with good appetite and the old woman watches, smiling. We give her something in return for her hospitality and move on, a little stiff now after resting.

Once we are back on the main track the route falls quickly down to the Ratong Chu, a rough-and-tumble torrent. The rotting wooden suspension bridge is draped with prayer flags, as thin and wispy as the clinging valley mist. I finger one which drips the spray from the river. The material is gauze or filmy undyed muslin. Most of the flags are the same size, about 30 by 40 centimetres, and printed with regular designs in black. On the older flags the designs are faded, almost invisible. Each flag is a Tibetan Buddhist prayer, Tashi tells me, invoked by every passing breeze.

Bakhim, where we will sleep tonight, is a 600 metre climb above the river, up a long gradual ridge. We will follow this ridge for two days more to avoid the Ratong gorge. The *chowkidar* at Yuksam gave us a key to the Bakhim resthouse. The resthouse is not hard to find, being Bakhim's only building. We stop in front of it and lever off our rucksacks from backs wet with sweat. I rub my aching shoulders in relief: it is a long time since I last carried a heavy pack all day. As I relax it is suddenly unpleasantly cool and I dig into my rucksack for a sweater and trousers and change out of my walking shorts. We build a fire on the ground outside to cook our evening meal and potter about the resthouse, laying out our sleeping bags.

There is something slightly depressing about our situation. It could be the damp cloud which came in during the afternoon, cutting off the view south to the plains, or perhaps it is the isolation of this lonely building, perched on a flat scrap of ridge in the tall dripping forest. Whatever it is, we are all subdued. I think of Ann in Kathmandu, knowing she would rather be here trekking, wondering what she is doing right now. Night falls before our meal is completed. The six of us slump on rucksacks and boulders about the open fire. Our eyes are on the flames and our backs to the forest, pools of darkness and silence between us. Once we have eaten, our desultory attempts at conversation fail completely. One by one we go quietly inside to bed.

In the morning Tashi brews sweet tea on the primus and we breakfast on the last of our small yeasty loaves of bread from the bazaar at Darjeeling. I cut thick, awkward slices with my pen-knife. Soon fingers, knife and sleeping bag are scattered with crumbs and sticky with pink apple jam, imported from Bhutan.

We discuss today's objective. Bakhim is at 3300 metres and from here on we have to consider the question of altitude. Our bodies need time to adjust to the reduced amounts of oxygen in the atmosphere above 3000 metres, to acclimatise to the thin mountain air. Our blood will thicken, manufacturing more red corpuscles to transport the oxygen more effectively round the body. Our hearts will work harder. If we rush our rate of ascent, climbing more quickly than our rate of acclimatisation, we risk oedema, a swelling in the lungs or skull cavity. Descent is the only remedy. Oedema can prove fatal if ignored. There are many early warning signs of altitude sickness, however — headaches, nausea and dizziness all indicate the need to slow down and rest before further climbing. Some minor breathlessness or reduced energy is virtually unavoidable in the interim, however, no matter how well one acclimatises.

At any event, that is the theory, about which I have read extensively. My practical experience, on the other hand, is virtually nil. I climbed Mount Kinabalu (4102 metres) in Borneo with my father and brother when I was 13, and suffered no ill effects from the altitude. That climb involved only two days above 3000 metres, however, hardly long enough for the symptoms to occur. Besides, that was a long time ago. I worry about whether I shall manage at altitude here in the Himalaya.

The usual travel stage from here, for the local people, is to continue up the ridge to Dzongri, a hamlet at 4300 metres. Tashi is concerned that this rate of ascent may be too rapid for us. The alternative seems to be the summer village of Shoka, which is barely at 3600 metres. This would mean a gain of only 300 metres today, which seems too little progress to Ding and Pete.

In the end I suggest a compromise, that we go above Shoka and camp at 3900 metres, where the forest ends. The next day we can go on through Dzongri and continue up over the Dzongri La at 4600 metres. Then we can descend from the pass to camp that night in the upper Ratong valley at about 3600 metres. Tashi approves of this plan and it is accepted, for the theory of acclimatising says that it is good for the body to climb during the day to heights greater than those at which you return to sleep at night.

It is easy to tell when we are approaching Shoka, for the forest undergrowth has been cleared and trampled by grazing cattle. Closer to the houses there are gaping areas where all the large trees have been felled. One family lives in Shoka all year round, keeping watch over the other houses which are shuttered and locked for the winter. Soon our friends from the forest below will return from their winter camps, sweating and puffing with their loads up this long ridge. They will herd their cattle before them, laden down also with mounds of cooking pots and containers, precariously balanced on top of the woven matting rolled for re-use.

Then Shoka will be briefly full of bustle and chatter. Once the crops are planted many of the villagers will move even higher with their animals, seeking out the lush fresh grazing of the alpine pastures, living in temporary summer shelters. Transhumance, advancing and retreating with the seasons, is a hard and semi-nomadic life. No wonder the hill people look with amazement upon people who come to the mountains to accept discomfort through choice. Who, they must wonder, could have too much comfort?

At a Buddhist *stupa* in the middle of the village we pause for the view, looking south through clear blue skies to where the myriad foothills fold green and brown into the dun coloured plains behind us.

The *stupa* is a curious structure. Each side presents the same image to me as I walk around it, clockwise at Tashi's insistence. The base is a five metre square, about two metres high. From this rises a half-dome nearly two metres high again, topped by another smaller stone square. Above all towers a pillar of diminishing diameter, nearly three metres high, and crowned with bamboo wands and prayer flags. The dome of the *stupa* has been smoothed with mud and white-washed to a creamy sheen, representing water; the square below represents earth; the pillar above, fire. On the sides of the top-most square the all-seeing eyes of Buddha have been painted in black, with striking blue and white pupils. They gaze north, south, east and west over the Sikkim countryside, protecting the village from evil spirits. The *stupa* (or *chorten* as it is sometimes called) is often hollow, Tashi says, containing holy relics of the Buddhist faith, such as printed scriptures or mementos of local pietists.

We go on quickly through the last of the remaining houses, bleak and full of echoes, back into the forest. As we climb higher the vegetation alters. There are no tall trees now. Oak gives way completely to rhododendron. I pick my path carefully on dirty grey frozen snow that has drifted under the shoulder-height shrubs, where the sun hardly penetrates. Then, abruptly, the angle of the ridge eases, and we emerge on a level shoulder where there are two rough wooden shelters. This is the best place for tents, Tashi tells us.

One shelter has its roof almost intact and we drop our packs there on a bench against the wall, separating for the chores of setting up camp. Pete starts clearing our two tent sites, scraping away old snow and clearing a level area from the jumble of mossy rocks. SP and Ding return to the forest edge, to gather wood from where the heavy winter snows have fractured the young rhododendron branches. I am the water carrier for the night and I day-dream over the task, scooping out the crystal clear liquid from a shallow pool nearby. It tinkles with shards of ice as I carry back the billy and water-bottles, brimming full.

The second tent is pitched just as the familiar afternoon cloud arrives and we retreat inside the relatively roomy shelter to while away the rest of the afternoon, huddled on the bench, dodging the swirling smoke of Tashi's fire and drinking cup after cup of black sweet tea.

Again it is dark before we finish our evening meal but the sea of cloud ebbs quickly as the temperature drops. Across the valley to the north-east a line of peaks, parallel to our ridge, stands clear in the starlight. Tashi points them out: lowest of all is Jopuno (5936 metres), then Tinche Gang (6010 metres) and furthest to the north looms the chunky unclimbed bulk of Pandim (6691 metres).

Luminescence in the sky behind Jopuno heralds the rise of the full moon. It inches clear almost imperceptibly and then seems to rush upwards, leaping free of the concealing ridge. Down in the valley and north over the Chinese border, Tibetans are praying: they will burn candles and juniper incense for Losar, Tashi says, to honour this first full moon in their lunar New Year. Do they see the moon as clearly down there, I wonder? Here it seems so close that I could reach out and touch it, huge and bright.

Next morning Tashi is anxious to get away quickly. If we reach the next high point on the ridge before the cloud comes in we will be rewarded with a view of Kangchenjunga. This, the third highest mountain in the world, is the symbolic marker for the beginning of our journey. In Nepal we will approach Mount Everest, the highest point on earth, and at the year's end, when we reach the foot of K2 in Pakistan, the second highest mountain in the world, we will have reached the end of our journey.

Our track becomes a climb, on rough-hewn rock steps up from our campsite. The sun warms the rocks and breath is short, halting conversation. A steep bluff falls away near the track, heralded by the sharp crack of prayer flags in the wind. I urge myself on and out into the welcome breeze. To the north, clearly visible, the sprawling mass of Kangchenjunga straddles the horizon. We stare across at the sheer south-east flank of the mountain, split by a single granite ridge, narrow and fluted, forcing its way up to the ridge of many summits.

On that summit ridge a gale is blowing. Long dark lenticular clouds curve and tumble over each other, roaring southward out of Tibet. Tashi explains the various names of the mountain. The Sikkimese call it Kangchenjongna, 'Five Mountain Fort'. Tibetans call it Khangchenchena, 'Fifteen Mountain Peaks'. Some Tibetans translate the name to mean 'Five Treasures of the Eternal Snows' and believe that the god of wealth stores the five treasures there. What are the five treasures? Corn, copper, silver, gold and, last but not least, sacred books.

A huge Himalayan griffon comes gliding down on a tongue of wind, a fugitive from the storm out of Tibet. Feathers humming and its huge wings outstretched to their full span of nearly two metres, this griffon is the biggest bird I have ever seen. I watch as it soars with a stately ponderous grace out over the bluff, away from the peaks; it is outlined for a long time against the haze of the plains behind. We move on too, heading along the bluff for Dzongri, feeling now that we are truly in the Himalaya at last.

Dzongri is not like other villages we have walked through. Being the most northerly village on our route through Sikkim and at the highest altitude, it is built to withstand severe winters. Shoka had wooden buildings; here, far above the forest, wood is either too flimsy or too precious and the houses are low, solid stone structures with walls nearly a metre thick. Yet, instead of banding together for warmth or for company, this village is also the most dispersed and no house is built within sight of another.

The headman of Dzongri invites us in and we stop briefly to snack on biscuits and to shelter from the searching wind. During our halt the headman's powerful Tibetan mastiff stands slightly uphill from the door and barks furiously at us without pause. By accident or perhaps by design the headman sits with the light behind him, his face in darkness. He is very interested in our planned traverse of the Himalaya and offers some advice. He holds his hand out, palm up.

'On the Tibetan side,' he says, pointing to his outstretched palm while Tashi translates for me, 'it is all flat, easy going. On the Nepali side,' he points to the gaps between his fingers, 'it is all broken by great rivers and you go up and down, up and down, all the time. You should,' he says, 'traverse on the Tibetan side.'

It is hard to argue with either his geography or his logic. The only flaw in his argument is that he himself only lives here because he had to flee from Tibet at the time of the Chinese invasion. Perhaps he thinks that we can travel there freely.

Above the village we steadily gain height through what will shortly be summer pasture. Today the ground is spongy underfoot, the grass yellowed and pressed flat. Winter snow has not been off this slope for long.

Just north of the Dzongri La is Kabur (4810 metres), a squat, black rock peak of no apparent difficulty. It has been included for religious reasons on the Indian Government list of prohibited ascents. Notwithstanding that, Tashi says it has been climbed once by a local man and 'one English'. The pass itself is a jumble of black rock fallen from the south face of Kabur and we pick our way amongst the confusion, seeking out the best vantage point. I pause for breath and a flock of brilliant blue birds settles around me. The only sounds are the chatter of the birds and behind me, on the pass, the crack of prayer flags in the wind. Then something alarms the birds and they are off, lifting their wings in a flash of deep aquamarine.

For once we have a view of our day's objective below us, the hanging valley of the upper Ratong river. At the head of the valley, to the north-west, I can see the terminal moraine of the East Ratong glacier. Above that, somewhere, lies our destination, the Ratong La which crosses the Singalila ridge at 5197 metres on the border of Sikkim and Nepal. There are two Ratong glaciers; one flows east towards us and India, the other flows west into Nepal.

The track stays high on the eastern side of the Ratong, heading for the glacier. We are not going to that altitude today, however, and soon leave the track, forcing a path straight downhill through short scrubby juniper to the river flat. Tashi knows of a shepherd's hut on the other side of the river where we will camp.

The cold here is intense, straight from the snow, and I am dampened by rain from the thick mist which has crept over the pass behind us. We stop to pull on anoraks, then press on in the mist. Tashi finds the bridge — two squared-off tree trunks laid side by side over a bouldery river bed. A wary crossing and a five minute search bring us to the shelter.

We call it the 'yak hut'. There is a thick carpet of yak dung over the old floor covering of juniper branches. One wall is formed by a huge boulder one metre high and the other walls are built in dry stone to the same height. The roof consists of rough lengths of split timber that overlap the central ridge-pole. The entrance is a hole, through which we must crawl, in the uphill wall of the hut. Chill breezes whistle through every crevice. We all work at clearing the floor, piling the dung in one corner to save it for the fires of the summer residents. Then Tashi and I go looking for firewood to eke out the dung for our fire. We are lucky; hidden under an overhanging rock we find a cache of dry wood already broken into kindling sized pieces.

I pass the rest of the afternoon catching up on my diary and beginning a letter home to my mother. A blackened billy of rice and stew bubbles on the flames.

Outside, the valley is lost in mist and steady drizzle.

Perhaps it is because we are all together in the one shelter, but we talk with more enthusiasm than usual after dinner. With a last mug of tea clasped in our hands, the five of us sit bunched up together in our sleeping bags, warmed by the cheery glow of the firelight. SP explains to us how the Indians threw the British out of India. We have an idea that it was not quite so one-sided as this and a spirited debate takes place in which we defend the British. I hope they are grateful.

When I venture outside to relieve myself any illusion of warmth is quickly dispelled by a wind that cuts through three layers of clothing. The peaks at the head of the Ratong are clear and their summits catch the first glancing beams from the rising moon. I hurry back inside to my sleeping bag. Settling down, I try to shuffle into a comfortable position on my thin foam sleeping mat spread out on the juniper. Perhaps it is those branches beneath me but I cannot sleep. Neither can Rivising, the porter. He has only his threadbare blanket and the loan of our jackets for the night. He squats at the edge of the fire, outlined by what is left of the light, feeding in small chips of dung and wood and chain-smoking.

I lie awake, reviewing everything I can remember about altitude and worrying whether I will perform well over the next few days. What a mess this trip will become if it turns out that I react badly to altitude. Specks of ash from the fire float in the air and for long hours I lie watching them hover in shafts of moonlight that plunge through gaps in the roof. Slowly, ever so slowly, the angle of the moonbeams steepens to the vertical; slowly, ever so slowly, it subsides.

I doze at last, dreaming terrible dreams. I am at home and walk into a room full of friends. An old girlfriend stares at me with a look of unspeakable horror as if I knew a word that would bring the whole world crashing down in ruins — and might speak it. I struggle awake. Tiredness is better than sleep like that. Through the door, looking north, I can see sunlight on the peaks, golden and warm. But the yak hut is deep in the valley, locked in frost until after eight, when, in imitation of last night's moonbeams, bright sunlight finally comes splintering through chinks in the roof.

We eat our breakfast in the sun and, as the frost evaporates, spread our sleeping bags on the roof to air. SP does his *puja* out on the grass. Ding and Pete have decided to stay down here today to write their first 'expedition progress' articles to send home for the newspapers. SP, Tashi, Rivising and I will carry loads to about 4800 metres by the foot of the East Ratong glacier. Tashi has explained that the Mountaineering Institute has a fixed base camp there, where we may sleep when we are ready to move up to that height. We will leave today's loads there and return to the yak hut tonight, in an attempt to further acclimatise before carrying the last loads to the base camp tomorrow.

Tashi and I walk together, chatting in the sun. His full name is Chewang Tashi. 'Chewang' means 'blessings' and 'tashi' means 'good luck' or 'fortunate'. 'And I have been fortunate,' he says. 'I survived being a soldier and on many expeditions.' Home now is a cottage in Darjeeling with his wife and three daughters and his elderly widowed mother.

'Why did your family move from Nepal to India?' I ask.

'Like all the others,' he chuckles, 'to find work. Now I am an Indian citizen and work for the Government. My young brother is an officer in the Indian army, in the Bengal Tigers Regiment. I am a Tibetan Buddhist Indian; there are Hindu Indians, such as Mr Chamoli; there are Christian Indians; Muslim Indians — oh, there are all sorts. Now tell me this,' he says with a smile, 'how is it that there are three of you New Zealanders and you are the only one with a religion?'

I think about that for a while. 'I'm not sure, Tashi,' I say at last. 'Maybe I'm old-fashioned.'

He nods his head. 'I have met many foreigners,' he replies. 'I have found them most interesting, but not many are old-fashioned.'

The base camp sits on a flat shoulder of old moraine. In the centre of it is a cylindrical aluminium Nissen hut. 'This is the Silver Hut, from the New Zealand Wintering-Over Expedition of 1960 led by Peter's father, Sir Edmund Hillary,' Tashi explains. 'You must have heard about it?'

'Yes, I have, but I thought they built the hut near Ama Dablam, in Nepal?' I reply.

'They did, but it was carried here for the Institute's base camp. These other small stone huts have been built by the instructors. We sleep in them during the courses, but the students camp there on the flat in tents.'

We stow our loads in one of the huts and lie back against its warm rock walls, soaking up the midday winter sun. SP and Rivising join us. I pull out a packet of biscuits and suggest that we nibble on these for lunch. 'Surely we are going to go back down to the yak hut and cook something?' says SP. 'We must have three cooked meals each day in the mountains.'

'Wouldn't that slow us down a bit, if we did it every day?' I wonder.

'That is the way we always do it on our expeditions. The cooks prefer it that way also.'

'Well, we're the only cooks on this expedition, SP, so we'd better talk this over later, when we get back down to the yak hut.' I continue. 'I've got a feeling that three cooked meals a day might be just a bit unrealistic for this trip.'

We do share the packet of biscuits, but I suspect that SP is still reluctant to call a few cold biscuits 'lunch'.

Early in the afternoon we stroll back down the valley, packs empty, to reach the yak hut just before the cloud. Rivising has now delivered his load to base camp, as agreed. We pay him and he leaves quickly, a small figure heading directly up the far side of the valley towards the track, hoping to reach Dzongri tonight.

Next morning the five of us clean out the yak hut, leaving a small dump of food for SP and me on our return this way from the La. We travel in a leisurely fashion up the valley, pausing often to take photographs of the mountains.

When we reach the base camp, just after midday, Tashi and I go to fetch water from a stream beyond a nearby ridge. As we climb over a rib of moraine, we are startled by an abrupt clatter of stones and watch as four Himalayan blue sheep, *bharal,* bound up the moraine wall away from us. They are in beautiful condition, lean but not starved, and look more like goats than sheep. These are young animals and they move on the loose ground with enviable, easy grace. They group again, high up the moraine, and look back at us. In spite we call out like wolves, yelping and howling. They disappear away over the skyline with a flash of their pale silver rumps, leaving us alone with our foolishness. Tashi grins, 'Snow leopard has been seen here once but no bharal for a long time. People do not usually come here this soon after winter — we are lucky.'

That evening I am suddenly feverish and take to my sleeping bag, racked by bouts of painful coughing. Ding, Pete and I have all had various degrees of chest infection in the last few weeks and I blame it on living in the thick, filthy air of Delhi for too long. Our base camp hut feels draughty and cold and I toss and turn in acute misery until, long after midnight, I wear myself out and sleep.

The next day is designated a rest day and for me it passes in a blur of fever. I lie out in the sun, dozing and taking large handfuls of pills. Today is Tuesday, so first there is my regular weekly Maloprim, to guard against malaria; then there are multi-vitamins and mineral pills; and finally, there are decongestants and pain killers. Tashi brings me tea from time to time and by nightfall I seem to have sweated out the worst of the infection. I am even more apprehensive now, however, about our trip to the pass tomorrow, because the effects of altitude can be even worse if one's lungs are already congested.

Our original plan had been that Ding, Pete and Tashi would cross the western Sikkim border at the Ratong La, just above us, into Nepal. SP and I were to help by carrying part of their food and equipment for them to the pass and were then to return this way to Darjeeling. During the rest day Ding and Pete decide against this plan, because of their concern that they might later get into difficulties in Nepal if it became known that they had made an illegal border crossing. From the Ratong La, they and Tashi will strike directly south, along the crest of the Singalila ridge that follows the border between Sikkim and Nepal virtually to Darjeeling. There they can formally enter Nepal and then head north again, on the western side of the border, to recommence their westward route. From the point of view of acclimatisation this new plan is better — it means that none of us will have heavy loads to carry to the pass tomorrow. I think I am not the only one who is relieved.

We breakfast on *tsampa,* plain Tibetan and Sherpa food. It is Tashi's favourite. You make a cup of sweet tea, stir in the *tsampa* (dry roasted barley, ground into a flour) until the tea is as thick as porridge, and then eat it. Old hands like Tashi have it even drier. He makes it into a ball of dry dough that he can bounce in the palm of his hand and he eats it happily like that. I find it a trifle bland but am not sure if Pete's solution is much better — he stirs jam into it.

After this quick breakfast we stuff biscuits, wind suits and gloves into otherwise empty packs and set off up the glacier toward the pass. We keep to the moraine, the long low ridge of rock pushed up at the edge of the glacier, as long as we can, finding our own way among weathered grey boulders. The north faces of Frey's Peak (5830 metres) and Koktang rear up on our left, Frey's Peak split by a long curving snow gully. Across the glacier, the south faces of Forked Peak (6108 metres) and Kabru Dome (6600 metres) cast long shadows over our progress. Ahead, and to the right, is the south face of Ratong (6679 metres), steep and loose with poor rock showing under new snow. The pass must lie at its foot.

When the moraine wall becomes too broken for easy travel we take to the dry white ice of the glacier, picking our way carefully without crampons. I stick close behind Tashi, and Ding and Pete pick their own route. My chest is heaving. Do I feel a slight headache? Or do I just imagine it? The more I think about it the less certain I am. I stop thinking about it and feel better straightaway.

Just below the pass we have to zigzag, moving back and forth across the crumbling rock. There is a small step where I need to use my hands for balance and after it I pause, dripping with sweat. Tashi turns to encourage me. 'Come on,' he says, 'not far.' I force myself on and, minutes later, I am walking on to the pass where Tashi gestures to a widening and deepening horizon of snow and ice, the Nepal Himalaya.

On the crest there is a small cairn of stones and Tashi picks up another to add to them, calling out in a sing-song voice, 'So so so, la la doh.'

'What does that mean?' I ask him.

'It is something like this,' he tells me. ' "So so so" means "at last we are at the top and we don't have to climb any more". "La la doh" gives thanks that we have all reached here safely.' We each add a stone and I mutter a small prayer of my own.

Before us the West Ratong glacier tumbles down to merge with the Yalung which flows, rock-heaped and ugly, in a great curve away to the south-west. Beyond it are the peaks of Boktoh (5932 metres) and the southern end of the Jannu range, where Ding and other New Zealanders climbed in 1975. These are jagged lumps of rock and ice, thrusting up into a cloudless sky.

The wind is keen on the pass, despite the clear sky and sun, and I put on my anorak and gloves. Pete and Ding and I take gleeful and illegal steps into Nepal, childishly mocking the invisible border. We are islanders and these borders seem a little unreal to us. Tashi takes the situation more seriously. 'In my time,' he tells me, 'I have seen both Pakistani and Chinese soldiers cross such lines as this into India.'

The afternoon is advancing and the time comes for us to turn back. I am elated by the day's effort. I have been all the way to 5197 metres and have suffered no ill effects. My concerns about altitude sickness evaporate, and I find myself looking forward to the remaining climbs on our journey with eager anticipation and reasonable confidence. Our descent on the rubble-strewn glacier turns into a race against the fading light. I pick my way, weary but immensely satisfied, back to the base camp in the last of the twilight.

Ding, Pete and Tashi return to Darjeeling by way of the Singalila ridge. They ask if we would like to go with them; I am keen but SP has only light walking boots and does not wish to go with the others because late winter snow is still expected along the high ridge. Someone must go with SP, so SP and I end up retracing our route through Dzongri and Yuksam to Darjeeling. Still, it is a pleasant walk.

Relaxing into the rhythm of the trail, SP and I halt wherever night finds us. At one camp below Dzongri it is so cold that a small stream freezes solid during the night. We wake to find ourselves above a sea of cloud stretching white and fluffy and unbroken for hundreds of kilometres across the plains to the south. Our tent lies in deep shadow and the cold reduces my hands to useless blocks. Tears of pain come to my eyes as I fumble to undo the clasps on our tent poles.

Two days later we are cursing the heat. We have to walk from the road end at Yuksam to Pelling, to find a vehicle, and we hire a porter to take some of our load. He shows us the local short-cuts and saves us several hours of unnecessary road walking. Along the way we pass our porter's home and he invites us in. We are offered hospitality by his father and the family serves us glasses of fresh boiled milk. The old man shows us the scars of three Japanese bullets, legacy of his service as a Gurkha soldier with the British army in the second world war.

I tell him that my father, his brother and his cousins fought in that war also. His eyes light up. A child is dispatched into their mud-walled hut and returns with a small cloth-wrapped package of grandfather's mementos: a heavy army pocket-knife on a thick lanyard, a round of .303 ammunition, a much folded section of a British Army map of Burma and five war medals. There is a '39-45' Award, a 'Good Conduct', a 'Burma Star', and two that I cannot identify. The old man points out places to me on the map and I nod sagely. His family smile ... and I, suddenly, could be at home with my own father and my family.

As we are about to leave the old man shows me a form that he has received in the post, advising him of the time and places at which war pensions will be paid. The notice states that police stations have also been instructed to ensure that at all fairs and big market days an announcement of the time and place will be made and that attention shall be attracted to the announcement 'by beating a drum as in times past'.

Late in the day, hot and grubby, SP and I shuffle the last 1000 metres up a hillside into Pelling. The only hotel is full, but taking our measure from our scruffy appearance they offer to let us sleep on the floor of the restaurant. We pay at once, eager to snatch some rest. The bus for Darjeeling leaves at sunrise.

In the early morning dark, hardly awake, we carry our loads in failing torchlight to the bus. I stand by the bus, waiting for SP, stamping my feet in the pre-dawn cold. A man pads silently along the road, a pair of thin bare legs beneath an immense load of brushwood. He leaves the tarmac and descends through dew-damp fields into the valley. The barking of dogs follows him from one darkened house to the next. As if on a signal the sun begins to rise. All is blue on blue — the light blue of the far mountains and the folded ridges before them, then deeper and deeper shades in the valleys between, until the final, deep, dark blue of the valley below me.

The sun picks out the snow-covered peaks at last, yellow and pink. The white wall of Kangchenjunga stands sharply etched against the pale sky, frozen, clear and cold. In my mind's eye a tiny figure is moving along the summit ridge, slowly but surely, up from the shadows into the light.

Sikkim provided us with our first test of the expedition's strength: SP and Tashi had their first opportunity to assess us in the field, and we them. Tashi's first impressions, as I recall, were rather unfavourable. He thought that New Zealanders, with their somewhat extreme brand of egalitarianism, were a rather rough and rude bunch, and were excessively familiar with SP. SP had (courtesy of the IMF) the title of joint leader of our joint expedition, a position which remained entirely titular, since the real decisions were made by Pete and Ding. However, in true Indian style, Tashi was invariably (and sincerely) polite, attentive and deferential to SP. In 10 months I never heard him refer to SP, either directly or to one of us, as anything other than Mr Chamoli, and he always checked to see that SP's wants were met.

We were, in the eyes of the Indians, blunt to a fault as well as quarrelsome. The march into the Ratong La was marked by disagreements between Ding and Pete regarding the role of the support party and its size. This had been a bone of contention between them before we ever left New Zealand and I had thought it had been resolved in our final expedition agreement.

The earliest expedition plan had been that Ding and Pete would be supported by their respective companions of the time, Corrina and Nena. Then Nena left Pete, to go and live with Reinhold Messner, whom she'd met after Pete's accident on Ama Dablam (6856 metres) in 1979. As Pete's and Ding's hopes for the traverse expedition became more certain (and the full extent of the work involved more definite), they decided that they would need more than two in their support team anyway. They cast around for people who could augment Corrina in support, and that was when they came to see Ann and me.

Ann and I agreed to join them and duly prepared for the trip, borrowing $4000 to pay into the expedition fund and participating fully in the later expedition negotiations. It was clear, however, that both Ding and Pete were occasionally racked by doubts as to the cost of the whole venture. Five airfares would cost more than four or three, and internal travel and living costs for a year for five would be expensive. What if the expedition didn't succeed and all we had to show for it were big debts? What if there were an accident and a helicopter rescue were necessary? Who would pay? Our thesis was that the five members should bear all losses equally. It seemed the most equitable solution.

Increasingly, however, as the expedition planning progressed, Ann and I sensed doubt on Ding's and Pete's part about our involvement in the expedition. It began to seem as if we were at the root of any problem of expedition cost. In October, after a lot of discussion, Ann and I decided to resign from the expedition, three months before it was due to leave. We had had other plans for 1981 that could easily be put back into place. We wanted to climb Mount McKinley in Alaska, and had planned to travel back through North America: infinitely preferable to being unsure whether you are wanted or needed on someone else's expedition. We gave Ding and Pete time to think about our offer to resign, and suggested alternative members for the support team, in case cost wasn't the only factor.

Happily Ding and Pete weren't interested in alternatives. Together they assured us we were needed: the bulk of the expedition cost was inevitable anyway; they wished to be the proprietors of the expedition (sharing profits or losses equally between themselves); and they didn't want to leave without us. Ann and I still wanted to go to the Himalaya; we still got on fine with the other three; we went.

But the support team issue plainly still troubled Pete. I remember sitting by the track in the rhododendron forest, below Bakhim, waiting for Ding and Pete and hearing their raised voices long before I saw them. Pete was insisting that the support party was too large, that one New Zealander and one Indian would be ample. As it turned out, he was probably right, since Ann and I managed on our own on a couple of occasions in the early stages when Corrina was ill and when the Indian members were unavailable. Later the three of us would take turns carrying out the support team's tasks. But he and Ding had invited three New Zealanders and had also decided that the expedition should be a joint one with additional Indian members. Having asked us to contribute to the expedition and come to India, Pete had, to my mind, left it rather late to repent of that decision.

This time the arguments went on over several days until, worn down by Pete's determination — and feverish from a lingering chest infection similar to the one I later contracted — Ding agreed, for the sake of peace, that the expedition purse should be charged with only one third of the total cost of the New Zealand support team, that he would pay the rest of our costs out of his share of any expedition profits. Ding told me later that he had agreed to this in the hope that it might remove the last cause of friction between him and Pete. What it did instead was establish an undesirable precedent for the future. It encouraged Pete to think that he could reopen any part of the expedition agreement which he might find irksome.

SP and Tashi found our capacity to argue in public about such matters quite extraordinary. I am sure they never got used to it. Then, on a more prosaic level, they had our style of mountain travel to adjust to as well. The Indian tradition is that of the grand expedition — a sort of royal progress with cooks, porters, bearers, three cooked meals a day and folding camp furniture.

Tashi, I am sure, had roughed it in the hills more than any of us, but SP found it hard to adjust to the fact that we expedition members did our own cooking, morning and night (meagre meals they were too), and lunched off biscuits, cheese and cold water. As a result of this style of travel we covered two or three times more ground than a big party would have. And yet, at this stage, I doubt that any of us really appreciated just how much further our traverse had to go. SP got the distinct feeling from this first trek that he had been let in for a year of extreme hunger and discomfort, and would be required, as he put it, to live like a lizard, under rocks. Maybe he wasn't far wrong, as things turned out.

SP had another justifiable complaint. He was a vegetarian and, without forewarning, we had not been able to cater well for him. He had had to subsist on the first stage through Sikkim on a rather boring diet of plain noodles and macaroni cheese after our rice and fresh vegetables were finished on the walk in. I know expeditions that have failed with less provocation than this.

But there must have been something attractive about our progress. The traverse team, Ding, Pete and Tashi, arrived back in Darjeeling on 5 March. SP and Tashi conferred and were, for whatever reasons, prepared to continue with us. I had felt at the time that there was a real risk that they would withdraw there, making our chances of success on the traverse even less likely.

On 6 March the five of us took a bus to Nepal, crossing the border at Kaka Bhitta where we got the problematical entry stamp in our passports. On the Nepal side of the border we separated into two parties again. Ding, Pete and Tashi set off by road for Ilam, to pick up their route as close to the Sikkim border as they could. The traverse line would then take them up the Barun valley, past the Makalu base camp and then westward over high passes into the Everest region.

SP and I took another bus westward for 18 hours into Kathmandu, to rejoin Ann and Corrina. My reunion with Ann was highly emotional. It was exciting to be together again, elated, swapping experiences, touching each other once more. It took a while to get around to the question of why she'd decided not to come to Sikkim. 'Decided!' Ann exploded at me. 'What do you mean?' As it turned out Ding had, on virtually the last day before their planned departure for Darjeeling, suddenly called the three of them together for a meeting. He said that he and Corrina had decided that Corrina would stay in Kathmandu and he had decided that the expedition would not need Ann's help either for the Sikkim stage of the traverse. She tried to change his mind but there was nothing she could do, since Ding was the leader, with final say. So, when Ann heard that we had needed to hire a porter in Sikkim, her response was predictable and not altogether quiet.

'You mean I missed out on trekking in Sikkim, and the expedition had to pay for my accommodation here in Kathmandu, and then had to pay for a porter to join the support team to replace us?' We changed the topic a few hours later and I heard what she and Corrina had been up to.

Corrina and Ann had finished in rapid time the tasks Ding had left them to do in Kathmandu. Realising that there wasn't much point hanging around waiting for us, they decided they could at least be the first of the expedition to trek in Nepal. On 7 March, when SP and I arrived, they had just returned from a round-trip in the Helambu and Malemchi districts north-east of Kathmandu.

Our base in Kathmandu was an apartment owned by the Himalayan Trust, which Pete's father had set up to undertake aid work in the Sherpa region of Nepal. We had a week of chores to do in Kathmandu before setting off for our first resupply point in Nepal. SP, Corrina, Ann and I shared out the many small tasks and took it in turn to do a bit of sightseeing. Since Ann and I spent more time alone together during our time in Kathmandu, we have written this account of our activities only. SP and Corrina were at Dilli Bazaar too, but there was so much to do and see that we tended to meet up only at dinner time.

When Ann, Corrina and Ding had first come to Kathmandu they arrived, like SP and I, at the central bus station. I had never seen chaos like it. As I was to discover during the next few months, this chaos was more apparent than real.

4. Kathmandu

Our bus turns down off the road into an enclosed compound, 100 metres square and absolutely choked with buses. We climb down stiffly into a sea of dark mud. Ragged porters and rickshaw walas besiege us, wanting to unload our bags, offering us hotel rooms and hash. 'No, thank you, we have a place to stay,' Ann says firmly and they lose interest in us immediately, passing on to more likely customers.

Ann clambers up the metal frame at the rear of the bus along with the porters and villagers, all keen to remove their baggage from the roof. She lowers our rucksacks and kitbags one by one. I find a dry space for the pile and guard them until she gets down. Then I go off to find a taxi that can take this much luggage.

When I return with a driver, Ann is gaily chatting with a couple of rickshaw walas. The pile of bright new looking gear had convinced them that we must be yet more foreigners going to climb Mount Everest.

Our taxi is a small, nearly new, Japanese car. Despite its newness it takes two

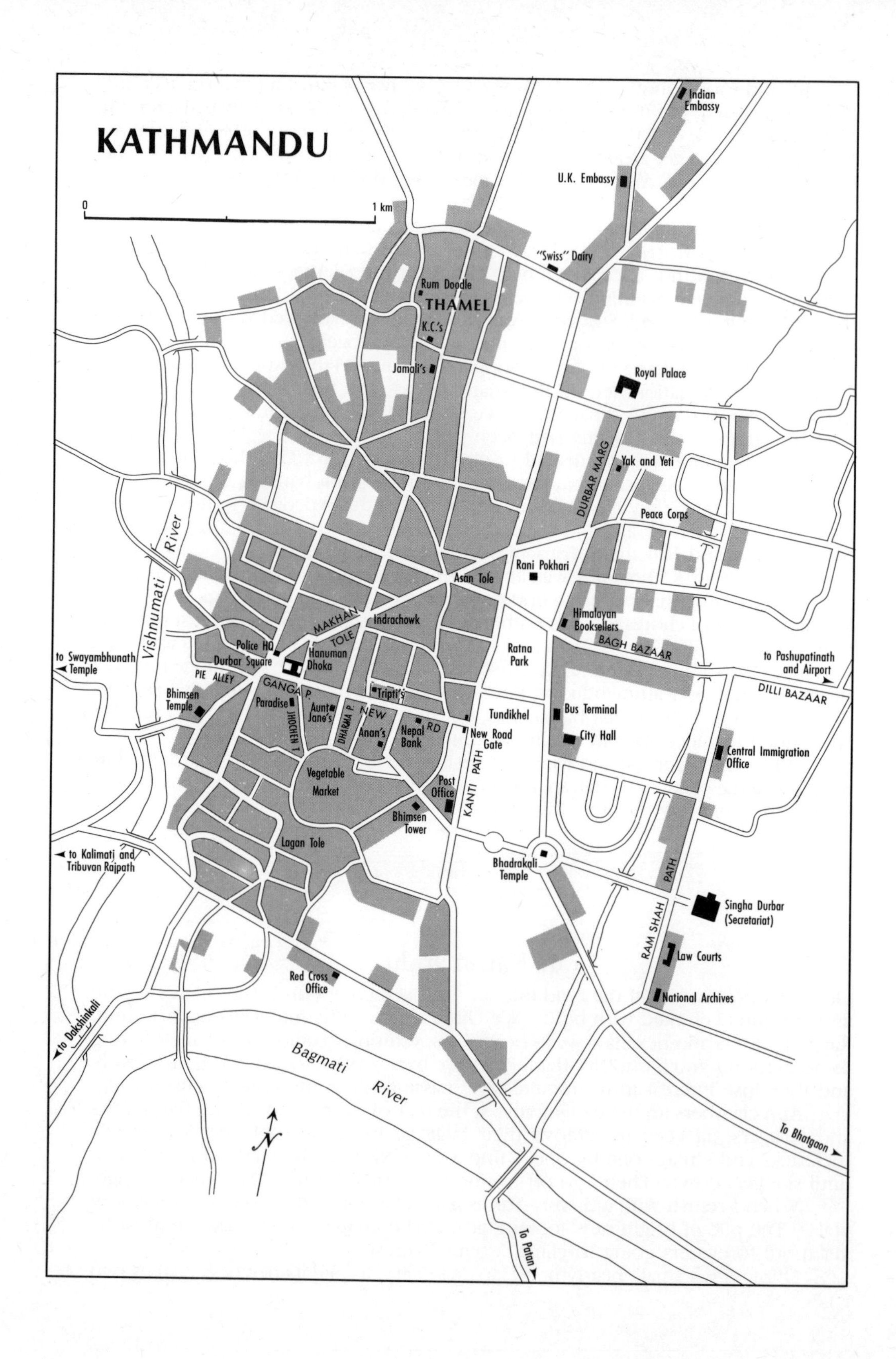

KATHMANDU
0
1 km
Indian Embassy
U.K. Embassy
"Swiss" Dairy
Rum Doodle
THAMEL
K.C.'s
Jamali's
Royal Palace
DURBAR MARG
Yak and Yeti
Peace Corps
Vishnumati River
Rani Pokhari
Asan Tole
MAKHAN TOLE
Indrachowk
Himalayan Booksellers
BAGH BAZAAR
Police HQ
Durbar Square
Hanuman Dhoka
Ratna Park
to Swayambhunath Temple
to Pashupatinath and Airport
PIE ALLEY
GANGA P.
Tripti's
DILLI BAZAAR
Bhimsen Temple
Paradise
Aunt Jane's
NEW RD
Tundikhel
Bus Terminal
JHOCHEN T.
DHARMA P.
Anan's
Nepal Bank
New Road Gate
City Hall
Central Immigration Office
Vegetable Market
Post Office
KANTI PATH
Bhimsen Tower
Lagan Tole
to Kalimati and Tribuvan Rajpath
Bhadrakali Temple
PATH
RAM SHAH
Singha Durbar (Secretariat)
Law Courts
Red Cross Office
National Archives
to Dakshinkali
Bagmati River
N
To Bhatgaon
To Patan

Rotis cooked by the roadside are available at five for a rupee on the porter route south from Okhaldhunga to the east-west Nepal highway.

SP tries a 60kg load of wool for size. 'Super porters' carry these double-size loads for double pay.

Stones hold down the rough wood shingles of this house at Bharadang village in the upper Marsyangdi valley.

Cotton-clad porters, waiting for work at Sete village in eastern Nepal, rest in a balanced position upon their feet – the most comfortable position in a society where chairs are scarce.

Sumi, a Sherpani from Sete village, carries home a tumpline load of prickly oak foliage as fodder for her family's goats.

Khunde village after a late spring snowfall. Namche Bazaar lies over the wooded ridge in the background, opposite the steep north face of Kongde Ri (6187m) on the skyline.

Ann shelters from the sun at a chiya shop in Shivalaya village, eastern Nepal.

Thatchers in the Marsyangdi valley repair the roofs of Khudi village before the onset of the monsoon rains.

attempts to negotiate the muddy ramp which leads up into the street. The driver pilots us casually into the teeming traffic, a torrent of buses, trucks, bullock drays, rickshaws and cyclists. In a few minutes we turn off from the cobbles of Dilli Bazaar, pass through a gate manned by a *chowkidar* and come to rest in a peaceful courtyard.

Five or six houses share this entrance and ours is the closest to the street. It is a white concrete house of European design, two-storeyed, set back in a well-tended garden, fringed by trees.

Friends have arranged the loan of this apartment for us, close to the centre of Kathmandu. We are to store expedition equipment here and use it as a base between treks. But we did not expect it to be quite so grand. I am conscious of how travel-worn and dishevelled we are as we carry our bags up the path from the taxi to the verandah.

The door is opened for us by a tall slender man in his late twenties, dressed all in white with a shaven head. 'My name is Sri,' he says, pressing his palms together and bowing his head to us in 'Namaste'. We return his 'Namaste' and explain who we are. He nods shyly. 'Yes, we have been expecting you. Please come in.'

He ushers us in through the screen door, into a cool shaded sitting room with comfortable cane furniture. It is full of colourful rugs and loaded bookshelves, a haven after our long bus journey.

'You must be very tired,' he says. 'Will you take tea?' We collapse into the waiting armchairs.

'We would love a cup of tea.'

Sri serves it to us almost immediately, from china cups and saucers on a tray with teapot and milk jug. He explains that we will have the use of this downstairs apartment. He is responsible for this part of the house and will cook for us if we wish. He takes us round, showing us the cool white-washed bedrooms, the bathroom with its 'real' toilet and bath and shower. A faint scent of roses and jasmine adds the final touch of peaceful luxury to our temporary home. There are flower boxes outside each bedroom window as well as bright flower beds at the front of the house.

'Who looks after the garden, Sri?' Ann asks.

'That is my responsibility also, memsahib.'

'Well, it's beautiful,' she says. 'I haven't seen such a lovely garden for a long time.' Sri's eyes light up.

'Thank you, memsahib. I am always happy in the garden.'

Ann nobly lets me have the first bath while she goes through our bags for clean clothes.

'How do you feel?' she asks, when we are both washed and changed.

'Okay. Why?'

'I just wondered if you'd like to go for a look at the Shivaratri festival that we read about. I heard from the rickshaw walas that it's on today. I feel too excited just to catch up on sleep.'

Sri gives us a vague idea of where the festival is held and how to get there but it soon becomes apparent that directions are unnecessary. All Nepal must be heading the same way for we are quickly caught up in a swelling crowd of pilgrims making their way to Pashupatinath temple.

There are *sadhus,* the itinerant holy men of Hinduism, barefoot wanderers with matted hair, faces smeared with ashes, and a twist of orange cloth around their loins. Each carries the same meagre possessions — a small brass pot for alms, tongs for the temple fires, a sealed brass vessel of holy water. Apparently oblivious of the turmoil around them, the blaring of vehicle horns and the passage of residents about their daily business, these *sadhus* stride along the narrow footpaths, almost fierce in their intensity.

Women form the bulk of the crowd and they have that same intense look of expectation on their faces. Many of them are orthodox Hindu Shiva worshippers from the south of India, lean and dark. Their saris and bangles flash pink, yellow, cerise and lime. Calico-wrapped bundles and brass water jars balance easily on their heads. Only the younger women raise an occasional hand to steady their load.

This festive ceremony is to greet the first moonless night in the first month of the Hindu New Year. Many pilgrims walk from India, journeying for weeks towards Pashupatinath. The Hindus believe that past evil deeds or instances of caste-pollution can be cleansed through ritual immersion in holy rivers or at other sites of religious importance. The Ganga (or Ganges river) in India is the most important of these but Pashupatinath, on the banks of the Bagmati river near Kathmandu, is another. Tonight the prayers and offerings to the *lingam* and images of Shiva will continue until dawn, as worshippers pray for an improved incarnation in their next life.

The push and jostle of the crowd on the footpath ease for a moment and in a temporary lull we come out above the Bagmati river. Further progress is barred by the teeming throng gathered along its banks. The number of people is staggering — thousands and thousands of them; every hill and hollow is packed with worshippers.

I catch a fleeting glimpse of pilgrims immersing themselves in the shallows of the river, before we are swept on again, swallowed up in the ebb and flow of people. Every person around us is intent on involvement in these rituals that we cannot see and certainly know nothing about. The temple might as well be on the moon for all the prospect we have of getting to it and finding out what is happening.

Giving up our attempts to get closer, Ann and I push our way back to the outskirts of the crowd, to hover irresolutely for a few minutes more. Buses and vans pull up, overflowing with people who further swell the crowd. It seems suddenly imprudent, possibly offensive, for us to jostle our way into this throng, merely in the hope of a view of the temple or a photograph perhaps. We came here on an impulse, in the hope of seeing something exciting and new, a spectacle, and this expectation has set us apart from the people with whom we are rubbing shoulders.

The crowd itself is the spectacle we should be looking at: the families settling down to lunch on the pavement, the hawkers selling bamboo whistles and plastic multi-coloured windmills, the mix of faces and fashions, the chatter of many tongues. These are the accessible events of Shivaratri for us, but Ann and I have been struggling to see past them, to some central event that is possibly not there at all.

The fatigue from our bus journey begins to weigh upon me and I realise I am too tired to go on in this crowd. 'Let's go home,' I suggest and we turn back towards Dilli Bazaar.

Early the next morning we go out to buy some yoghurt from the bazaar for breakfast and have a chance to take stock of the neighbourhood. Dilli Bazaar is lent a flavour of antiquity by its cobbled roadway and tall narrow three-storey houses. Most of the houses are built entirely of wood, nearly black with age. Row upon row of tiny wooden apartment balconies and verandahs are lavishly embellished with intricate carving. Even the pillars that support each storey have been decorated with inlaid tiles, mosaic or, occasionally, carvings in stone.

In a gap between two rows of wooden houses a new building is springing up. On the footpath in front of it a youth is making concrete by diverting the flow of water from the gutter to moisten his sandy mixture. He then scoops it up on his broken shovel-blade and tosses it neatly up through the open wall to the first floor. There two plasterers hurriedly smoothe the paste over freshly laid brick walls.

I see that some of the rear apartments of the building are already occupied.

Bright sky-blue shutters against the plain grey of the new concrete building provide a happy contrast to the rich dark brown of the older wooden houses next door. New and old buildings alike sport flowering plants, red geraniums and marigolds, nodding from window boxes. Colourful household washing, bright sari-lengths and hanks of wool, also drape these upper floors.

At street-level most of the houses are subdivided into tiny cubicles, hardly more than a metre wide, rented out to craftspeople and shopkeepers. In rapid succession we pass a cobbler, a draper and two tailors. A caged lark whistles and chirrups above the hum of a treadle sewing machine. Next door is a fruit and vegetable shop. A tall young man waits for business, sitting cross-legged on a raised platform with his meagre stock arranged around him. His brass balance-scales are suspended from the rafters within easy reach. There are three photography studios in less than a hundred metres, 'hole in the wall' shops, each with a few folds of black cloth to curtain off the darkroom in the rear. Fading black and white portraits peel back from the windows — school photos, sports teams, family groups, all familiar genres.

On the corner, past a jeweller's store, is a tiny grocery. Sweets and bread, biscuits and soap powders, bottles of coloured drink and tins of food are stacked precariously on shelves reaching to the roof. Most of the floor space is taken up by old kerosene tins with the tops sliced off. These hold green and yellow *dahl,* brown lentils, two grades of white rice and coarse ground rock salt. In one corner a yellowing old refrigerator stands silent, packed with foil-wrapped pats of butter, trays of eggs, cheeses and earthenware bowls of *dahi* or yoghurt.

'Not going this morning,' the plump shopkeeper apologises, waving a hand at the fridge. 'No electricity, many cuts. Not good.'

'The *dahi* would still be fresh though, wouldn't it?' Ann asks.

'Oh yes, yes, very good *dahi.* Swiss dairy *dahi.* Every day coming,' she assures us.

In a mixture of English, hand signals and Hindi we arrange for some *dahi* to be kept for us each night. We buy one large flat bowl of it now for our breakfast. The grocer sees us off home with a cheerful 'Namaste'.

After breakfast we set out to explore Kathmandu. Sri reminds us to set our watches forward. So conscious is Nepal of the presence of India to the south, that Nepal rather ostentatiously keeps its time 10 minutes ahead of Indian time. Sri says we will need bicycles for exploring and that the best place to hire them is at the Durbar Square end of New Road. It is a 20 minute walk along Dilli Bazaar and Bagh Bazaar into town, so we make our first stop at a bookseller at the end of Bagh Bazaar in the hope of buying a map.

The bookshop is painted white, immaculate, and has one side open to the street. The rest of the shop is filled, ceiling to floor, with an impressive range of books. Ann asks for a map while I browse through some of the stock — mountaineering books, history books, wildlife studies and fiction by authors from all over the world. I pick out a slim volume.

'Ann, here's a Nepali phrase book that looks okay.' The owner of the shop has spread a selection of maps on the counter for Ann to choose from but he turns, at my voice, to look at the phrase book.

'It is the best of a bad bunch,' he jokes, 'like my trekking maps.' I glance at him, with some surprise at the possibility that this small bookshop proprietor might also be a publisher. He looks to be a Newar, one of the most common tribal groups in Kathmandu, possibly in his early thirties, slightly built and dressed in neat western clothing, not much different from the other merchants we have seen so far.

He explains that he himself has drawn several of the maps he stocks. 'So many foreigners came to my shop asking for trekking maps, that I decided to try one trek with a company to see what it was all about. I enjoyed it so much that I have since walked most of the major trekking routes with that same company. But there is always a problem. If there is a map available, it has the names wrong or the villages in the wrong spot or it forgets to tell you about the hills. I decided I could do better myself.'

He shows Ann a map of the Marsyangdi/Kali Gandaki trekking area, around the Annapurna massif west of Kathmandu. 'This one I made. You know the area?'

'We'll be trekking there in a month,' she tells him. 'So far I've only read about it.'

'You will enjoy it,' he responds. 'Next for me is eastern Nepal. That will be for nearly a month and maybe I will make a new map there too.'

Ann goes on to tell him about our role as support crew to Ding's and Pete's expedition, describing the traverse to him.

'Well, you may be surprised again but I am knowing Peter Hillary too. He used to come in here sometimes with his family when he was just a boy. I have even ordered some copies of his first book to sell in my shop. That one is about climbing in Nepal too, but this new traverse, it sounds different. I think it will be a wonderful journey,' he says. Then, on impulse, he hands Ann one of his trekking maps. 'Take it with you,' he says. 'I would like to know the corrections; it needs many! You two will be in a good position to find them.' Then, unselfconsciously, he signs it for us 'with all the best compliments from the publisher, Madhab Lal Maharjan'.

Opposite Madhab's bookshop the cobbles of Bagh Bazaar intersect with the Durbar Marg, a busy four lane highway that stretches broad and flat to the gate of the King's Palace, a kilometre away to the north. A traffic woman in a black uniform waves the traffic to a halt at her roundabout and with a blast on her whistle signals to us to cross.

Our new map marks a short cut to New Road through Ratna Park, a large grassy *maidan* between Durbar Marg and the Kanti Path (the King's Way), the two main city streets. Shoe-shine and shoe-repair boys line the foot track, each one with a low wooden box containing tins of Kiwi polish, a few tools, strips of tyre-rubber and a few pieces of leather. Flocks of piebald goats are tethered to the railings by the Kanti Path, chewing leaves under the appraising gaze of prospective buyers. Beyond them, at the southern end of the park, squads of Nepali soldiers are drilling, rank after rank of green-clad troops parading to shouted commands.

We dash across another busy roundabout towards the tall wide arch which spans the beginning of New Road. Its pillars support small images of Ganesh, the elephant-headed Hindu god, and the lintel has what appear to be the heads of growling Buddhist dragons skulking at each end of the beam. We enter New Road through a pedestrian passageway at the side of the gate.

Durbar Square is a bewildering area of temples and palaces with a few shops on its outskirts; in front of these shops there are ranks of dozens of bicycles, heavy leather-seated steeds. A few are blue, some green, but most are black: 'Flying Duck', 'Buffalo' and 'Hero' brand, all made in India. At one shop a handpainted sign advertises the going rate 'bisycle *(sic)* FOR Hire Five rupees per day'.

We check the bicycles carefully and eliminate a large number before we find two that have seats, pedals and handlebars solidly attached and in the right places, a wheel-lock and key, a noisy bell and brakes that work. When we make our choice we are taken to Bhaikagi Sowal's to write our names, addresses and passport numbers in his 'Bicycles Hired' book. Bhaikagi runs a chemist supply business at the back of Durbar Square. As a sideline he employs a young fellow to act as general handyman around the shop and maintain a small fleet of bicycles for hire to tourists.

Having completed the business formalities of hiring us bicycles, Bhaikagi invites us to take tea with him and his friend, Bal Krisna. Bhaikagi sends his boy for *char chiya,* four teas. Bal Krisna sits, puffy-eyed and grey-faced, behind the jumble of paper work and empty cartons on Bhaikagi's office desk and mournfully informs us that he has hepatitis, 'very bad'. He has not been able to eat for three days on account of the pain in his stomach.

'Have you been to the hospital?' Ann asks.

'There is no need.' Bal Krisna produces a brown glass vial from his shirt pocket, 'See, I have some excellent Tibetan medicine.' Ann tries not to look too dubious as Bhaikagi assures us, 'There is really no need to worry.'

The tea is delicious, sweet as usual, but with a hint of spice, possibly cardamom.

'If you would like to buy it for yourselves any time, just ask for "special *chiya*". Not *chai,* of course, for *chai* is Hindi,' says Bhaikagi. 'You have learned some Hindi, I think, for I heard you speaking it to my boy.'

'Yes,' Ann replies, 'but just this morning we bought a Nepali phrase book. I haven't had a chance to use it yet. Is Nepali much different from Hindi?'

'There are basic similarities, but you will find the people do not like to use Hindi here. We like to keep our own language. But if you can speak some Hindi you will find it easy to speak some Nepali.'

Bhaikagi notes our map of the city and tells us that it is a good one. 'It will help you with seeing the main sights,' he tells us as we take our leave to go and have lunch. 'If you need any help, just come by and ask me. I can arrange a guide or I will take you myself. It will be my pleasure.'

It is a long time since I last pedalled a bicycle and I wobble precariously over the cobblestones, weaving in and out between rickshaws and porters, ferociously jangling my bell at unwary pedestrians. We turn down a side street and spot a sign saying 'Paradise Restaurant'. Having heard much from other travellers of the wonderful food in Kathmandu we decide that this sounds a good place for lunch. Guide books wax lyrical about the range of food that can be bought in Kathmandu for only a few rupees per meal — Indian, French, American, Russian, Tibetan, Chinese, Italian — all nationalities are catered for by restaurants and street-side stalls that line the main streets of old Kathmandu.

As we wobble to a halt two young boys approach us, offering drugs. 'Cocaine, cocaine, maybe you want some good hash? Charas, man, we got the best charas.' They tug at our hands, gaily inviting us upstairs in the next alleyway to meet their *dajiu,* their 'elder brother', who will supply us with whatever we ask.

We shake them off our hands with a smile, then park and lock our bicycles on the sidewalk. Two of the small alcove shops between us and the restaurant sell drug equipment: hash pipes and fancy silver cigarette-holders, licorice and chocolate flavoured rolling-papers, ornate tiny spoons for the sniffing of powders, all labelled and priced. This preoccupation with the paraphernalia of drug use is a purely Western trait. Only very rarely have we seen local people indulging. The stall keepers, whom we saw on the railway station platform in India, have proven the exception rather than the rule so far.

Paradise Restaurant is half underground, right at the end of the lane. Like many of the more impressive restaurants that we've heard about on New Road, this one serves European food. We both have a big bowl of spinach soup, then order a stack of pancakes with honey and yoghurt and finish off with peanut brownies. What a treat!

As we eat we discuss our tasks for the afternoon. The first priority is to apply for our trekking permits, so we need to go to the Central Immigration Office. Ann checks the map for directions.

'Ah,' she says, 'that explains the kids outside. This area is called Jhochen Tole. Look, the notes say it's usually called Freak Street, the most famous hippy street in the world in the flower-power days. According to this, the drug trade is a lot less blatant than it used to be.'

'Well,' I reply, 'it must have been quite something when it was blatant.'

The Central Immigration Office is a pale yellow building on Ram Shah Path, just around the corner from Dilli Bazaar. Leaving our bicycles in the rack outside we go up worn stone stairs to the first floor. Here we make enquiries about trekking permits and visas.

The Nepali entry visa allows a foreigner to stay in Kathmandu, Pokhara and just a few other places for one week. It is not a permit to wander all over the country. To leave these specified areas special trekking permits have to be obtained. These can be issued for any of the major trekking routes but are usually only granted for the period of time it would take a normal trekker to do that route.

All foreigners must possess either a current tourist visa or trekking permit. The fee for a trekking permit is less per day than the fee for a visa, and so many people have been taking out trekking permits and then remaining in the city. In response the authorities have conducted dawn raids on tourist hotels, checking that the occupants hold the correct papers. Those who are caught have to pay the difference for the whole period of the trekking permit.

Ann and I are given application forms and asked to fill them in. We each hand over a passport photo with our completed applications and have our personal details copied from our passports. 'Which trek do you wish to take?' the officer asks us.

'To Namche Bazaar,' I reply, 'but we do not wish to return by the east-west route. We wish to return south, travelling all the way to the flat *terai* before coming back to Kathmandu.'

'Ah, that will be a good trek,' says the officer. 'You will see much more of our country. I will make a special note because this rubber stamp for Namche does not list all the police checkposts you will need clearance for. I will have to add some.' He consults a large wall map. 'You will go through Phaphlu, Beding and Okhaldhunga. Not many foreigners trek that route. But the *terai* is not too hot yet, and you will enjoy seeing the forests.'

'Namaste!' A young immigration official has come up behind us, and greets Ann.

'Sanjay, namaste, what a surprise,' she says. 'What are you doing here?'

'Transfer,' he says, grinning happily.

Ann introduces us, explaining that she had met Sanjay at the border crossing at Birganj on her way to Nepal with Ding and Corrina. 'It was really late at night but Sanjay was up in the office still, playing chess with a friend. He interrupted his game to stamp our passports.' She turns to Sanjay. 'We talked for a long time while we waited for a bus from there, and you mentioned that you might be transferring to Kathmandu, Sanjay. Time to get married, you said.'

He laughs. 'A very distant town, Birganj. Here I can meet people. Perhaps you and Mr Douglas would like to go out and see some sights with me? I have a holiday on Saturday.'

'That sounds great,' I reply.

'Yep,' says Ann, 'we should have most of the day free. We plan to start our trek on Monday so we should have finished most of our jobs by Saturday.'

'Your permit will be ready tomorrow,' the first officer tells us. 'You may collect it after midday.'

In the evening we go out to dinner in Thamel, a northern suburb of Kathmandu with cheap restaurants and modest hotels where many trekkers stay. On the way into Thamel we cycle past a tall old gum tree festooned with black bats. It takes a moment to realise what the small angular, neatly draped bundles hanging in rows along each branch are. The bats share their roost with graceful white cattle egrets and a flock of big black crows that squawk rudely as they clap their wings in delight over the pickings in sidewalk rubbish-heaps.

This northern area has many trekking supply shops run by Sherpas and Tibetans. Each of them displays used expedition equipment such as boots, packs, stoves, frying pans, down clothing and sleeping bags. These are for hire as well as for sale. The prices seem very cheap but I still don't buy. I have enough equipment for now and I don't want to risk running out of money. There are too many months yet to go.

Along with trekking supplies, the narrow streets of Thamel are dotted with souvenir shops. The souvenirs are invariably described as 'genuine' Tibetan artefacts or 'antique' jewellery. Antique or not, the materials are beautiful and we stop to look. There are hand-tooled silver prayer wheels, brass bells, bone ornaments and the complementary colours of turquoise and coral, amber and jade in jewellery. Some vendors have black and white *yin-yang* signs made of bone. These are a simple yet elegant Buddhist symbol of the spiritual balance of positive and negative forces in the world. Another shop has sheets of almost transparent paper, hand-made from the bark of the daphne bush, plus carved bronze statues, anklets, silver rings and nose-studs.

There are homespun carpets too which one enterprising shop owner has hoisted up on racks in the street. The striking colours of Indian dyes enhance traditional Tibetan designs, bold geometric patterns etched deeply into the thick pile of the wool. My favourite is a dark almost midnight blue carpet, with a narrow border and central motifs in crimson and gold. There are a few smaller ones, seat-squabs possibly, which Ann prefers, woven with designs of dragons and yaks in the muted creams and browns of natural fleeces.

K.C.'s restaurant in Thamel has a huge blackboard menu in multicoloured chalks that covers half a wall in the main room. Under the grand heading SUPER FANTASTIC FOODS is a list that includes pancakes with lemon and banana, French onion and tomato soups, filet mignon and Wiener schnitzel, Swiss rosti and pizza, then 'succulent salads' and 'ambrosial drinks'. I wonder to myself if it could beat 'Paradise's' cooking.

The electricity is off tonight in Thamel, owing to demand far exceeding supply. Sri told us that it goes off in each suburb for six out of every 24 hours on average, and will continue to do so until the next of Nepal's hydro-electric schemes is commissioned. This lack of electricity is something everyone seems used to and we dine by candlelight while the cooks work over gas primus cookers. A parade of sizzling steaks and pizzas keeps on coming out of the kitchen.

We give our order to the cheeky young waiter, a boy of about ten, swamped in an over-sized butcher's apron. K.C. comes over to our table and joins us for a *lassi,* a salted drink made from yoghurt or whey.

'Ke garné?' he asks with a flourish, translating for us in the same breath, 'What to do?'

'Lots', says Ann emphatically, pointing at his menu, 'especially eating.'

'Ah, yes,' he smiles, 'but wait one moment — I have a saying that I like to tell newcomers. You listen.' He stands by Ann's chair and assumes a dramatic pose. ' "No money, no honey, no wife, no children; no problem what to do in Kathmandu." Now don't ever complain to me that you two are bored here, please. Life costs nothing to enjoy.' Our order arrives. 'Ah,' he says, 'eat up, you need the strength for your trekking.'

'Ke garne' has become virtually the stock response to problems in Kathmandu. The phrase is embroidered on many of the jackets and shirts for sale in tourist haunts, and we constantly hear it in reply to enquiries, usually when nothing can be done. If one wants tickets for a bus and they are sold out, the ticket seller may shrug expressively and say 'Ke garne', meaning not 'what to do?' but 'what can be done?' The answer is usually 'nothing'.

We enjoy these few days in Kathmandu. They are undoubtedly a peaceful and idyllic interlude compared to most of the rest of this year. Sri brings tea to our bedside at about seven and by the time we are dressed and washed he has a massive breakfast on the table. Wholemeal bread for toast, with peanut butter bought at 'Aunt Jane's' restaurant and honey from a trekking supplies shop in Thamel; then a two-egg omelette, with lashings of garlic in deference to Ann's belief that garlic will be a good aid to acclimatisation. We have mangoes and bananas and tangerines that we buy from the young green-grocer in Dilli Bazaar, along with the bowls of *dahi* saved for us by the grocer on the corner. The earthenware *dahi* bowls are not returnable and Sri uses them for plant cuttings from the garden. Breakfast is followed with endless cups of tea made to our taste, without sugar.

Mornings are cool enough to take our paperwork out on to the verandah where, with Corrina and SP, we talk our way through long lists of estimates and supplies for each of the planned Nepal resupply treks. How much food can we expect to find along the way? Will we need our tent? Stove? What first-aid equipment? Will we need any climbing gear? How much expedition equipment will the traverse party need? Will that mean we'll need a porter? What sort of clothing is required? Do we need more maps? How much film will we use in six weeks? Which lenses? The answers are different for each trek. Three out of the four resupplies in Nepal are a long way from the road, which suits us just fine. The more ground we cover the better.

Sri, our faithful house-servant, wears a small flat Nepali *topi* and under it his head is shaven. The *topi* is white, like the rest of his clothing.

'Why do you always wear white, Sri?' Ann asks him one morning as he brings us a cup of tea on the verandah.

'Ah, memsahib, my mother died,' he replies. 'It was not long ago. All this year I wear only white and I keep my head shaven. It is the custom.'

'I am sorry, Sri,' Ann replies.

'Well, we are all going off from this life to the next sometime, memsahib. I am doing special *pujas* and ceremonies during this year also; they help.'

Sri introduces us to the other servants from upstairs: Ram Krisna, the round-faced cook, who brings us his latest batch of *achaar* or chutney, and sweet 'biscoots' to taste; Kumar, the tall sombre looking clerk; and Krisnaman, who serves the drinks and walks 'Tigger', the legendary and ferocious Lhasa apso lap-dog who rules the neighbourhood from his spy post upstairs. Where 'Tigger' goes, frayed ankles are sure to follow.

There are a few items from our resupply list that Ann and I have had difficulty locating: contact adhesive glue, flea powder and supplementary dried foods are the most elusive of these. Ram Krisna offers to come into the old city with us to help look for them. He thinks that we might get dried foods in the 'Fresh House' and he shows us the way.

He takes us past the main vegetable market near the post office. Aubergines and radishes, cauliflowers and artichokes, sweet potatoes and clumps of garlic, red onions and magnificent long marrows, green beans, corn and peppers are available in profusion, arranged in neat piles and rows under woven grass sunshades.

Next comes the butchers' lane near Dharma Path, not quite so much to our taste but definitely colourful. The joints of unidentifiable beasts are displayed on front doorsteps, and goats' heads, skinned and trimmed, are suspended in strings from the door lintels. Above the grisly blood-filled gutters rises a slender white tower, seemingly of marble and close to 60 metres high.

'That is Bhimsen watchtower,' Ram Krisna tells us. 'We are not needing it much now but, before, it was used all the time. Then there were always wars between Kathmandu and the other cities of the valley — Patan and Bhatgaon. From the top the army could spy upon all our enemies.'

Travelling west still, along the Dharma Path from Bhimsen tower, we come to the 'Fresh House', a store house of imported delicacies from around the world, tinned, dried and frozen — apricots and walnuts, noodles and salmon, jam and preserves. There are a few dried foods which we need and we add these to our rucksacks.

'Great, now how about plastic bags, Ram Krisna,' says Ann. 'That's something I've had no luck with at all.'

'Okay, memsahib. Plastic bags. I think on the other side of Makhan Tole there is a place.'

'All right, let's go. But on the way can you tell me what a *tole* is,' she requests.

'Certainly,' says Ram Krisna. 'A *tole* is a small community within the city. Usually there is a square at the centre and the people who live around it all belong to that *tole.* So, there is Makhan Tole, Lagan Tole, Asan Tole. But it is confusing for you, because not all areas are named that way. So, some are named as the Indians do it — as a *chauk* or bazaar.'

In Makhan Tole he shows us a wooden post into which you can hammer a nail if you want to rid yourself of toothache. The wood is almost invisible under thousands of nails. Behind it is a small gilded image of Vaisha Dev, the god of toothache. 'If the pain does not go,' Ram Krisna observes with a smile, 'there are many dentists to help you in this street.'

We finally track down plastic bags in a tiny store in Indrachowk Bazaar. Hemmed in by a long row of dressmakers and hardware suppliers is a little cubicle hardly larger than a cupboard and lined entirely with rolls of plastic in all different weights, sizes and colours.

'Could we have 20 medium-sized bags, please?' Ann indicates the approximate shape in the air.

'We are having two qualities in that size, madam, this weight and this.' The retailer points to each from his cross-legged sitting position in the centre of the cubicle. Ann chooses the heavier weight and we watch as he pulls off about 10 metres of doubled plastic from a roll and cuts it into 20 pieces of equal length.

He fumbles on the back shelf for what turns out to be a packet of matches and a candle. A young lad who squats behind him folds up about two centimetres along the bottom edge of each tube of plastic. He holds it while his master passes the lighted candle back and forth along the fold, melting the plastic just enough to seal it. A measured, practised ritual — hand-made plastic bags.

In India we grew accustomed to long waits in banks. Each branch operates an elaborate system of checks, most apparently designed to ensure the honesty of their employees. Cashing one traveller's cheque anywhere in India would often take 30 minutes. We discover that Nepal by contrast has a number of small foreign-exchange counters that give quick, accurate service. The handiest is in New Road and we go there one morning to cash a traveller's cheque each for our trekking expenses, feeling departure at last close upon us.

Ann puts her bag down beside her on a bench to sign a cheque and I watch as the teller counts out the thick pile of rupees, Rs 1190 to US$100. Then Ann counts them carefully also. The custom is to do this out loud so that everyone is satisfied that you really are getting the correct money. There can then be no criticism later. It takes a little while to count Rs 1190.

Moving aside, Ann suddenly notices with disbelief that her bag has gone. It must have dropped. No. I race out into the street but cannot recognise anyone who has been in the bank. I cannot even remember if anyone was in there with us. The teller shakes his head. He saw no one, not a thing.

Shocked and angry we search the nearest sidestreets and alleyways, over the back of rubbish heaps, gutters, hoping that the thief might have taken the valuables and discarded the rest. There wasn't much in her bag — toiletries, suncream, letter-writing kit and three of my traveller's cheques, totalling US$220, all replaceable.

If that were all, it would be nothing, but just that morning Ann had put my Sikkim diary, all 80 pages of it, in there too. She was hoping to get a chance to read it between errands. Now that is gone. I blame Ann for her carelessness and she me for not watching the bag while she was busy at the counter. We pedal home to Dilli Bazaar, furious, hot, snapping irritably at each other and yet hoping beyond hope that maybe we are only imagining it, maybe the diary is still at home, waiting for us.

Only Sri is there, seeing our distress and offering a cup of tea. My initial anger passes but a hollow, stomach-churning sense of loss remains. It will be such an effort to re-create the diary and try to remember everything that happened, everything that was so special about Sikkim. Ann is contrite, allowing me to have the last word when I am moved to recriminate once more. I decide we must act quickly to salvage what we can from the loss.

I go to the bank which holds the agency for our traveller's cheques and enquire about the procedure to get replacement cheques. First we need a form from the police to certify the theft. Police headquarters is around the back of the Hanuman Dhoka temple in Durbar Square, not far from Bhaikagi's shop.

A side-entrance and four flights of stairs bring us to an office with a sign stating 'Interpole' fixed to the door. Inside there are two hard benches, one cupboard, one official and seven foreigners, all of whom have been robbed in the last few days. The police officer on duty is only relieving; he knows the necessary forms are in the cupboard but does not know who has the keys.

Ann and I sit and wait on a hard bench, exchanging our tale of woe with the others present. A friendly German woman who is about two hours ahead of us in the queue tells us that we will need a one rupee stamp to attach to the police form. Ann offers to go to the post office to get one for me, but the German woman has a spare and gives it to us.

The permanent official arrives and apologises for any inconvenience. He explains that these thefts are most unusual for Kathmandu. Every year the ranks of those million or so pilgrims who come for Shivaratri are swelled by camp-followers of all sorts, including pickpockets and thieves. More thefts occur in Kathmandu during this three week period of Shivaratri than throughout all the rest of the year.

'It is very bad for Nepal,' says the police officer with evident sincerity. 'They give us a very bad name.' Delays are still necessary, however, for the police are bothered also by unscrupulous tourists who hide their own traveller's cheques and then report them stolen.

'Only this morning I have been detained by a search in the rooms of some of these victims and have found two of them having their cheques hidden with them in the mattress. You will understand that we must be doing our job properly.'

I had taken the precaution when we were back at Dilli Bazaar of changing into my tidiest clothes and this conservative dress, together with the vinyl camera bag slung over my shoulder, seems to have a beneficial effect. The officer decides I look like a genuine, honest tourist, not a hippy.

'And, after all, you have only lost US$220, which is not much more than nothing. You are still having most of the rest of your traveller's cheques with you and your wife. I am thinking this will be permissible.'

I get my form the next morning. Some of the travellers in that office have been waiting more than a week. Perhaps it is a coincidence, but they tend to be the ones dressed like freaks.

'Would you like to go to the Dakshinkali Temple?' Sanjay asks, when we meet him on Saturday. 'They have sacrifices there — it is a very holy place.' The excursion is all arranged. We hire a taxi and drive south from the city. Its location gives the temple its name, the Dakshin or 'southern' Kali temple. Kali is a Hindu goddess and is worshipped for her awesome and occasionally destructive powers. The site of her temple is flanked by two mountains and close up by forested hills. Our taxi parks, to wait for us, at the top of a long flight of steps that lead down to a pool where two streams meet. We watch people washing two struggling goats there in the dark water, shaded by tall over-hanging trees. 'Here the animal is prepared,' Sanjay tells us. 'First it is washed, then powders are placed on the forehead.'

A woman precedes us up a stairway on the far side, leading a dripping goat on a short length of hemp rope. Ahead is a complex of walled enclosures with a raised roof sheltering the innermost area. The roof is supported by four long leaning pillars in the form of golden snakes. A crowd bustles about the enclosures and the woman is soon lost from view. The air is full with the hubbub of conversation, the bleating of animals and the intermittent chiming of bells.

In the inner courtyard two slaughtermen are at work. They stand on a marble floor, inlaid with an intricate pattern of tiles and overlaid with a film of blood. A small family group pushes forward through the crowd with their young goat held high. The slaughterman takes it and stands facing them. The father is in the middle, mother at one side and son at the other. With a practised movement the young goat is flipped on its side and the slaughterman places his feet on its legs. Then, with a swift slice, the throat is cut and the head removed. Blood spurts strongly for a moment, then ebbs to a gentle flow. The head is swung before the main statue of Kali, the six-armed goddess, one of the consorts of Shiva, standing on a trampled male human. Blood drips from the wall and down over the statue. Offerings are placed with the head on the ground in front of the statue — hibiscus flowers, herbs, small bowls of *dahl* and sugar cane, a scattering of rice.

The slaughterman passes on to the next worshippers, moving easily in and out of the crowd. Not only goats are being sacrificed. There are chickens, ducks and lambs. Beggars wait on the outskirts, hoping that a morsel of flesh will be spared them from this sacrificial bounty.

I have seen enough and at my suggestion we go back to the entry area. There are *chiya* shops here and we take tea beneath a large sign which advises us, in both Nepali and English, to 'beware of pickpocketer'.

'Are there such sacrifices in your country?' Sanjay asks.

'No', Ann shakes her head. 'They're described early on in the Bible, but they're not part of Christian worship.'

Sanjay nods. 'That is what I thought. Many foreigners come here but some of them find it distasteful.' He sips his *chiya*. 'Of course, for us it is very holy. The sacrifice is costly and there is merit in that. But also, we believe that there is, what is the English — reincarnation?' Ann nods. 'Yes, I thought so — so that the poor soul trapped in the sacrificed animal gets another birth — another chance to be re-born as a human.'

About halfway back to Kathmandu we are delayed by a traffic accident and wait while the road ahead is cleared. After a time soldiers permit us to drive forward and we slowly pass the spot where two heavily laden Tata trucks have collided. The wrecks are off to the side of the road. Blood covers the bonnet of one truck and patches of it have splashed on the road. 'This sort of sacrifice is more common in our country,' I tell Sanjay. 'To the god of transportation.' He nods uncertainly. I am afraid he thinks I am making fun of him.

Before we leave Kathmandu we need booster inoculations against hepatitis. No one really knows whether the drug, gamma globulin, works or not, but experienced travellers maintain that it lessens the symptoms of hepatitis — should you catch it — to the level of a mild influenza. The Kalimatic Clinic, staffed mainly by the wives of members of the Diplomatic Corps, is recommended to us as the best place to go. We cycle there on one of our last days in Kathmandu, to be inoculated with decidedly professional dispatch. Then Ann spoils the effect by collapsing to the floor as she turns to leave. The nurses help me to pick her up and lay her on a bench.

'Did she have any lunch?' the nurse asks as we bend over her. I try to remember. 'No, she didn't have time.'

'There is nothing to worry about, then,' she reassures me. 'This happens quite often.'

Ann comes to while we are talking. 'Oh no, I didn't really faint, did I? I've never done that before. I don't even mind injections,' she protests from the bench. She looks decidedly relieved when the nurse assures her that it is just because she came out here without having had enough to eat.

'What a weakling I felt,' she mutters, after a rest, when she is allowed to take the risk of cycling home.

On the way back we get a tantalising glimpse of the mountains. The peaks are usually hidden from view by the wall of the Kathmandu valley. It is difficult to judge distances in the clear air and the peaks could be many days' walk away. Yet, even at this distance, they fill a broad segment of the horizon, miniature snowy peaks to the north-east and a huge jagged black rock ridge, looming due north. Its summit must be close to 5000 metres. The black rock is scarred with gullies, marked by thin lines of old winter snow.

I take Ann for a late lunch at 'Anan's' where they have freshly made vegetable spring rolls. Afterwards we cycle home through narrow streets in Lagan Tole. We hear snatches of music from open shop fronts. Sometimes a Hindi movie-score or sitar music, but often it is Western music. Ann stops to see if she can identify some rock music but, laughing, pedals on.

'The lyrics seem to be in Japanese,' she says.

The streets become narrower. We pass through a square where potters are working with small wheels, flat on the ground in front of them, rotated by foot pressure. Some are turning out row after row of small eating plates and bowls. Others are specialising in ornate terracotta work, clay statues and fanciful garden ornaments — lions, rhinos and elephants with open backs in which a herb garden could be planted: they are attractive and cost only a few rupees each, but are too fragile to survive shipping home to New Zealand.

On the steps of a small temple three women arrange strips of cloth, embroidered in fiery oranges and reds and dotted with small appliqueed mirrors.

Back home again, our last task is to stuff additional down into our sleeping bags. They are a specially designed lightweight model that has so far proved rather cold. The problem seems to be that they are filled with a high quality 'expedition' down which has tended to compact itself too readily, leaving empty spots in the baffles. We decide to add some lower quality down to prevent the balling effect and we acquire an old down sleeping bag to pull apart for the raw material. We spend a hilarious morning at Dilli Bazaar on the job, under Sri and Ram Krisna's encouraging gaze.

The old sleeping bag is unstitched at one seam and Ann sinks her arm deep into each baffle to extract the down which we collect in a plastic bag. Then follows what feels like sacrilege, taking to our own sleeping bags. I cut them open along the zipper's edge, one baffle at a time, and we reverse the morning's process. My hands are too large so I hold the baffles open as Ann forces three small fistfuls of feathers into each baffle. It is slow going because the feathers are so prone to fly away if not handled carefully.

'Aaaaah, bliss,' Ann says as she visualises us, during the rest of the trip, luxuriating in snug warm pits. I put a simple tacking stitch along the seam we opened and that evening we take the bags to a tailor who finishes the seam off for us with a machine.

That night we go out for final treats, rolling from one restaurant to another, having one course at each. In 'Tripti's' we have *masala dosa,* stuffed spiced potato pancakes, about 30 centimetres long, golden and crisp, a southern Indian speciality.

For dessert we go to 'Jamali's' in Thamel where there is a good range of 'just baked today' cakes — apple strudel and chocolate cake, marshmallow pies and cinnamon rolls. 'Jamali's' plays Western music from a huge pile of tapes behind the counter. A girl comes up and talks to Ann. They were at college together in New Zealand and last saw each other ten years ago. That's Kathmandu.

As we ride home from dinner, the tiny bats of Thamel flit and glide over a compound of pagoda-roofed temples opposite, silhouetted in a blue-bronze twilight. Tomorrow we start trekking to Everest.

GRISHMA

hot
season

SP, Ann, Corrina and I left Kathmandu on 13 March. The support party's objective was to trek into the Khumbu (or Everest) region, in time to meet Ding, Pete and Tashi on their way from Ilam near the Nepal border with Sikkim. We were to trek eastwards to Khunde village, and they were coming west.

The route into the Khumbu from Kathmandu is well known and hundreds of tourists trek it every year. There are villages all the way and food is plentiful. For that reason we had far less to pack than we had in Sikkim; our personal gear fitted easily into our rucksacks, with room to spare for treats for the traversers and on top of that we piled in some of the spare equipment, camera gear and freeze dried food that would supply the traverse team for their next stage westwards from the Khumbu. But we were definitely going to need a porter to carry the rest of the equipment that might be needed, about another 20 kg of it.

Back we went to the Kathmandu bus terminal and found seats on a creaking old bus heading north to the Everest-trek road end at Karantichap. We were on our way to Everest, new country for all of us, and we bubbled over with the excitement of heading into the hills again. Feeling so happy, we thrived on the increased exercise of the trail. Our only health problem on this section occurred when Corrina contracted a bad stomach infection that did not respond well to treatment. She withstood its rigours with stoic good humour, however, and continued to carry her full load.

People, Pete and Ding included, had told us that we would not need to take our boots, that sneakers were all the trip required. We disbelieved them, even after my experience in Sikkim where sneakers would have been perfectly adequate, at least up to our height ceiling of 5200 metres on the Ratong La trip. We were going to see Everest, for goodness sake, and climbing boots must obviously be required at some stage. We each had a pair with us, stuck in our packs 'for later'. In fact, there was no 'later', and, apart from one snowy day in Khunde, our boots stayed in our packs and had a free ride in and out of the Khumbu.

This Everest trek was the first time we functioned properly as a support party, meeting the traverse team at a pre-arranged rendezvous. It was going to be interesting to see how it worked. How accurate would the estimated time of each party's arrival be? What would we do if they did not arrive? After what length of time should we set out in search?

The proposed route for the traverse party involved the crossing of three high passes from the Makalu base camp — Far East Col, West Col and the Amphu Laptsa (5780 metres). This would involve them in some of the most significant 'mountaineering' of the traverse. Such a small party could easily run into trouble if they were low on food or if any one of them became too ill to proceed.

There were two problems I foresaw arising if they didn't come. First, we did not have enough technical climbing equipment to attempt to cross out of the Everest region by those same high passes, even if the whole support party had had the necessary skill, which we didn't. The second was that if the traverse party was turned back from the high pass route there were several alternative routes further south which they might choose to come by. If we went haring off from the Khumbu to try and intercept them we were liable to miss them.

Ding and Pete had cautioned me on their departure for Ilam that we would have to decide on a plan of action in case of their non-arrival. We worried away at it until forced to conclude that the only practical plan was just to sit tight and let them sort out any problems themselves. If they did get into real trouble they were the only ones that could get themselves out of it — at that altitude and with little reserve food they wouldn't last until outside 'help' came. So much for the support party concept on this section of the traverse.

In the event, the traversers arrived eight days later than their estimate. By that time SP's concern was mounting, and Ann and I had taken to going down to Shyangboche air strip below Khunde each day to try and find a pilot who was prepared to risk a short flight over their proposed route into Khumbu — ten minutes in an aircraft but about a week on the ground.

Meanwhile, on their way up the Barun valley, Ding, Pete and Tashi had realised how far they were behind schedule and posted several cards to us care of Khunde village, asking us not to meet them there, but to go up a side valley and camp below the Amphu Laptsa, about a day closer to them. Of course the postcards never arrived and when the traverse team came down from the Amphu Laptsa we were unaccountably (in their eyes) absent. They reached us after another half day's forced march: thin, hungry, tired, with only five rupees left between them. That was in Khunde on 6 April 1981.

5. The Everest Trek

Karantichap is small and undistinguished by much except its relatively high temperatures. It is about 1000 metres above sea level, even lower than Kathmandu. We find seats around the porter-rest beneath the pipal tree and explain our business to the inquisitive locals. First we wish to obtain a porter.

'That will be difficult, sahib,' I am told. 'One Japanese expedition passed this way not so long ago and hired 300 porters.' It is time for ploughing and labour is in short supply but still the information is passed on: 'There are sahibs in the village wanting one porter to go all the way to Namche Bazaar.'

It is time for *chiya* and food; that is more easily arranged. Then I settle myself on a rickety *charpoy* or rope bed. Time passes. We doze in the shade while swallows flit about the branches of the pipal tree above us. We are learning: a month or so ago we might have been pacing up and down, getting excited; now we enjoy the rest. A porter will come some time — everybody knows we want one.

And one does come. Vaim Bahadur is his name and he wears the homespun cotton jacket of a lowland Rai or Chhetri Nepali.

'You are a coolie?' Ann asks.

'Yes, memsahib, I am a coolie,' he replies. I was reluctant to use the word 'coolie' when I first had to deal with porters, but have come to accept that it has no derogatory overtones. To Vaim Bahadur it is simply the technical description of his occupation: he carries loads for others.

'Namche?' he asks.

'Yes, we are going to Namche Bazaar. Have you been there before?'

'No, not before.'

Vaim Bahadur tries his load for size. It is one green khaki kitbag, carefully packed by us in Kathmandu to ensure that it weighs less than 20 kg. SP discusses

From anywhere south of the Khumbu glacier, all but the topmost triangle of Everest is obscured by the immense mountain wall, 4000 metres high, that runs eastward from Nuptse (7879m) to Lhotse (8501m). The westernmost end of that icy wall is visible in the right foreground. The peak behind the Lho La (6006m), in the left centre of photo, is in Tibet. Everest's west ridge begins at the Lho La and continues diagonally right over the high point in the centre of the photo before reappearing as the left-hand edge of the rocky summit of Everest.

An overhanging rock supplies the back wall for this home at Goromcho, Trisuli valley, central Nepal.

The vegetable market in Katari bazaar, a town on the route south from Khumbu to the east-west Nepal highway.

A Sherpani from Machermo carries firewood north with her yaks to Gokyo village in search of fresh pasture until autumn.

Our book of plant photos provoked much interest from this farming family at Bupsa on the summer route between Jubing and Surkye in the Dudh Kosi valley, Nepal.

Manidingma village on the Everest trail: tall prayer flags are topped by tridents, the symbol of the Hindu god, Shiva.

Ann catches up on the washing at Jomosom.

Dhaulagiri (8167m) in the background, east face to left and north face to right, and Tukuche peak (6920m) from the Muktinath pilgrimage site near the Tibetan border with central Nepal.

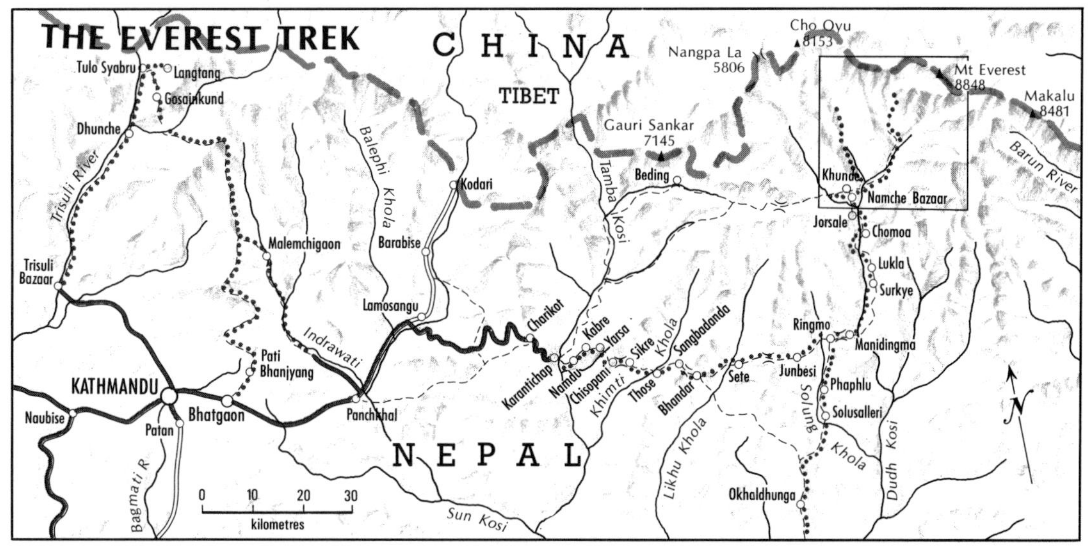
THE EVEREST TREK
CHINA
TIBET
Cho Oyu
8153
Nangpa La
5806
Mt Everest
8848
Makalu
8481
Gauri Sankar
7145
Beding
Barun River
Tulo Syabru
Langtang
Gosainkund
Dhunche
Trisuli River
Balephi Khola
Kodari
Tamba Kosi
Khunde
Namche Bazaar
Jorsale
Chomoa
Lukla
Surkye
Malemchigaon
Barabise
Trisuli
Bazaar
Lamosangu
Charikot
Indrawati
Ringmo
Manidingma
Kabre
Yarsa
Sikre
Khimti Khola
Sangbadanda
Namdu
Chisapani
Karantichap
Those
Bhandar
Sete
Junbesi
Phaphlu
Solusalleri
Solung Khola
Pati
Bhanjyang
KATHMANDU
Naubise
Patan
Bhatgaon
Panchkhal
NEPAL
Likhu Khola
Dudh Kosi
Okhaldhunga
Sun Kosi
Bagmati R
0 10 20 30
kilometres

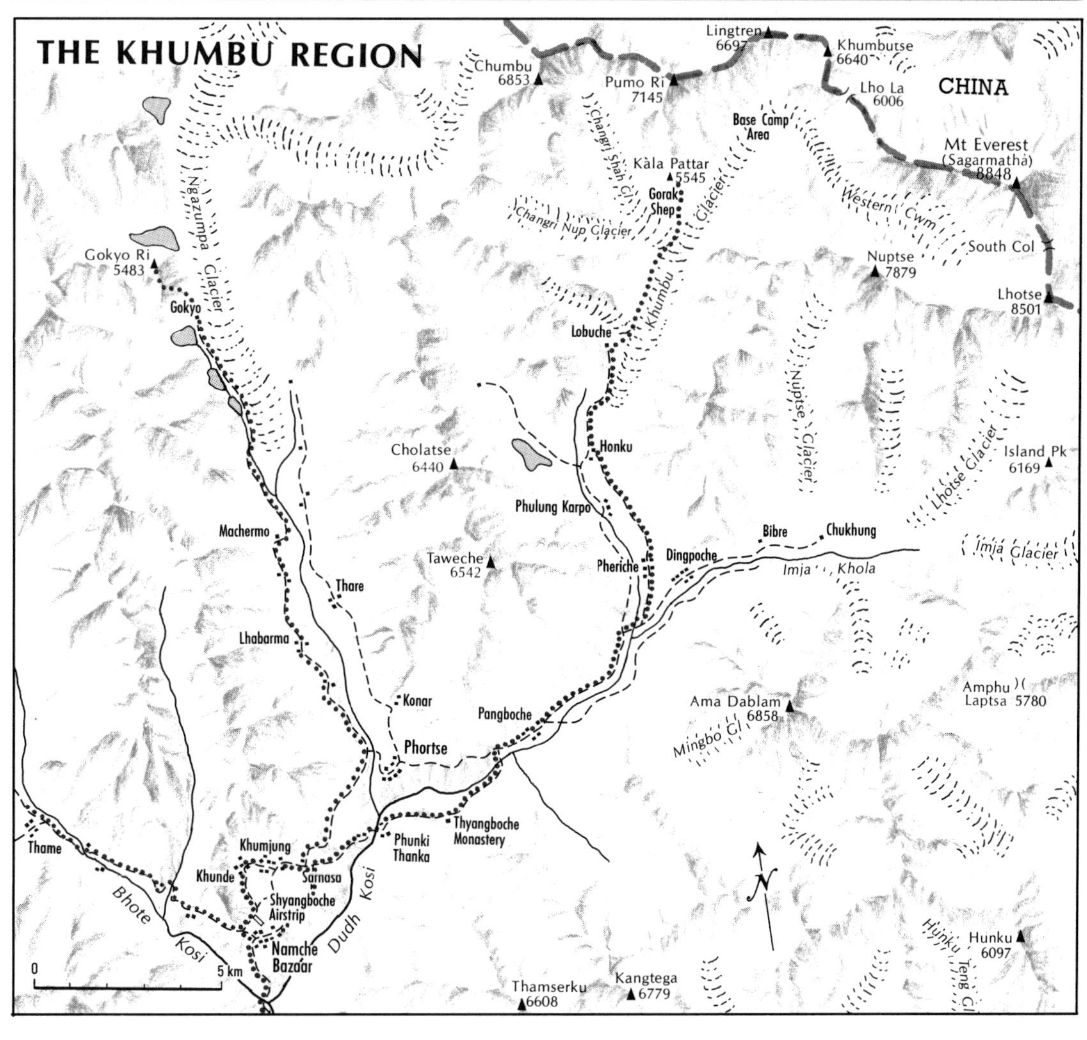
THE KHUMBU REGION
Lingtren
6697
Khumbutse
6640
Chumbu
6853
Pumo Ri
7145
Lho La
6006
CHINA
Base Camp
Area
Changri Shar Gl
Kàla Pattar
5545
Mt Everest
(Sagarmathà)
8848
Gorak
Shep
Changri Nup Glacier
Western Cwm
Khumbu Glacier
South Col
Nuptse
7879
Gokyo Ri
5483
Ngazumpa Glacier
Gokyo
Lhotse
8501
Lobuche
Nuptse Glacier
Honku
Cholatse
6440
Island Pk
6169
Lhotse Glacier
Phulung Karpo
Machermo
Bibre
Chukhung
Taweche
6542
Dingpoche
Pheriche
Imja Khola
Imja Glacier
Thare
Lhabarma
Konar
Pangboche
Ama Dablam
6858
Amphu
Laptsa 5780
Mingbo Gl
Phortse
Thame
Khumjung
Phunki
Thanka
Thyangboche
Monastery
Khunde
Sarnasa
Shyangboche
Airstrip
Bhote Kosi
Dudh Kosi
Namche
Bazaar
Hunku
6097
Hunku Teng Gl
0
5 km
Thamserku
6608
Kangtega
6779

the rate with Vaim: some porters prefer a set daily rate plus food paid for by the employer; others charge a slightly higher rate but provide their own food. Vaim Bahadur decides that he will come with us, and settles on Rs 20 per day with us paying for his food. It is a sensible choice: the guidebook warns that as we go further from the road the food becomes more expensive.

Vaim Bahadur excuses himself for a moment and returns with a cloth-wrapped package of rice which he will carry with him, carefully hoarding it for his return journey. He asks a friend from his village nearby to tell his wife that he will be back in about two weeks.

'I am ready now, sahib,' he tells me.

The crowd is all smiles. See how easy it is at Karantichap, they seem to say. You can eat, rest and find a porter, all in a few hours which is, after all, not much more than a blink of the eye. We shake hands all around. Vaim Bahadur wraps a cloth around his head, takes a woven fibre rope and slings it low around the kitbag. Getting his back snug up against the kitbag, he drops the top of the rope on to his forehead, where the cloth is wrapped, and as he stands up the rope comes tight in one long band, over his forehead, down and around the kitbag. We follow Vaim as he sets off from the village at SP's command.

Our way lies downwards first, through shady rhododendrons just in bud, towards the Tamba Kosi river.

'This is better than buses,' calls Ann from behind me. It is close to midday now and even this short distance down to the river is enough to leave us dripping with sweat in the heat. On the far side we pause and rest for a while. At first we escape the worst of the heat on the porch of the *chiya* shop at Busti, but later Corrina has an even better idea.

'How about a swim?' she suggests. SP looks surprised.

'But there may be fish,' he protests. We decide to risk it. The Tamba Kosi is slow moving, broad and clean. We find a small patch of sand edged with warm round boulders by the water's edge and I strip down to my shorts and dive in. The water feels great and I swim lazily towards the centre of the river with languid, water-dripping strokes, then float on my back, cool and refreshed, looking up into the pale blue sky.

Afterwards we drip dry on rocks in the sun. Downstream, puffs of smoke and the dull thud of explosives mark the advance of the road builders. Soon the road will pass here. Will a swim at Busti feel the same to anyone who has not walked there?

Beyond Busti there is a two hour climb up the side of the valley, through the small hamlet of Namdu where more road construction is under way. Skirting the roadworks we move out into the fields again, following three Tamang women. They each have a large triangular *doko* or basket on their back, secured (like Vaim Bahadur's load) by a single *tump* line around the forehead.

Cabbages and the flat leaves of the sal tree, used for plates, are visible through the wicker. The women are singing a melodic chant, first one takes a line, then another. SP translates the words:

'Oh the way is very long
and my little baby is crying at home
I am overcome with sadness
I feel like crying
My eyes fill with tears.'

In fact they seem anything but sad and when not singing they joke and tease each other with great spirit. Three times the woman in front turns and chases the one behind her into the fields, both shrieking with laughter, pulling one another's hair, ignoring their heavy loads.

Just near dusk we enter Kabre where we will sleep tonight. There is no such thing as a hotel in Kabre, or at least not as we have previously understood the term. What there is, however, is a well developed custom regarding casual lodging for travellers. Someone in the village will take us in to their home, provide us with a place to sleep, feed us as part of the family and provide us with *chiya.* So, tonight, after our enquiries for lodging are made, cackling chickens are swept off the narrow verandah of a house and mats are spread there, for us to sleep on.

The diet in the hills is very varied, like Mr Ford's car: you can have anything you want, provided that you want *dahl bhat,* rice and lentils. This is perfectly understandable when one considers the circumstances. Humble farmhouses between Karantichap and Namche Bazaar cannot stock the peculiar foods that foreign sahibs may be accustomed to. Foreigners can eat local food if they wish, or bring their own.

Rice and lentils are filling and nutritious and we grow to like the combination. The rice is fairly uniform but the lentils are seldom the same twice, ranging from thick brews of red beans or pulses and dried peas, to rich dark green broths. Each cook has his or her own mix of spices or flavouring. If we are lucky there may be a little vegetable, such as spinach, or a luxury item such as eggs. Meat is very rare, since there are no refrigerators and these lowland areas are too humid to store dried meat.

We pay a modest fee for our food and lodging: a place to sleep, say two cups of tea in the evening, an evening meal of *dahl bhat* and a cup of tea in the morning costs us about Rs 8 each. On the major trekking routes, such as this, one could travel for weeks with little more than the clothes on one's back, a sleeping bag and a plentiful supply of small denomination notes.

We try not to get in the way of the family or disturb their household too much and, equally, we try not to offend by requesting things which are unusual. There is, for example, no hot water for washing and if we wish to wash we can go to the stream as the villagers do. There are no toilets in the village either and we are expected to use the fields, according to custom. Although nothing is said it is obvious that wind blown pieces of the strange foreign paper can give offence, so they should be burned if possible or otherwise buried.

Our meal is completed before 7.30 pm and after that there is nothing to stay up for. I blow out the candle and we lie down on the verandah to sleep, coughing in the smoke which comes drifting up from the kitchen. Just below us there are brief snatches of conversation as the last few villagers go up and down the street completing their tasks for the day. The chickens have been secured tonight beneath an upturned *doko* and they cluck away softly at the end of my sleeping bag.

We are awake early and breakfast on cold boiled *aloo* or potatoes and, a special treat, cold boiled *phul* or eggs. This breakfast is an extra, which we requested that they prepare last night. It allows us to eat quickly and get moving on the trail before the heat of the day. It fits in well with local routine also, as the villagers will seldom have much of a fire going in the morning, just enough for tea perhaps. They work in the fields for four hours or so and then, late in the morning when the kitchen is fired up and rice has cooked, they stop for the first of two substantial meals in the day. We are weaning ourselves slowly from our customary breakfast habits so these cold snacks fit our requirements admirably. We pay for our food and lodging, pack up, and by 7 am we are on the trail again.

In the cool of the morning we walk through fields green with wheat. Each little stream has a small mill built over it where a grindstone, less than a metre across, is turned on an axle driven by a carefully directed stream of water that spins a broad-bladed paddle wheel. In one of these mills a girl is grinding wheat, scooping handfuls of it into the hole in the centre of the upper stone. Flour comes spinning out in a fine spray where the two stones meet and with an old can she scrapes up the flour from the clay floor into a large square tin. The whirr of the turning stones is almost drowned out by the slosh of water against the paddle wheel.

We cross the river beyond Yarsa and follow a track through poplars and maples towards Chisopani, which means 'cold water'. By 10.30 am cold water is certainly on our minds; in these populated areas, however, unlike the virtually empty hills of Sikkim, the water is not safe to drink and we must content ourselves with endless cups of tea whenever a *chiya* shop is passed.

A *chiya* shop up in these hills may be an alcove beside a verandah, with a single cupboard in which tea, sugar and biscuits are kept, or a small area where a *chiya wala* has stretched an old scrap of canvas as an awning against the sun and built a seat by laying a plank across a few stones. In each case there will be a tiny fire inside a clay oven, with an ancient blackened kettle steaming gently in the top.

I order tea in Chisopani and the *chiya wala* produces it in seconds, with great economy of movement. He takes a glass, rinses it in cold water and spoons raw sugar into it; then he takes a strainer, shakes thick tea dust into it and places it over the top of the glass. He lifts the steaming kettle and pours boiling water through the tea dust, clean water above the strainer then thick dark *chiya* beneath. From a second pot he adds boiling milk.

'Ek mohar (50 paisa, or about US 3 cents), sahib.'

Tea dust makes the tea of the common people. When tea is processed into the pieces which are sold as leaf tea, there is always a considerable residue of dust, pieces too small for sale as leaves; this 'dust' is collected and sold, packaged in bright gold and crimson packets. It is very cheap by comparison with the better quality leaf tea. Like all Indian tea, however, its price is subsidised. The Indian tea industry has a high wage structure in comparison with competitors such as Sri Lanka and Bangladesh, and only government support prevents the Indian tea producers from being priced out of existence. But tea dust makes fine *chiya* regardless, especially after a four-hour walk in the steadily growing heat of the day.

This hot season before the monsoon is the time for the villagers to put things in order. Thatchers are working on a house across the path from us, tearing out clumps of old thatch to expose the roof's frame of branches beneath. When the whole side of the roof is stripped, they begin carefully to tie down the new thatch, starting with the bottom strip, above the eaves, and working slowly in overlapping rows to the peak of the roof.

After lunch there is a short climb to a pass. The rough rock track of the Chisopani side turns into a steep dusty red clay track on the other side. Parallel ridges of dark green hills stretch across the horizon ahead of us. Banked up one against the other, each ridge seems a little higher than the last and their outlines shimmer gently in the heat. We can see clearly where our trail zigzags down through two small villages to the Khimti Khola, then again up the other side of the valley to the next ridge. Side trails branch off to other villages, meandering off into the fields, following the contours around the hillside and on out of sight.

SP and I pause at the pass to take photographs and rest. A man comes up the trail towards us, looking quite cool beneath the shade of his black umbrella.

'I think we should have brought umbrellas, SP,' I remark, gazing wistfully at it.

'That is quite correct,' agrees SP, mopping his brow. 'This heat, it is something fantastic. You know, even this pass we are just crossing, it is only 2000 metres above sea level. Ah, if only we were at my place at Mussoorie, this is so green and cool.' I stuff my camera back in my pack; the black metal is almost too hot to touch.

'I am looking forward to it already,' I reply. SP has described to us in great detail his large old home in the Indian Himalayan foothills and it assumes an even more attractive aspect in this heat. We raise puffs of red dust behind us as we pad down towards the river to catch up with Ann and Corrina.

We pass through Sikre and climb again towards Those, walking through smaller fields where a man is ploughing behind two buffaloes. Near the crest of the ridge we walk through a good stand of pine, which harbours vicious biting midges. When we come over the top from the west-facing slope and drop down to the east, the pine forest is completely devastated and we walk through a sea of fresh, ugly stumps.

'But this is terrible,' SP laments to me, 'these people are cutting wood and cutting wood, but where is the planting? They are not doing any planting at all.'

'It certainly doesn't look like it,' I reply. 'Remember by Darjeeling there was a big re-afforestation project? We haven't seen anything like that here.'

'You will find the Indian Himalaya quite different, Douglas. The Government has kept much better control than this and the forests have been preserved. These people will be suffering terribly from erosion and, besides, what can they do when the wood is gone? They are not able to afford kerosene.' SP shakes his head sadly. 'You know in the Veda, one of our scriptures, it says that he who plants a tree will have his reward — shade, food, fruit and forage. These people are not knowing their scriptures.'

Those is the first town on the trek with any obvious Tibetan or Sherpa influence. Roofs are made of slate, rather than thatch, and the small windows have wooden shutters. The houses are built to withstand a real winter and mark the transition to the cooler mountain regions. We stay the night here and depart early next morning in the face of threatening rain. The foot trail winds along between closely-packed houses at first, the upper floors jutting out above us and closing out the sky. At the edge of the town a rough hand-painted sign says 'Way to Everest' and we take that track.

A fine rain begins to fall and in the soft mist we climb steadily through pine forest and rhododendrons to a village called Sangbadanda, and on to an un-named pass at a height of 3124 metres. Porters are squelching down towards us from the pass and we step aside to let a group come through. One loses his footing in the tricky clay and slips to the ground, struggling to keep his load upright. He and his friends chuckle mightily when Ann repeats for him the local saying, *'Rato mato — chiplo bato',* which Vaim has just taught her; it means 'red ground — slippery path', and it sums up accurately the awkward footing provided by this ochrous clay when wet.

Bhandar is the next village, beyond the pass. We sleep the night there in a barn and rise early. Vaim Bahadur is always ready first and I set off behind him, picking my way carefully between puddles and patches of mud. A farmer comes past driving two bullocks. He has a light stick in one hand and taps them occasionally, more from habit than from necessity. Over his shoulder he carries the yoke for the bullocks, a simple baulk of timber with four sticks driven into it — two sticks to fix on the shoulders of one animal and two for the other animal. His wooden plough, not even metal tipped, rests up against the low stone wall of the field.

I pause to wait for the others. Bhandar is a beautiful place with the morning sun streaming down. There is a chuckle of running water and the earth is damp and cool after the rain; the village houses are dotted about the terraced fields and over by the ridge to the south is a fringe of forest. But the thing which is most noticeable is the absence of machines — no growl and roar of trucks and buses, no screaming radio. It is beautifully, deeply, quiet. The only sound I hear is the chuck-chuck of the ploughing farmer, turning his buffalo. A child follows him, reaching into a bag and then scattering seed.

The day passes just like the previous ones: a long descent, down the side of the valley to the river, followed by a long climb up the opposite side. The river is the Likhu Khola and the next village is Kenja. We lunch at Kenja and go on up the ridge towards Sete.

As the prayer flags of Sete approach we are circled by an enormous flock of birds, over a hundred jungle crows that rise wheeling and cawing to float back against the cloud. They seem like birds of ill omen and perhaps that makes us feel ill at ease: Sete, damp and wrapped in mist, is depressing. We find a room to sleep in and I unpack, hanging my damp clothing on a line on the porch where the upper floor will shelter it if it rains tonight. I look down to where a farmer has slaughtered a goat on the path outside; he has the carcass spread out on a board and is cutting it into pieces with a *kukri,* the famous curved knife of the Nepalis. Porters queue up to buy the meat, and the farmer's companion weighs chunks of the bloody flesh on hand-held scales.

Each day as we trek we encounter convoys of porters, as many as 40 at a time, going up and down the trail. The porters carry in items that cannot be grown or made in the hills and carry out local produce to trade at the lowland markets. When outward bound the porters' loads are usually fairly manageable, mostly comprising agricultural produce, but inbound porters may carry heavy loads such as tins of cooking oil or long unwieldy sheets of corrugated iron. Before Bhandar we had to wait a long time before the trail was wide enough to overtake one unfortunate porter, who was carrying an entire four-drawer filing cabinet to some government office or other in the hills.

The porters do not sleep in the villages. They camp instead at well-used sites between, where there is water or fuel close by, without too much fetching to be done or payment made. The porters' day has a similar pattern to that of the farmers. Up early with little or nothing to eat, they are on the trail for four hours or so before a long halt in mid morning to cook a substantial meal of rice and *dahl,* and then another four or five hours of load-carrying before the night's camp where the second and final meal of the day is prepared.

The lowland porters wear no special clothing as they journey up into the hills. The women are clad in the same bright cotton sarongs and velvet jerkins of the *terai,* the men in their cotton thigh-length jackets and shorts. Almost all of them have, in addition, a broad sash of cotton or gauze, wound many times around the waist. It cushions their backs against the heavy *doko* load and makes a convenient pocket for the *kukri.*

In the morning we leave Sete and continue up the ridge, our objective today the Lamjura *bhanjyang* or pass. After two hours' steady going we come to an isolated farmhouse which has a sign outside saying, 'fooding and eating'. A child pokes her head out the window, dislodging a cat, which stalks off indignantly.

'Chiya milega? (Is tea available?)' Ann asks.

'Milega (It is available),' the child responds.

'Tikchha. Aat chiya dinehos, baini.' *Baini* is the complement of *didi,* it means younger sister, and the girl goes off smiling to fetch our eight teas.

The four of us tend to spread out along the trail as we trek, stopping for photographs or a view or a secluded toilet stop. We congregate again at tea shops, however, and the first to arrive will usually order enough tea for all four — usually two cups each. This can cause a few raised eyebrows and require some explanations when an apparently solo trekker wanders in off the trail and asks for eight teas.

As Ann and I sit and wait for the others, the owner comes out of the farmhouse to collect payment from a Dutch couple who have finished their *chiya* and are about to leave. The Dutchman tries to pay with a torn bank note and the owner will not take it. I have seen this happen in India as well as Nepal. No one will accept torn notes because a note with a tear in any of its sides is virtually valueless. There is no apparent reason for this; it is just the custom. Yet banks secure bundles of bank notes by punching a needle through the centre of them and tying the bundle with string. Almost every note I see has this hole through the centre, but that is ignored.

Before we learnt to be careful we unwittingly acquired some torn notes and I had to go to the head cashier of a major New Delhi bank to dispose of them. These village people, however, will seldom if ever be inside a bank, so they will argue strenuously before accepting even a partially torn note mended with tape. And if by chance they should have such a note, some of them are not above getting rid of it by trying to secrete it in the change they give some careless foreigner.

The Dutchman argues the toss for a long time, but eventually gives in and pays with another note. The owner then gives him careful directions on how to get to the Lamjura *bhanjyang.* The track forks here and he sends the couple off along the left hand fork. Later, our teas finished and paid for, we ask for directions ourselves, just to confirm the way. Ann addresses the farmhouse owner as *dajiu* and asks our 'older brother' the way to the Lamjura *bhanjyang.*

'Lamjura bhanjyang, dajiu, kun bato?'

'Yo bato,' he says, 'uppar, uppar,' indicating the right hand track which climbs high with the ridge. We are surprised — not the lower track, to the left? We check — no. I think the Dutch have received 'special' treatment for their pains.

We climb on towards the pass, through a forest full of the noise of wood cutters, shouts and the echoing ring of an axe. In a forest clearing we walk around a hole where two men are pit-sawing tree trunks into slabs and long square beams for building; one man is above, balanced on the trunk itself, and one below — one at each end of the long saw which glides up and down as they push and bend, golden sawdust spilling from the teeth.

The Lamjura *bhanjyang,* at an altitude of 3530 metres, is the highest pass which we cross on the eastward route before we turn north for Khumbu. It is only a few hundred metres lower than the highest mountain in New Zealand, Mt Cook, but there we would have had to do hours of difficult climbing to reach this height. Here, we are hardly above the forest line. We reach the *mani* wall on the pass, stoop under strings of flapping, ragged prayer flags, and drop down a little over the crest to rest out of the wind. Two ponies are grazing here, but no one is guarding them. While we rest Ann looks over the map and works out the route ahead. We are using one of the local trekking maps but not one of Madhab's. He does have plans to draw a map for the Everest track, but says he wants to walk the route himself at least once first.

'May I see?' asks SP, and Ann passes the map to him. 'Ah, so we are to go down the valley to Junbesi.'

'Looks like it,' says Ann. 'It's a bit hard to tell when the map's all printed in the one colour, but at least you can get an idea of the geography.'

'Quite so,' he replies. 'I am used to much better Indian maps too, in many colours, showing the vegetation and with better contours. But of course those maps are restricted in India, they are only available to the services.'

'Why is that, SP?' Corrina asks.

'Because of security. We cannot be dishing out detailed maps to foreigners; they might be coming into the hands of our enemies. Then they would use them against us if they invaded us.'

'So that explains what happened at the Survey of India,' says Corrina, turning to me.

'You went to the Survey of India?' SP raises his eyebrows in surprise.

'Yes,' I reply. 'I wanted to buy maps of the Indian mountain areas where we'll be trekking later in the year. The chap said that they had those maps but weren't selling them. He wouldn't explain why.'

'Good gracious me,' says SP. 'You shouldn't have done that, now they will be very suspicious.'

What 'they' had to be suspicious about was never made clear.

'According to the guidebook we get our first view of Everest around the next corner,' Ann tells me. 'I'm going ahead to get a photo — do you want to come?' I decide to stay back and keep Corrina company; she has picked up some kind of stomach infection, probably in Those, and since then has found the trekking hard going. Frequent toilet stops have slowed her down and she tells me she hasn't had much sleep the last two nights. We discuss her symptoms for a while and I suggest she try some antibiotics as a last resort. Corrina seems better already, at the expression of my concern, and I wish I'd had the sense to question her sooner. We stroll along the trail together and come around a corner of the ridge to find Ann sitting by a long *mani* wall, putting her camera away.

'It's a great view,' I suggest, looking north-east into a confused mass of cloud.

'Isn't it,' she laughs, 'I've taken a picture of the cloud anyway. I'll frame it and call it "First View of Everest".'

We stay the night at Junbesi, sleeping in the schoolhouse because the hotel is closed. A sign in the village promised hot showers, apples and cheese but none of these are available. Corrina is eating only plain boiled rice in the hope that it will settle her stomach. Both she and SP are total vegetarians and they are noticing the lack of green vegetables in their diet; not that Ann and I are eating meat either but at least we are feeling well.

In the morning we follow the track as it sidles around the base of the Shingshere Danda ridge. I walk with SP for a while, through the tall pines that lead us down to the Solung Khola.

'Are you enjoying this trekking?' SP suddenly asks me.

'Very much,' I reply. 'It's quite different to the areas we go walking in at home.'

'Of course, you would not be having such wilderness in your country.'

'Well, a wilderness to me is a place where there is no cultivation and no people living. Now this,' I encompass the view with a wave of my arm, 'this is all cultivated. Terraced fields as far as you can see, and hundreds of people live hereabouts. Why, in the last village there was a little red post box and you posted a letter — a wilderness doesn't have post boxes in it.'

'In that case,' replies SP, after a considered pause, 'what is wilderness like in your country?'

'A bit like Sikkim was beyond Dzongri,' I decide. 'No permanent habitation and no cultivation. Just the valleys and the mountains and a few people walking through. We have quite a lot of that sort of terrain.'

'But how do you find your way and buy your food?'

'Well, there are very good maps, like we were talking about the other day, and we carry all our own food because no one lives there from whom we could buy it.'

'So you must be using porters?'

'No, we can carry enough dehydrated food for a trip of 10 to 14 days and we don't often get the chance to do a journey longer than that.'

'Well', he says, 'if this is not a wilderness for you, what do you find interesting here? For myself I was going to tell you how much I am coming to like this kind of trekking. It is good not to have to worry about porters and cook boys and how far they will not want to walk today. I wasn't sure how you and the others felt though, so that was why I was asking.'

'I think it's the social experience that I appreciate the most, SP,' I reply, adding, 'and I'm not sure that I've thought this through fully yet. You see, this village life and method of agriculture don't exist at home. The life of these people is very like the daily life of people described in Biblical times. Of course it has changed here for the better in many ways, but in others it remains the same. So this shows me a way of life that I can't experience back home.'

'It is very primitive, I agree,' he says.

'I don't think it is primitive, SP; it's just a different level of technology. Within its limits it's quite sophisticated. Take that bridge we crossed yesterday: it was a cantilevered bridge built out of pitsawn timber, with dry-stone foundations, yet it was all properly square and level. It was perfectly adequate for the traffic it carries.'

'I'll think about that,' SP replies, smiling.

We pass through the bare apple orchards at Ringmo and climb again, cross the Trakshindu La and descend once more to Manidingma, where we halt for the night. Our hotel is called the Danphe Restaurant, after Nepal's national bird. A colourful picture of the pheasant is painted on the hotel sign which hangs above the door; this was how inns and lodging places in Europe identified themselves when most of the population was illiterate.

'We're hardly likely to see pheasants here though,' Corrina comments. 'According to that book of yours, Ann, this is within their altitude range but you don't see them in the more cultivated areas.'

Ann and Corrina talk to a young girl, Ang Yange, whose family owns the hotel. She goes to school four days each week in Junbesi — over the pass we've just crossed, three hours there and three hours back. Ang Yange is keen to practise her English on us and sticks right by us throughout our stay.

Ang Yange's grandmother spends most of the evening in the corner of the main room by the fire, nodding and smiling as the conversation continues and twirling the handle of a Buddhist prayer wheel in her left hand. The silver drum at the head of the prayer wheel is tightly packed with written prayers and each time she spins the drum, the prayers ascend to heaven. The old woman reaches out suddenly, to steer one of the younger grandchildren away from the fire, and she swaps the prayer wheel from one hand to the other without interrupting its spinning.

The hearth is wide and open and a metal frame for the pots stands tall enough to enable small logs to be slipped in underneath. Fixed to the flagstones is a small circular bellows, its nozzle pointing into the centre of the fire. A boy stoops to take the handle, cranking it around and around, and a jet of air fans flames from the embers. Our *dahl bhat* comes with a little cooked spinach or *saag* tonight and we sit packed in tight amongst the family while we eat. The three grandsons crouch down by the fireside, clutching their bowls of rice and wriggling their toes in the cooling outer ashes, their heads outlined against the firelight.

We sleep on a raised wooden platform in the storeroom behind the kitchen and I am bothered by fleas. Then I think I hear rats getting into the block of cheese we bought from the cheese factory below the Trakshindu La. Carrying the 2 kg of fresh cheese in to the traversers at Khunde seemed worth the extra weight in my pack. Now I have to get up, late in the night, to repack all my gear more securely by the flickering light of a candle.

It is cool in the morning and I am awake early. I take my camera back to the edge of the forest to photograph the village. There are snowy peaks visible to the east, sharp in the sunlight and on either side of the track stand tall flag poles with prayer flags hanging limp. The flag poles are topped with crowns pierced by broad-bladed tridents and I try to compose a picture with them showing clear against the early morning light. The houses of Manidingma are still in shade, walls of white-washed mud over stone, with black-edged wooden-shuttered windows. The roofs are of split pine laths weighted down with stones.

I come back from my walk dissatisfied. How can you photograph the smell of wood smoke, or the sound of cock-crow in the still morning air, the feel of a sleeping village when you have walked seven days to reach it? Where in the photograph will the discomfort of the flea bites appear, or the pleasure that we shared when the rest of the cheese survived the night?

From Manidingma we descend into a broad valley and by mid morning we are at the Dudh Kosi river. *Dudh* is the Nepali and Hindi word for milk and the Dudh Kosi is aptly named. It boils past, green-white with glacial dust from the mountains thousands of metres above. We cross cautiously, one by one, on a wire suspension bridge and turn off our eastward track at last, heading north up the gorge of the Dudh Kosi into the heart of Sherpa country. It is only two or three days now to Namche Bazaar.

Descending porters have told Vaim Bahadur of a summer track which takes a more direct route north along the walls of the gorge. This saves a day's travel compared with the safer all-weather route which skirts the ridges far above. We elect to try it and all day we follow an impressive track cut from rock slabs, perched on the sheer cliff walls barely two or three bounces above the river. At one point what little there is of the track has slipped away: a traveller before us has attempted a makeshift repair by shoving the ends of branches as far as possible into the narrow crannies in the otherwise bare rock, then laying a half-split log over the top to bridge the gap in the trail. I don't know how it bears our weight, nor how we convince ourselves to trust it. Five hours after we enter the gorge, our track is still confined to the cliff walls. Since none of us has any idea how far it is till we can expect to emerge on to flat land again, I find myself carefully assessing dry spots beneath overhanging rocks as the afternoon wears on, in case we must camp.

Then, just after 4 pm, we come suddenly around a corner to a beautiful and welcome view. In the foreground a small blue pine stands beside a clear waterfall, among yellow flowering primulas and rhododendrons. Behind that the corner of a shingled roof projects, a curling plume of smoke catching the last of the afternoon sun.

The smoke comes from the New Hotel and Lodge at Surkye. We haul ourselves up the long flight of steps at the front of the house and file in through the open doorway. We are definitely in Sherpa country now: the doorways are low. This is not because the Sherpas are short (although compared with me they frequently are), for even a Sherpa must stoop to enter his or her own home, but largely to conserve heat in the winter. It takes me some time to adjust to these doorways, and until I do I thump myself on the forehead several times a day.

The kitchen walls in this Surkye home have been pasted over with pages torn from magazines. Among the pages are Nepali health posters, warning of the dangers of spitting and worms, one entire section devoted to western comics and another section representing a Red Chinese opera in pictures. Above the kitchen door hang two climbing helmets and a framed photograph of the King and Queen of Nepal.

'There was a photo of the King and Queen in Ang Yange's house, too, at Manidingma,' Ann tells me, 'and in Bhandar.'

'I also have one in my house,' says Vaim Bahadur shyly. 'Most people are having them.'

Threatening clouds have made the evening muggy and hot and now, once we are safely inside, rain begins in earnest. I race upstairs to the dormitory to rearrange our sleeping bags away from the worst of the leaks. After dinner I sit up for a while to write my diary, using the light of a homemade lamp — a simple cotton wick punched through the screw-on lid of a small jar of kerosene.

From Surkye we continue north up the Dudh Kosi valley by the normal route. A Spanish expedition is on its way to Ama Dablam and all day we share the track with their baggage train. They have many porters, but the bulk of their kit is carried by yak-cattle crossbreeds. These resilient animals are invaluable for load-carrying in the warmer temperatures of sub-alpine areas. Behind their bony shoulder humps they are fitted with small wooden saddles and on each flank hangs a bag or plastic drum of supplies. At higher altitudes the pure-bred yak comes into its own: thick shaggy coats protect them against the cold and their powerful legs can forge a steady path through thick snow.

Both yaks and crossbreeds travel a little slower than us, and they are not easy animals to overtake. They swing their heads as they amble along and their wide horns sweep the path from side to side. They are unhappy about being passed on the inside, an instinctive reaction of most mountain dwellers. I try to pass on the outside, with the edge of the track dropping steeply away to the river below, and I appreciate their feelings.

We duck in and out between them later, on the river flats, where the Dudh Kosi flows almost calm between sandy banks and tall pines. The Japanese Restaurant Hotel at Chomoa is famous for its home-grown vegetables so we decide to spend the night there, only to find there are no Japanese there at present, only Sherpas, and no sign of the famous vegetables. All night rats scurry back and forth in the roof; rain falls steadily and when the temperature drops during the night there is intermittent snow.

We are away early in the morning, leaving Chomoa and following the Dudh Kosi to Jorsale. At Jorsale we pass through the Sagarmatha (Mt Everest) National Park checkpost and pay the national park entry fee of Rs 60. Then we go on, crossing the Bhote Kosi river as it comes in from the left, and from there a stiff climb of 600 metres brings us to Namche Bazaar.

Namche is smaller than I expected, a scattering of white-walled stone houses on the lower terraces of a natural amphitheatre at an altitude of 3440 metres. The ring of surrounding hills is given a dark and sombre aspect by a patch of cloud which hangs below the crest. There is ice on the ground in the shade, but in the sun the surface of the trail has quickly turned to mud.

In mountaineering history Namche has always appeared as an outpost at the far edge of civilisation, the last sizeable village before the wilds of Everest. It is still a small village, but now it has a post office, police post, national park headquarters and a bank that will cash travellers' cheques. A geographical survey reported 483 trekkers in the area in a single month (October 1978).

We have to go on past Namche to our resupply base in Khunde, a Sherpa village about 400 metres higher, where we are to stay with friends. We walk up the last hill together, Vaim Bahadur in front, steadily climbing past the tiny Shyangboche airstrip, over a last ridge and on to the top of the hill which is crowned by a long solid *mani* wall. We pass by the *mani* wall into bare rock-walled fields and make our winding way up to the big house where Mingma and Ang Dooli live.

Mingma is away bringing in a group of Ed Hillary's Himalayan Trust workers for a schoolhouse project, but Ang Dooli is here to greet us with her beaming smile. We met Ang Dooli in Kathmandu when she came to visit her youngest son at boarding school there. 'Cup of tea, yes?' she asks. She knows us well.

Ang Dooli's kitchen is upstairs above the dark yak barn where their five beasts are stabled each night, safe from snow leopards, *yetis* and thieves. In the cosy room that does duty as a living, sleeping and kitchen area, we sit on benches cushioned with rugs of faded rich wool, eating *chapatis* with our *chiya.* There are other rooms but life congregates here, in the warmest spot. The walls are lined with shelves of beautiful porcelain china and delicately patterned silver plates and utensils.

Ann and I sit in the window alcove near the fireplace and look out over the fields. The main crop at this altitude is *rigis* (potatoes) and we have pitched our tent on the dusty surface of a *rigi* field in front of the house. At the edge of the field a group of *Sherpanis* (Sherpa women) are unearthing pits of seed potatoes, buried deep to survive the winter frosts, and are sorting them for planting.

The women are dressed as Ang Dooli is, in a patterned blouse beneath the dark grey or blue *ingi,* a long woollen crossover-front robe, worn with a colourful apron. The wool for the apron has been woven in 20-centimetre-long strips of different colours, joined together and held up by a cummerbund secured with a solid silver buckle. Ang Dooli wears a necklace of thick nuggets of turquoise and coral and her long black hair is tightly braided and protected from the wind by a woven headscarf.

Tomorrow is Saturday, weekly market day in Namche, Ang Dooli tells us. She checks with us whether we will eat the local diet of *chapatis* and potatoes, explaining that *dahl bhat* is not always available at this altitude. Every market day she walks 400 metres down to the market to shop and then walks 400 metres back up the hill with the supplies. We go with her to help out and have a closer look at Namche.

In the morning we pay Vaim Bahadur his due for the portering work to Khunde. Vaim has been very encouraged by successfully making this trip into the Khumbu and he has told us of his hope to get work as an expedition porter. He asks if we will write something for him that he can show to expedition sirdars when they are hiring porters.

'Of course,' I reply and I write out a reference for him. It reads: 'Vaim Bahadur carried a load for us from Karantichap to Khunde. He proved to be a hardworking, cheerful, reliable and honest porter. I have no hesitation in recommending him for further employment.' Then I sign it.

SP translates it for Vaim, who blushes distinctly.

'Thank you, sahib,' he says.

'It is all true,' I say, smiling. We are sorry to see him go. Moving quickly back along our route without a load, he expects to be home in about four days.

Khunde faces east on to one of the finest views in the world. Below us, where the ridge falls away steeply to the upper Dudh Kosi, there is often a still bank of cloud in the early mornings. Above that, sharply outlined by the sun behind, is a ring of mountains, from Ama Dablam's distinctive peak in the north, east to Kangtega (6779 metres) and Thamserku (6608 metres) in the south. The western flanks of the mountains are still and calm in deep shadow, but soon the sun creeps higher and its warmth loosens the frozen snow and ice. Then the daily bombardment begins, small whispering slides of snow growing into avalanches, falling ice and rock hurtling down the faces.

There is plenty of opportunity to familiarise ourselves with this view as we settle in for a few days, catching up on yet more trekking chores. At the front of Ang Dooli's house is an area of paved stone, and along the edge of it stands a 20-metre long by two-metre-high pile of wood, stored against the long winter, the widest logs at the bottom and gradually smaller sticks towards the top. After washing our grubby trekking clothes we lay them on this wall to dry. Behind the wall is the toilet, a little shack on poles, built out from the courtyard over the first *rigi* field. There is a hole in the floor and around it a deep pile of pine needles, rhododendron leaves and foliage. Each person who uses the toilet drops a handful of leaves down the hole and, periodically, the mixture below is taken out and spread on the *rigi* fields. This is the first time I have seen such a deliberate attempt to use waste to fertilise the fields; one of the other houses we stayed in had a similar toilet structure but it had a waterway running beneath it.

Manure is taken from the yak barn also and Ang Dooli's eldest son, Temba, is working there today. The floor is carpeted one metre deep below ground level with a similar mix of foliage and droppings accumulated during the winter. Temba is digging it out with a shovel and two women employed by Ang Dooli are taking *doko* loads of it out into the fields.

The Himalayan Trust party arrive and for a while the Khumbu seems to be full of New Zealanders. After a few days' acclimatisation at Khunde, Ann and I team up with Peg Gosden, a friend from Mt Cook, and we set off one afternoon to complete the trek to the Everest base camp.

The trail leads down through Khumjung, where shouting children are quietened by a ringing school bell, to Sarnasa, where the Khunde track joins the main track north from Namche. There are only two or three buildings at the crossroads but on each fine day in the trekking season traders, some of them Tibetan refugees, come down from the surrounding villages to sell souvenirs to tourists. The traders have laid crimson cloth along the side of the track by a *chiya* shop and carefully spread out their stocks — *kukri* knives, chunks of turquoise, rings, belt buckles, small stone Buddhas, lockets, earrings, brass buttons.

'Old Tibetan, sahib, very old.'

'Yes, of course.'

There are woollen hats in grey homespun and after some negotiation I buy one for Rs 25. There is nothing either traditionally Sherpa or Tibetan about a wool hat but they are warm and this one has a nice design of yak horns around it. I notice that the Tibetans here count not on the fingertips but on the joints of their fingers. So, provided they have been careful while wood cutting, they can count up to 14 on one hand. Perhaps the metric system is not the only 'natural' one after all.

From Sarnasa we trundle on, dropping steadily towards the upper Dudh Kosi. We cross the river at Phunki Thanka and climb 1000 metres above it to where Thyangboche monastery sits on a jutting promontory, presiding over the approach to Mount Everest. Everest is visible from here, the very top of the mountain poking above the long rugged ridge between Nuptse and Lhotse, but it is too far away, and too little of it is visible, to be inspiring. Thyangboche is famous for other reasons: partly the *gompa* or monastery itself, a large building of traditional Tibetan design, with small huts clustered about its walls, and partly the view behind the monastery of the Mingbo face of Ama Dablam which rears up from a curtain of ice-fluted ridges. *Ama* means 'mother', *dablam* 'locket', and the mountain takes its name from the locket, an immense projecting glacier which hangs over and threatens the Mingbo face of the mountain. At 6858 metres Ama Dablam is not among the highest peaks but it has a reputation for difficulty: it was below that locket that Pete's 1979 expedition was hit by falling ice, and one member of the team was killed, and two (including Pete) badly injured. The survivors had a difficult retreat from the face before beginning their long lonely trip home.

There is hardly a book on Nepal which omits a photograph of this view and from my reading I know the scene intimately. Yet nothing has prepared me for the reality. The mountain dominates the human element in the landscape and it was perhaps for that reason that the monastery was sited here. But there is something inspiring, something suggesting resilience, in the fact that the human element is noticeable in this landscape at all: the monastery does not intrude or retreat; it seems to belong, to be as natural here as the mountain itself.

We make it all the way to Pangboche with Peg that afternoon, leaving a scruffy trail behind us through falling snow. We stop for the night at a two-room hotel called the New Teahouse where they prepare *chiya* while we stand by the door cooling down after our exertion. Two yaks are in the field just below the steps, steaming gently like us in the cold despite the snow settling on their backs. A boy was unloading firewood from them as we came in, and now one yak is licking a patch on the other's back where the saddle has been rubbing.

Inside, the three of us have been given the main room of the teahouse, which has narrow sleeping benches around three walls. A little light comes in through a single unshuttered window high in the wall.

As in most of the Khumbu there are only a few women and children left with the infirm or elderly of the village. The rest of the residents, female and male, are away working while the summer permits: they may be camped with their yak-beasts in a high pasture or trekking with tourists or, highest paid and riskiest of all, they may be amongst the elite high altitude porters and away with an expedition to some mountain. Wherever they are, for most families, this isolation will continue until autumn.

The woman who attends us is polite and speaks some English, but seems a little distracted when she shows us into our room. As the evening passes there is increasing coming and going in the kitchen, with people popping briefly into our room and then out again. Just after our *dhal* and rice are served a woman slips in through the door to the kitchen and a distressed wailing breaks out; something terrible must have happened. We finish our meal in uneasy silence and Ann goes to the kitchen door as the crying dies down but comes back none the wiser. There seems little we can do except go to bed.

Later, when we are quiet, villagers come into our room in twos and threes. We are lying on the benches and they squat on the floor until the room is full. On the far side of the room someone's pressure lantern surges fitfully, casting shadows which deepen the darkness. The crowd is swayed by a restless murmuring which falls to a hush when a lama comes in, a grave lean-faced man robed in dark maroon wool. Space is made for the lama near the middle of the room and he places before him on the floor a bowl containing clay while someone passes a bowl of water to him through the crowd. Taking some water, he slowly builds a small human figure about hand-high and when it is completed he stands it on top of a tin and builds an elaborate structure like a mountain or a fantastic tiered cake around and up the sides of the tin. The figure stands at the top surrounded by tall spines of clay, and the 'mountain' is riven with deep fissures and decorated with stones. The lama sits behind the figure and reaches for a small drum. Tapping it gently he leads the crowd in a sing-song chant which rises and falls in tempo, murmuring and then clamouring. Through it all, and the last thing I remember before sleep, is the sound of someone weeping.

In the middle of the night I suddenly start awake, disorientated. The ceiling of our room has been lined with flattened expedition cartons and on their surface confused shadows are dancing. A drum is tapping slowly in the midst of chanting voices and I half sit up, perplexed. An old man is squatting on the floor beside me and seeing my confusion he reaches out gently and pats my hand. I do not know what he says, but memory comes rushing back and my puzzlement recedes. I nod to him slowly and he smiles, cracked teeth shining in the lamplight. I roll over again and sleep.

In the morning there are a few scattered grains of rice on the floor, but nothing else to show what passed last night. We are served tea, but the Sherpani who let us into the house tells us that they cannot provide food today. She explains that her brother lives in Pheriche, and that yesterday his baby died and the mother is still very sick. Just telling us is too much for her and she begins to cry, leaning forward sobbing until her head rests on the narrow table. Ann takes the Sherpani's hand in her own and puts her arm around her shoulders, hugging her awkwardly on the rough bench.

Outside all is light, bright sun on new snow, the air crisp. We move quickly over the flat ground of the broad valley floor, through Pheriche and then up the Khumbu glacier moraine to Honku. In the early afternoon we arrive at Lobuche, which is wrapped in damp mist. It does not take long to explore Lobuche: there is a national park lodge, a few huts, about a dozen trekking-group tents in orderly lines, and a huge rubbish dump, the refuse of countless trekkers and expeditions. Lobuche is the traditional overnight stop before the Everest base camp, last stop on the Khumbu trail. But few trekkers go to the base camp: the usual trip is to climb to Kala Pattar (5545 metres), which is higher than the base camp, and from which a better view of Everest can be gained. Ann, Peg and I decide that we too will climb to Kala Pattar tomorrow and then descend as far as we can towards Khunde in the afternoon, so that Peg can get back in time to her work for the Himalayan Trust.

Although yaks can be seen grazing high up on the pastures there is obviously not enough feed for them here, for the *sirdar* of one trekking group is supervising the feeding of hay to his yaks. Two of the yaks begin fighting with a sudden heavy rush and clash of horns. Porters drive them apart and proceed to tie them up to a low stone wall that runs out behind one of the tent lines. The porters tie ropes round the yaks' necks, pass the free ends through gaps low in the wall and tie them to sticks. As the yaks move away, their ropes are pulled taut and the sticks lodge fast against the wall, jerking the yaks to a halt.

Inside the national park lodge 20 or so trekkers are clustered around the fire, members of organised trekking groups from the rows of tents outside. Most of them are wearing down trousers, down jackets and double boots but complaints about the cold are clearly audible. Ann and Peg raise their eyebrows at this: the three of us are wearing old ski trousers with a jacket over a jersey each, and woollen hats and running shoes. During the afternoon we have to go for a walk on the moraine to keep warm but it works.

By 6.25 the next morning we are off up the trail to Kala Pattar, carrying only our cameras and storm clothing. It is cold and decidedly sunless at this hour so we are wearing gloves and we beat our hands together to warm them up as we go. The trekking groups have started before us and we follow their stabbing beams of torchlight as the faint starlight fades in the dawn. The track is well worn and easy to follow in the grassy trough, but becomes more difficult where the flows of the Changri Nup and Changri Shah glaciers come in to join the Khumbu and we have to traverse a well cairned route across the rubble of the glacier. Half an hour of this brings us down to the big sand pan of the old dried lake called Gorak Shep. We are at 5185 metres now, and the sun has reached us at last.

In the rocks beside the dried up lake is a low-walled shelter with a tarpaulin roof, where an enterprising Sherpani sells *chiya* and glucose biscuits. Three hundred and sixty metres above us is the black rubble of the peak called Kala Pattar (black stones). Pumo Ri (7145 metres) stands behind it, an elegant rock peak with a graceful cap of smooth snow and ice. The prospect draws us on.

Soon we are climbing again, zigzagging back and forth over the short turf, stirring dust under foot and watching the Khumbu glacier flatten out below us. I find myself pausing more and more frequently for breath, sucking in the thin air, but rather than admit it I use the time-honoured excuse of 'taking in the view'. I grow more breathless, however, and resort to other tricks such as 'checking the map' or 'taking a photo'. On each occasion the rest of the party is gracious enough to stop with me. To the north the Khumbu glacier's jagged ice fall curves in exit from the Western Cwm and just below the ice fall we can see the brightly coloured dots that are the tents of the Japanese expedition at Everest base camp. We take turns in watching these dots of colour through the 150 mm lens, but there are no signs of activity, no further excuses to linger, so we push on towards the black rocks above us.

It is mid morning when we reach the crest of Kala Pattar at last. In the foreground, on the far side of the Khumbu glacier, is the ridge that runs down southwards off Nuptse. On the other side of Nuptse this ridge runs eastward and then northward in a huge encircling curve, two kilometres high, through the summit of Lhotse, to Everest. It is this ridge which hides everything except the very summit of Everest from those who try to view the highest mountain in the world from the distant south. Only here, close at hand, can we see behind that curtain.

The sheer bulk of Everest's 8848 metres dwarfs everything. The south-west face of the mountain is black and forbidding. Only one tongue of snow can be seen, mid way up the face; all the rest is stripped bare by the searching wind. The jet stream, soaring in from Tibet, strikes the summit of Everest and glances off again into space, a huge plume of cloud, easily two kilometres long, blowing out to the north-east. Ann and Peg and I sit on the ridge and watch. For a long time nothing is said. Everest, 'the big E', is simply awesome.

Lush rice paddies and farmhouses below Besi Shahar village in the Marsyangdi valley east of Pokhara in central Nepal.

Buses are the main means of travel from Kathmandu and fares are cheap. For every person on top of a bus there'll be another four inside.

A Tamang woman and child above the Trisuli river, northwest of Kathmandu.

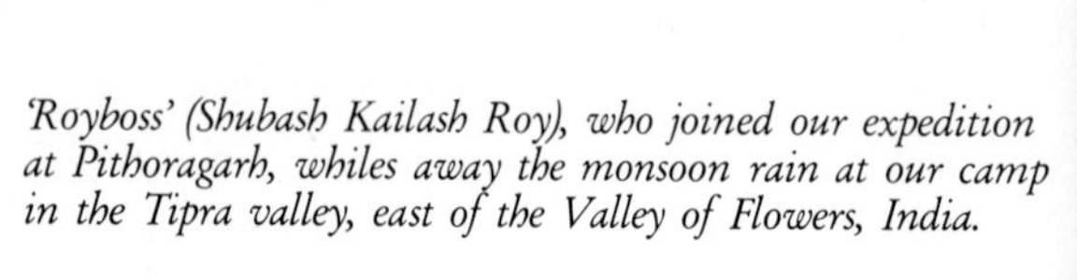

'Royboss' (Shubash Kailash Roy), who joined our expedition at Pithoragarh, whiles away the monsoon rain at our camp in the Tipra valley, east of the Valley of Flowers, India.

Luckily for our expedition, signs such as this one below Gangotri were not common.

Where travellers go, signs follow. This one graces the roadside at Rohtang La (3978m) above the Kulu-Manali valley in northern India.

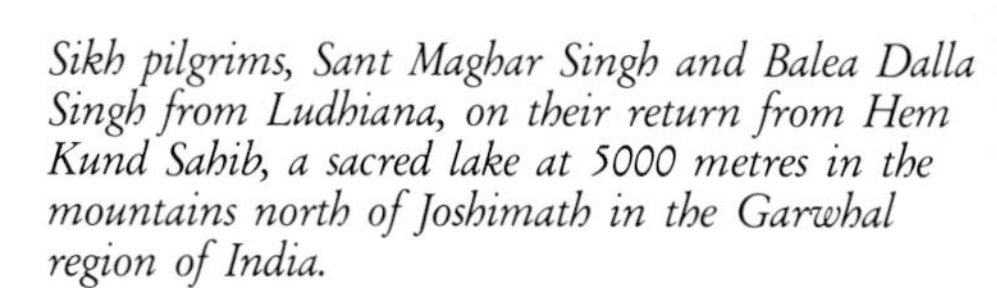

Sikh pilgrims, Sant Maghar Singh and Balea Dalla Singh from Ludhiana, on their return from Hem Kund Sahib, a sacred lake at 5000 metres in the mountains north of Joshimath in the Garwhal region of India.

In the early morning fog we prepare to leave Kathmandu for the last time.

The top of the bus is the coolest place to travel. Passengers settle their baggage at a bus-stop east of Pokhara.

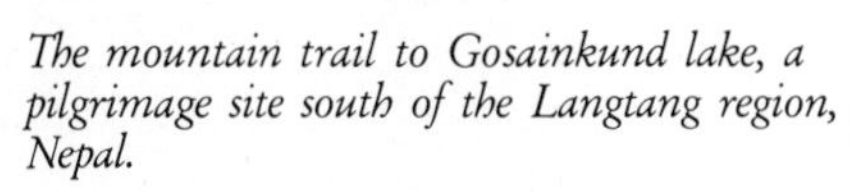

The mountain trail to Gosainkund lake, a pilgrimage site south of the Langtang region, Nepal.

Papadoms and subji (curried vegetables) provide lunch for this family group below Joshimath.

During our stay in the Khumbu we all managed to fit in several side trips. As well as our trip to Kala Pattar with Peg, Ann and I visited the Buddhist monastery at Thame (Thame Gompa) and climbed to the top of Gokyo Ri (5360 metres) for another view of Everest, this time from further west. Corrina's stomach trouble had abated sufficiently by the time the traversers arrived to accompany Ding, Tashi, Pete and SP on a quick visit to the Gokyo valley for an attempt on a peak there.

It was nearly two months since Ding and Corrina had last been together and their joy at seeing each other was evident. Tashi also was extremely pleased to be in the Khumbu, and he and SP had much news to swap. Luckily for Pete, within just a few days his father, his uncle, Rex, and then his aunt, June, arrived. They were joining the Himalayan Trust party which was adding an extension to the Khunde hospital. For a few days their presence delayed our assessment of the expedition's progress and future strategy — apart from the serious business of replenishing hungry stomachs, that is — but provided a welcome break for us all from the tension that once again threatened to build up amongst our team at Khunde.

Eventually, however, we had to have some planning sessions. Before we left New Zealand we had been invited by a British mountaineer, Doug Scott, to join him on an International Climbing Meet in the Gangotri region of India for a few weeks during June. This had seemed a welcome opportunity for a break from the traverse, giving us a chance to mix with other climbers and maybe even get some 'real' mountaineering done. Yet already it was April and only a small part of the traverse had been accomplished. With a long distance still to go, just to reach India, it was unlikely that we could get to the Gangotri in time to join up with Doug Scott. There was some disagreement about the appropriate way of dealing with this. Pete made it quite clear that, to him, this climbing section was a very important part of the expedition. It would give him a chance to wind down and spend some time with his own friends. If necessary, he felt, we should stop the traverse wherever we had got to in June and go from there to join the climbing meet. After six weeks of climbing we could go back and restart the traverse.

Ding and Corrina were keen on the climbing meet too, as Ann and I were, but Ding was worried about our present rate of progress. My view was quite clear. If we had not reached Gangotri by June and still took six weeks off for climbing, I doubted if we could finish the traverse in 1981. None of us particularly relished the thought of staying over for the next Himalayan winter, to finish off in the following year.

In the end I was asked to write to Doug Scott, saying that Ding and Pete would be there in June for the climbing meet. I did so, but added my own view that they were dreaming: if they finished the traverse itself, they would be doing well and, in my opinion, Doug should not count on their arrival. As it turned out, the month of June came and nearly went before the traverse party had managed to complete even the crossing of Nepal. By then, all thoughts of climbing in the Gangotri had been quietly forgotten.

Ann and I finally left the Khumbu, with SP, on 18 April, and Corrina flew out to Kathmandu a few days later. Our trekking route headed south through Phaphlu and brought us out to the main east-west Nepal highway, seven days after leaving

Khunde. We arrived in Kathmandu in time to celebrate Ann's 25th birthday on 4 May with a few of the friends we had made there (and huge helpings of borsch and baked alaska) at Boris's Russian Restaurant.

The next two months were full of activity. SP, Ann and I trekked for 26 days around the Annapurna mountain massif, crossing the Thorong La, a pass of 5416 metres, to resupply the traverse party in Jomosom in mid-western Nepal. At Jomosom another complication arose. Corrina had flown into Jomosom to meet us and there met up with Al and Adrian Burgess, English mountaineering twins. They had been on a British expedition which had attempted the West Ridge of Everest during the winter of 1980-81. They were in Jomosom now, having just climbed Dhaulagiri (8167 metres), across the valley from Jomosom, with a Canadian expedition. Also on Dhaulagiri was an Argentinian mountaineering team, who had suffered an accident in which their leader died. They had been using Dhaulagiri as a training ground for their attempt on the West Ridge of Everest in the 1981 post-monsoon period and it now looked as if they would default on their booking. In that case there would be a vacant slot for Everest and the twins were rushing to Kathmandu to see if they could take over the booking. They needed another pair. 'What about Ding and Pete?' Corrina suggested.

The twins knew Pete and promptly agreed. Leaving a hurriedly scribbled note behind them for the traversers, they dashed off to Kathmandu. When Ding, Pete and Tashi arrived in Jomosom on 26 May, the Everest invitation burst among them like a bombshell. After much discussion the positions resolved themselves. Ding felt that they should not go, much as he would have liked to. He felt that climbing Everest would require a three month break at least, and that would mean the traverse would probably not be finished at all. He didn't see how they could abandon the traverse and still keep faith with the sponsors. Pete felt that the sponsors would agree to such a prestigious change in our route, and that the traverse could be finished by August anyway, in time for Everest, or else it could be finished afterwards. Although SP and Tashi weren't directly concerned with our sponsors, they did feel that they would be let down if Ding and Pete took off for Everest.

Once again the support party became the expedition's communication system with the outside world. We were despatched urgently to Kathmandu to find out whether the twins had got the permit, Ding hoping fervently that they hadn't. When we caught up with the twins there, it was to discover that they had missed out. Two New Zealand mountaineers, Paddy Freaney and Russell Brice, had got wind of the Argentinians' problem and beaten the twins to the Ministry of Tourism by a day. So one more threat to our progress was safely out of the way.

When the support party was all back in Kathmandu we were joined by Michael Okkerse, a friend from New Zealand. Mike had flown over to accompany the support team for seven weeks or so of holiday. He was keen to see and do as much as possible and we planned some trekking and minor mountaineering together.

I now went down to New Delhi to try to uplift a new permit from the IMF that would allow us to commence the western portion of our journey, through the Indian Himalaya. The traversers had only a three-week section left in order to finish the Nepal portion of their traverse. What a disappointment that trip to Delhi was: the IMF had failed to obtain permission for our expedition to enter any of the mountain areas inside the Inner-line. The alternative route that they had allocated us made the traverse much longer and less interesting, often leading through the foothills of north-western India rather than through the mountains. It would be at leech level, too, when the monsoon came, and the monsoon was not far away. Since we had heard no definite news of the Indian Army expedition's progress, I tried to find out from the IMF how it was getting on. The IMF couldn't tell me, or so they said. I sifted carefully through the pile of old newspapers in the corner of the hostel where I was staying, but could find no news of their expedition there either. I hoped that this was a case of 'no news is good news' for us.

While I was in New Delhi, Ann took Mike trekking up into the Langtang valley, near the Tibetan border, returning via the Laurebina La (5144 metres). Corrina was recuperating from another bout of stomach infection in Kathmandu, so SP flew alone into Jumla, in western Nepal, to resupply the traverse team for their last Nepal stage. We had heard that on this stage the traversers would be passing through a region suffering from food shortages. So we sent in enough freeze-dried meals to last them two weeks. It was just enough. SP walked with the traversers on this last section, happy to reach the border with India at last — his own country. 'From here, everything will go smoothly,' he promised.

Corrina and Ann, together with Michael, made their own way out of Nepal and across to Pithoragarh, our first Indian rendezvous, by bus. I wasn't on that bus journey; I went to Pithoragarh by train from New Delhi. But, once again, I could as well have been there — incidents on that journey happened on others that I was on. So, since it is Ann's and my story that we decided to write, we have written me into this bus journey too, one similar to many others we experienced in that year together.

6. Nepal to India — A Bus Journey

None of the Kathmandu bus companies provide printed route schedules or timetables for their services. Destinations and departure times are painted on boards outside the booking offices of different bus companies at the central depot. First you have to find the right office, and hope that the information will be printed in English. There is no such information displayed at the bus company that we are directed to, so Ann tacks on to the end of a queue outside the ticket office.

'And to where is it that you are going, madam?'

'We have to meet some friends in a place called Pithoragarh. It's an Indian town on the western border of your country. Have you heard of it?'

'No, madam, I am not knowing the place of that name.'

'Could you tell me then, please, how often the buses run to the western border?'

'But no, madam, we are not having any buses going there. We are not having a road going there.'

'But isn't this a road marked on the map here?'

'Yes, madam, but we have not been building that road yet.' The clerk's head is nodding and shaking frenziedly. 'Please, madam, we have many people who are in the queueing. Perhaps you can be waiting?'

A man behind us in the queue volunteers assistance. He has a friend whose cousin once had to go to Pithoragarh on family business.

'I will bring him to you, tomorrow. He will help.'

I am more than a little sceptical and am not surprised when the cousin fails to materialise the next day. But the first man, Kumar, does and he has gone to the trouble of learning from his acquaintance the details of the route from Kathmandu to Pithoragarh.

Ann asks one of the young boys hanging around the depot to fetch us a glass of special *chiya* and some biscuits. The boy runs back, glasses clinking in the little rusty wire carrier from the shop around the corner. Kumar declines the biscuit and says he cannot stay, but asks Ann to write down the names of the towns along the route, in case she should forget.

'First to Pokhara by bus, as you say you have done once before, and then you are having Syangje by bus also. This is the District Headquarters, and the Angdi Khola river is next and Tansing and Butwal,' he recites for us. 'Then you will be having Betwari and Bhairawa which is the finish in Nepal. Gorakhpur is where you will be getting a train for Pithoragarh, but you must be getting another bus for the last part.'

'Do you have any idea of how long it took your friend?' Ann asks.

'We are thinking that two days will be more than sufficient for you.'

We arrive at the depot at four in the morning (two hours before the bus is scheduled to leave) with the hope of securing seats next to a window on one of the front benches. Although we are so early, there are three other passengers already inside, two men and a woman, probably a bit younger than Ann. They have the front bench and the men turn to smile as we sit behind.

'Namaste,' we greet each other. The woman peeks at us from under a fold of her sari, hastily pulled over her bare head as we arrived. The two men have a woollen shawl each, wrapped around their shoulders.

'My name is Chandra,' says the younger of the two, carefully enunciating the English phrases. 'My brother is named Yindra. Your name, sir?'

I tell them ours and Ann asks, 'Your sister's name?'

'No, no, my wife,' Chandra nudges her, 'Taragi.' Taragi promptly hides her face again at the mention of her name. 'First time in Kathmandu,' explains her husband. 'Very nice place. Home going now.' He says something to Taragi and she smiles and turns to Ann, showing her the decoration of scarlet powders along the central parting in her hair. 'Only the wife has this,' explains Chandra.

The first of Kathmandu's many vegetable sellers appears out of the darkness, carrying his creaking baskets of produce across the cobbled post office square. He vanishes in the fog in the direction of the Bhimsen tower.

Two boys are using a bucket to sluice off the layers of dust and, by the smell of it, vomit from the dark blue sides of our bus. I shiver at the splash of the water in the predawn chill. The ticket office is boarded up but at least half a dozen young boys, hardly in their teens, are busying themselves about the bus in the dark. They are dressed in a motley assortment of clothing — shabby trousers with cuffs ragged at the heel, nylon business shirts with, here and there, a button missing or undone. Most of the boys wear knitted acrylic vests in lurid patterns of pink and yellow over the top of their other clothes. Chandra and Yindra, I notice, have not forsaken their warmer homespun cotton and wool for the fashionable allure of polyester material.

As long as one of us stays on our seatbench in the bus for half an hour or so, we will have established a 'booking' for it. Then both of us will be free to walk around, leaving our jackets as proof of our claim while the rest of the bus fills up around them.

I get out for a stroll first, leaving Ann to occupy the seat. As I come around the front of the bus I see flames crackling away underneath. I dash back to the door.

'Hell's teeth, Ann, the bus is on fire, get out of there!' I shout.

'What!' she exclaims, leaping for the doorway. 'You must be joking, surely?' The words tumble out of her as she races down the steps, uncertain whether to take me seriously or not. The bus-boys certainly don't take me seriously — my shout is the signal for them to fall about laughing.

One of the boys comes up to me, wiping his eyes. 'No, no, sahib, *tikchha,*

tikchha (okay, okay),' he says, leading me around to the far side of the bus. He points at the flames and I see now that they come from two long poles wrapped in rags and obviously soaked in some sort of fuel, placed underneath the bus. 'Very cold this morning, sahib, diesel no good, warming up,' the boy explains. Then, taking a third pole, he shoves more rags in through the vent of the fuel tank, extracts them and then lowers that pole with its rags over the other two. The rags crackle into flame, curling up and around the fuel tank.

'You are making a fire under the fuel tank to warm the diesel, right?' I ask.

'Yes, sahib. All the time doing this, very safe, no problem.'

'I see,' I reply, wearily.

'Well, what do you think, Doug?' Ann asks me. 'Do you feel like getting back in?' The bus is beginning to fill up and none of the other passengers seems the least bit concerned.

'I suppose so,' I reply, adding, 'we haven't even left yet and these clowns already have me scared witless. I wish we could stay in the hills where it's safe.' A slightly older youth clambers into the driver's cab. I watch as he lights a bundle of incense and swings it in an arc over the steering-wheel, across the front under the windscreen and back to the driver's seat, muttering softly to himself. He completes his incantations and leaves the incense to burn in an old tin in the middle of the dashboard. Above it a string of small coloured light bulbs wink and glow by a picture of Ganesh, mounted between the front windows. Ganesh is the elephant-headed Hindu god of good judgment and prudence, his long curling trunk making him one of the easiest of the Hindu deities to recognise.

'Was that the driver?' Ann asks as the youth wanders away. Yindra shrugs eloquently, shaking his head.

'We shall see.'

The interior of our bus is wonderfully decorated. Psychedelic patterns of colour — pinks, yellows, greens and orange — have been woven around the edges of the front windscreen. Two small landscapes have been painted across the tops of the windows, one on either side of the picture of Ganesh. They are peaceful scenes — a reed fringed lake with implausibly large boats, and a view of mountains with a stream in the foreground and two animals, a deer and a panther I think.

Bold swirls of paint sweep back towards the rear of the bus. Above each of the side windows someone has carefully hung a row of yellow plastic baskets, about ten centimetres high, and filled with multi-hued bunches of plastic flowers. They sway and dance above our heads in the chill breeze that blows in through the open door. The sliding glass window panes beside us are cracked and dusty and the rear one cannot be budged.

'Hey, Doug, these look like bullet holes here.'

'Oh, come on, surely not?'

Ann has a closer look. 'Well, I don't know what else could have left such neat round holes in a window.'

Two men take down the boards from the front of the ticket cubicle and Ann goes to buy our tickets. After seeing how closely Taragi is attended by Chandra and his brother, I notice that Ann is the only woman outside in the queue. If she was a local woman she would be pitied now for the lack of a guardian male to buy her tickets for her; scorned even for such a deficient upbringing that she should mix, alone, with menfolk. But Ann is a foreigner, and friendly, and an exception is easily made for her.

Someone connects the transistor radio in the cab, and my ears are assailed with a mixture of high-pitched music and static. The noise jolts a passenger near the back into competition: on goes his radio vying with the first for airspace. What remains of the dawn hush is shattered by one of the bus-boys starting the engine: he revs it in neutral, time after time, until the bus is almost hidden from view by clouds of blue smoke.

Ann returns with the tickets and one of the two men who slipped into the empty spaces on our seat stands up straightaway to make room for her. She has the middle seat and I the window-seat on our unpadded wooden bench. It is a seat for three people although it is hardly more than a metre long. On the other side of the fifty centimetre wide aisle is an even shorter bench, only just wide enough for two people. Space has also been cut to a minimum between the rows of seats — there is just enough room for a person of average Nepali stature to sit comfortably. Ann and her neighbour, both not much over 160 centimetres tall, fit easily but I am nearer two metres and cannot fit my knees in front of me. First I have my legs crossed, then diagonally out to the side, but I am never comfortable and cannot get into a position where my legs support much of my weight. I have to cross and recross my legs to restore the circulation.

These Indian-made 'Tata' buses have been built short and narrow to cope with the extremely windy, narrow hill roads, and the bus company has given a lot of thought to gaining the maximum possible revenue for the limited amount of space. Despite this, fares are low: Ann paid US$4 for our trip and it could involve up to 18 hours' travel.

Little of the interior space of the bus is wasted on cargo. The roof of the bus has a platform with low walls around the edge of it, where baggage and freight are carried up on ladders at the rear of the bus and dumped. The bus shakes and groans as the porters crash about above our heads, wedging rucksacks, suitcases, tin trunks, *doko* loads of vegetables, bales of wire and building materials, into a stable load.

Each bench position inside our bus is numbered, but the company invariably sells more tickets than there are seats. As the bus fills, so does the aisle. The more prosperous-looking passengers get the seats. The porters board last, finishing their *bidis* before taking up their positions on sacks of grain in the aisle, squatting back-to-back for balance.

The incense man is the driver. Turning off the radio with an abrupt snap, he revs the engine and blasts on the horn to hurry along stragglers. He considers his load satisfactory when four more people have squashed on to the steps inside the front door. The bus dodges out into the congestion of pedestrians and bullock carts, billowing exhaust behind us. Farewell, Kathmandu. Bye, Sri.

Our driver looks incongruously small on his upholstered throne, perched behind the huge steering-wheel. His feet only just reach the pedals. Three of the young bus-boys have come aboard with him, roosting in uncomfortable corners of the cab. They watch in silence, as intent upon our driver as he is upon the road ahead and around them eddies a reassuring aura of care.

For the first hour we follow the long series of tight, sinuous corners of the Rajpath, as it climbs and descends over the Mahabharat range to the south of the Kathmandu valley. Our bus has 'SPEED 45 km' painted on its bumpers, but it seldom manages to travel more than 20 kilometres in any one hour. We stop frequently to pick up more passengers and unload produce. As new passengers clamber aboard, the bus-boys climb through the bus like monkeys above the crush of people, over the seat backs, hanging from the ceiling rail, issuing tickets and collecting payment. One of the bus-boys rides on the roof, supervising the passengers up there. At each stop he signals that the driver may start again, by delivering a sharp double hand-clap on the roof. White milestones announce the distance to the next destination. Some have been repainted with metric details, however, so it is not always easy to gauge our position.

The modest speed is uncomfortably fast for one of our fellow passengers and I flinch nervously at the sound of retching close by. It is one of the porters in the aisle, who is trying unsuccessfully to stop his mouth with his fingers. I would have rushed towards a window in his predicament, but then none of the ones that I tried earlier would open, so perhaps that would not have been such a good idea. The bus is so crowded, of course, that there is no question of cleaning up the mess. The sun is up now and the heat grows intense, but in a few hours we'll all be so ripe that no one will notice the smell.

At Naubise the driver switches off the engine, signalling a longer halt. Ann and I exit gratefully, although not gracefully, for there are many people to climb over. Chandra, Yindra and Taragi are leaving us for their village, another two days' walk to the west. Chandra climbs the ladder at the back of the bus and hands down their two cloth-wrapped bundles to Taragi. We exchange 'Namastes' a last time as they walk down the street, Taragi slightly behind, erect with both bundles balanced on her head.

Hawkers swoop on the bus, holding baskets of mangoes, bananas and cherries up to the windows for inspection while others push inside. 'Panch rupya, panch rupya, panch rupya Kg (Five rupees, five rupees, five rupees a Kg),' they chant, their calls rising and falling in singsong melody. 'Kera kera kera, tin rupya (Bananas bananas bananas, three rupees).' 'Panch rupya, panch rupya (Five rupees, five rupees).'

A full bus arrives from Birganj, the border town directly south of Kathmandu, ten hours' drive from this intersection. Nobody gets off it for our bus, so we depart again, scrambling aboard as the engine of our bus roars to life. Returning to our bench necessitates standing on the seat backs and swinging from the ceiling rails, like the bus-boys, with hardly a place to put our feet between people.

Three elderly villagers have moved on to the seats in front of us. One woman leans back to shout above the noise of the engine — where have we come from? Ann's immediate reply — Kathmandu — sends them into fits of cackles.

'Hoina hoina. Tapaiko ghar kaha ho? (No, no, where is your home?)' they press.

'Oh, mero ghar New Zealandma ho (New Zealand),' Ann replies.

'Kati tara chha? (How far is that?)' Our turn to laugh now.

'Dedi dedi tara chha. Dedi din lagchha,' Ann replies. They nod knowingly when Ann says it takes two days to get to India by this bus from Kathmandu, and when she goes on to explain that it would take one hundred days to get to New Zealand by the same bus, we all go 'ooooohh' together.

'Dedi dedi tara chha (very very far),' we agree in unison.

The elderly woman points to me and asks Ann if I am her husband. 'Yes', replies Ann, for simplicity's sake.

'Well,' comes the standard follow-up query, 'how come no children having?'

We have grown accustomed to this line of questioning and have developed a number of pat replies, which, depending on the audience, range from the serious through the humorous to the slightly off-colour. The serious reply, that we are delaying having children, is rarely given, because it requires so much explanation and description of options, plans and possibilities. Many of these ideas are hard to convey to people in a society where children are so important. This time I explain to the woman that I am *brahmacharya,* which is a Hindu term for a very pious man who practises celibacy out of religious conviction. Perhaps I do not look the part for general hysteria follows.

A bunch of cherries appears at my shoulder. I twist around looking for the donor, a man sitting a couple of rows behind us, who just smiles and gestures that we must eat them, that he bought them for us. We eat them with pleasure. Wherever we have travelled the local people have generally been polite and generous, especially outside of the cities. The tourist rip-offs are confined, by and large, to the major centres and even there they are the exception rather than the rule. In this environment Ann and I need to watch carefully to preserve our own veneer, at least, of politeness, to each other as well as to those around us, despite the heat or lack of sleep or any of the other myriad irritating, pinpricking aspects of travelling that can creep up on one. If either of us should show temper in public we would immediately lose a deal of respect, and appear to the people around us as ill-educated boors for our inability to control ourselves.

The daily living conditions of most Nepalis, whether in a village or a city, are a lot more crowded than those we are used to and their social structures and systems have evolved appropriate protective mechanisms and courteous behaviour to ensure privacy: in crowded conditions outbursts are provocative and the custom is to suppress them.

A good illustration of these social structures is the toilet system. I remember reading in New Delhi a description of a typical day in the life of a village dweller. It begins with ritual ablutions at dawn, followed by a visit to the field that is currently designated by the village elders as the village toilet. There may be 20 or more villagers squatting at one time in the same small field but eye-contact, greeting and any other form of social interaction are strictly avoided until these early morning rituals are completed. Each villager acts as if the others are not present and returns home to perform the morning *puja* before commencing work for the day.

Since it is practically impossible to be alone in these conditions, society has adapted to the point where virtually no one wants to be alone; it has become desirable always to have company. Groups of concerned locals, if they ever see me alone, immediately descend upon me, to help me 'endure' my stay with pleasant, if inconsequential, chit-chat; anything to help me avoid suffering alone-ness.

To us, of course, some time alone is highly desirable. I find I must guard myself carefully against showing irritation when besieged in this way.

From Naubise the road heads west, following the Trisuli river away from the Rajpath. The steep black rock walls of the river canyon support only a few patches of scrubby trees. Their meagre shade harbours motley herds of goats, watched carefully by agile goatherds.

The monsoon has not yet begun, but in this hot season before the rains there are occasional cloud-bursts and flash floods. The sky ahead has been black with cloud all morning and here, in this section of the gorge, the many small streams are running vigorously across the road. Suddenly our driver brakes and stops. Ahead of us a trickle of a stream flows over the road. As we crane to peer through the window, the trickle swells with loose soil and suddenly bursts into a metres wide flood of water-borne mud and rock. The horrible mudslide oozes across the road, minute after minute, as we sit watching. If we had not stopped, it might easily have caught the bus and swept it over the lip. We are only ten metres above the Trisuli and it races between its banks, dirty brown with the rain, fast and unforgiving. The Trisuli would have swallowed us without trace, bus and all.

Our driver reverses away from the landslide and we settle down to wait, wondering what will happen. A long line of buses and trucks builds up behind us; when I go for a walk I count over 50 before turning back towards our bus at the head of the queue.

Soldiers come, policemen and roadworkers. They labour away with crowbars, shovels and a bulldozer. The bulldozer lacks a fan belt, so it can only be used in short bursts before it overheats and goes out of action.

As the line of stationary traffic grows longer, the more impatient of the new arrivals in the queue begin driving forward up the right hand side of the road, to see what the problem is. Perhaps they imagine that several hundred trucks and buses, not as busy as themselves, have just stopped for no good reason. Whatever they think, it is clear that none of them will reverse back into the queue, so an immense double line of traffic builds up, completely blocking the road and preventing any more road-working vehicles from approaching. The same thing is happening on the far side of the slide, where the east-bound traffic stretches out in two similar road-choking lines, towards Pokhara. When the road is cleared will anyone be able to movc?

A *chiya wala* comes from out of nowhere and sets up a *chiya* shop so we take tea.

'Ke garne?' we ask each other. We take out our umbrellas and sit on the roadside and read, stopping to block our ears each time the roadworkers dynamite a rock.

Five hours later the road is open again. The bulldozer makes a triumphal journey to the far side and back again. A policeman then waves forward the first bus from the other side. It crosses empty, the passengers walking carefully behind it. The bus rocks and sways but arrives safely. There is a general blaring of horns, a hurried reshuffling and reversing into the queue, and a scramble of re-embarking passengers. Two more loaded vehicles cross from the far side, making their way with difficulty through the jam of vehicles on our side, and then it is our turn. Our slow speed gives more opportunity than I really want to see what we are in for. I have seen the other three cross safely before us, yet I still doubt our chances, and so does Ann apparently.

'I'd rather walk across,' she says, half hopefully — as if the driver would stop to pick her up again! The bus-frame creaks and flexes around us as we inch forward on to the landslide. Masses of unstable rock and gravel still hang poised above us, only 30 centimetres to the left of the bus windows, waiting to push us over the edge. The left rear wheel climbs over a rock and we lunge for the ceiling rail as the bus lurches and teeters to the right, towards the brink of the unimpeded drop into the Trisuli. The passengers heave a collective sigh of relief as the bus regains its equilibrium and we continue on across the breach, graunching and shuddering past the grinning road gang.

Another sideways lurch comes and Ann and I brace ourselves between the seat back and the window frame, gripping firmly and trying not to look out of the window right next to us. Everybody else seems to be grabbing us, but not just us I notice — our neighbours are holding on to each other, instinctively placing their trust in their fellow-creatures while Ann and I instead reach for the nearest piece of technology.

A nervous ripple of happy chatter marks the end of the rockslide and accentuates the frozen silence that had preceded it. Free of the canyon we thunder on at our steady 20 kilometres per hour again. The clouds of red dust sent up by the bus settle again on the scrawny chickens and wilting vegetation of tiny roadside hamlets. Children play on the tarseal, moving only the bare minimum necessary to let us pass. Tumlingtar, Anpo Khaireni — the names flash by, a straggle of mud-walled houses roofed with boards and thatch.

To the north, snow peaks are visible. Thc Annapurnas are easily recognised: we trekked around them in May, with SP, on our way to the Jomosom resupply. Machapuchare (6997 metres), the fishtail peak, is even easier to identify. Most trekking guides and picture books feature at least one photo of this attractive peak, at sunset usually, or reflected in the chill, calm lake waters of Phewa Tal below.

We turn off before Pokhara, the westernmost town on the highway, and strike south for the border at last.

'Arda ganta,' the bus driver yells, as we stop at a crossroads village.

'Half an hour. Dinner,' he translates, as Ann and I file past.

Virtually every one of the tiny shops here sells food. A row of wooden serveries, with a sheet of tin nailed over the top of each, faces the street. We pick one at random and go in. Several primus stoves loaded with pots of rice and vegetables are grouped at one end of the servery. In the middle waits a tin tray of wet glasses, ready for the *chiya* order. On a shelf underneath, fronted by a cracked pane of glass, round metal plates are heaped with cold sweetmeats, *samosas* and *jelebis*.

A young boy whisks sporadically at flies with a damp rag. Face impassive, he motions us to the wooden forms along the side wall and raises an eyebrow for our order. We are soon tucking into steaming mounds of pearly white rice and mix in by hand the side dishes of spiced lentils and pickled vegetables, and then yoghurt to cool it all down. Outside, the boy brings us a stainless steel tumbler of water each, to wash our hands with afterwards, and he pours the water over our hands on to the dirt, adjacent to the aluminium basin in which he tumbles the dishes with his fly-swat rag. Heat oozes out of the ground at us, sucking and wallowing around our legs. We retreat to the shelter of the *chiya* shop, ducking into its welcome shade. Rusting blue folding chairs and a table are set up outside but the metal is too hot to touch.

It is worse inside the bus again. I ask the driver if we may ride on the roof as some of the other passengers are doing. No problem, so up we clamber over *doko* loads of vegetables, sacks of pulses and grain, and even a basketful of clucking chickens. There is a conveniently sized hollow near the front of the roof where a large wooden box, filled with spare parts and tools, has been built across the top of the driver's cab. There is a tarpaulin there too, that we stretch out over a jumble of axles and what looks like a spare differential unit. We figured out earlier that these young bus-boys must be travelling mechanics too. I have yet to see a repair garage anywhere in Nepal, so any vehicle that breaks down must have to be fixed by its crew.

When SP, Ann and I walked out from the Khumbu in late April we ended up at a town called Katari, from where we hitched a ride across country in a truck to Bhandapur on the main east-west highway. The truck broke an axle while fording a stream, and we lay about under our umbrellas in the heat while the crew calmly knocked out the broken one and replaced it with one of the five spare axles they were carrying. We were on our way again in less than two hours.

It is the same with this bus. All the likely spares are carried with it and any repairs that are necessary will be performed on the roadside. It is not uncommon to see a truck parked by the side of the road, bonnet open, with its entrails spread out on the grass.

The refreshing breeze proves fierce when the bus picks up speed, knotting Ann's hair, whipping and cracking it across her eyes. I dig out a scarf and tie it turban fashion around my head; Ann secures hers over her hair beneath a sunshade brim. We plaster our faces and exposed skin with anti-sun cream and settle down to enjoy the scenery. The change is exhilarating: a 360 degree view to the far horizon, no longer restricted by the dirty windows of the bus. On either side of the road forested ridges fall steeply to bouldery riverbeds and dry gravel *nallas*. There are occasional patches of cleared land, where the brighter green of young wheat and rice paddy fills hand-made terraces. Farm houses rise harmoniously out of the soil from which they were fashioned; their doorways and windows are mere shadows in the ochre clay walls. Thatch and wooden shingles are weather-mellowed to tones of light grey and gold; a climbing rose adds a touch of pink where it sprawls over a verandah roof; then more forest, uncut and dark green.

'Duck!' Ann exclaims, and I do, followed by the others on top of the bus, as a low branch sweeps by, only centimetres above our heads.

The bus stops at a wayside temple dedicated, according to the golden trident above the roof, to Shiva, god of destruction and transformation. We watch as passengers disembark to make a brief *puja.* There is a roughly etched stone image of the god, about one metre high, sitting cross-legged just inside the barred gate of the inner temple. His head and shoulders are dusted with scarlet and yellow powders and white flower-petals are tumbled in his lap. The resident priest boards the bus with his tray to dispense *tikka,* the dots on the forehead for blessing for the journey. In four minutes his task is finished and he descends from the bus. I have been making many prayers of my own as we travel, about landslips, and accidents, and other such acts of God.

When we stop at Syangje, the mid-afternoon heat feels like a wall falling on me. No one is the least perturbed by my dousing my head, turban and all, under the spout of a hand-operated pump. As the administrative headquarters for the district, Syangje has an air of commerce and prosperity, not seen since we left Kathmandu. The closest *chiya* shop occupies the bottom floor of a three-storey concrete building, although, in keeping with ordinary *chiya* shops, the actual cooking is done in a lean-to shack outside.

In the gloom on the other side of the twin stone archways at the entrance we find rows of *charpoys,* rope-string beds, occupying most of the back half of the echoing chamber. There is plenty of room for the tables that are pushed to the front but there are no seats to go with them. It looks like a boarding house from which everyone has departed, taking their chairs, to watch an important cricket match perhaps. But at least the cooks are still here. So is their monkey, small, lean and ginger-haired. It leaps and prances with great energy from its chain at the door. Stretching down for a cabbage leaf off the ground, it then swings from the shirt tails of a passerby who jumps away in fright. A mirror hangs above a hand-basin by the door and consulting it is a shock — each individual pore of my face is black with dust.

The mountain view we had earlier has given way to endless foothills, through which we make a seemingly endless, winding descent. At one stop a young hawker sells bananas. A Nepali riding beside us on the roof asks for two and the lad deftly tosses them up to him.

'Ek rupya (one rupee),' the hawker calls. Just at that moment the bus-boy slaps the roof for the driver to leave. The Nepali smiles at the lad, not a nice smile, and the bus begins to pull away.

'Ek rupya, ek rupya,' calls the boy, but the man ignores him. The boy chases the bus for a few metres, then gives up, standing in the road waving his tiny fist. The Nepali laughs, as do one or two of the other roof-top passengers, but the chuckles are rather forced; there is a general air of disapproval.

Afternoon flows imperceptibly into evening. We sprawl out across the jumbled baggage, half-asleep, grimy with the dust and caked sweat. Pile upon pile of towering monsoon clouds are puffed up on the south-eastern horizon. Sunset comes as we follow the last ridge down the last foothill to the plains: they stretch away on all sides, flat to the sea, rivers standing out like chrome ribbon in the glare. The sun sets as a huge glowing ball of red, sliced by the black horizon, shimmering away into night.

Arrival at the border shatters our calm. The bus pulls up in Bhairawa with a long blast of the horn and the few remaining passengers from below erupt into what must be the main highway south. I cannot see much: pools of light ahead suggest kerosene lamps and buildings. We hastily lower our ten packs and kitbags on to the last patch of tarseal, before they are tossed off the roof with everyone else's baggage in the rush. Rickshaw walas hustle around the bus.

'Rickshaw, madam, rickshaw? Long way to India, madam. Sahib needing rickshaw?'

'Yes, please. I like the look of that guy, Ann — grab him.' We pile everything into the one rickshaw and walk alongside as the owner pedals, slowly. He's a helpful chap and tells us where we have to go.

'Nepali emigration, customs, border, Indian immigration, customs.' He lists them carefully, then asks, 'You need money change, sahib?'

'Yes, we will.' I had forgotten the minor ramifications of India's being another country; our Nepali rupees will be no use there. The rickshaw wala steers us into the first pool of light where we are dive-bombed by insects, flitting and bashing against the lamp-glass.

I step forward, straight into a puddle, and scramble up on to the verandah where two officials recline in the semi-darkness. We chat desultorily for a time about the weather, the mud, the monsoon's projected arrival, the heat. One of them pushes towards us yet another ragged-cornered exercise book to fill out; not many tourists exit this way, judging by the dates of the entries in the book. Ann writes in our names, nationality, passport numbers, last place of residence, home address, reason for visit, and we both sign it.

'New Zealand?' one of them notes. 'Sir Edmund Hillary Everest, yes?'

'Yes, that is the country.'

'Expedition?'

'No, no. No expedition. Just travelling, trekking,' we reply, thankful that our overladen rickshaw is hidden in the darkness beyond the lamplight. We had heard that expeditions can be heavily overcharged by officials in some areas and we planned to pass off our huge mound of luggage as 'trekking and touring equipment' wherever possible.

'You like Nepal?' he asks us.

'Nepal ekdam ramro chha! (Nepal is superlatively good!)' Ann states categorically. 'Positively glorious.' We are both a little concerned at what we may discover once trekking in the Indian hills, recalling the frustrating delays we suffered while waiting for Sikkim permits during our first month in India. Nepal has been four months of pleasure for us, unhindered by bureaucracy, a breeze by comparison with India.

'That is good,' they smile at us. We take this as our cue to push on. It is difficult to believe that it is half past seven at night, in the middle of nowhere, and yet we can sit there and chat about the weather as if we had been on that ramshackle verandah all week. We say our farewells and jump off, avoiding the puddles this time, and stride away with the rickshaw wala towards the next pool of light. A faded sign points the way to customs and we enter a concrete building, with bright blue painted walls, where three officials wait behind a long empty table. There are no forms visible, no cups of tea, not even a book — just a couple of kerosene lanterns and lots of fluttering moths. The eldest of the three men apologises to us.

'We are very sorry about the electricity, sir and madam. You have been to Kathmandu, yes?' We nod. 'In Kathmandu they are always having electricity. We are not having it here two nights in a row.' Ann attempts to reassure him that Kathmandu most definitely does have power cuts, but we take his point. Kathmandu must look as if it has everything when you are stationed in Bhairawa for two years, probably without even your family to accompany you. Some of Sanjay's comments about his tour of duty in Birganj come to mind.

'Now, some business.' The speaker's rather stern looking colleague produces a pad of forms to be completed in triplicate. There is no carbon. I offer my spare pens and they obligingly fill out the copies for us. There are four headings in bold type: Camera, Films, Money, Alcohol. Printed in large type across the bottom: IT IS AN OFFENSE TO EXPORT DRUGS. (Please declare your quantities). We declare: cameras, two each — Olympus; films, many — Kodak; money — 278 Nepali rupees and US$800 in travellers' cheques (it does not sound like much to last us another six months); alcohol, none; drugs, none.

'Where is your baggage?' the apologetic man asks. 'Please bring it inside, sir. We must search your baggage.' Ann looks at me and we both go outside, returning with our two big packs each. The official who produced the forms now raises his bushy eyebrows at us. 'You have more?' he says, half in jest. We carry in a couple of the kitbags this time.

'We have been in Nepal for a long time. We will travel for many more months,' I explain. 'We need a lot of baggage.'

Two assistants have materialised out of the darkness and they have started already to empty the first packs. Fibrepile jackets, Indian cotton shirts, a scarf, boots, jerseys, two rolls of toilet paper, toilet gear, a towel, five pairs of socks, underclothes, two books and, from the bottom, a flood of packets of freeze-dried meals pours from the pack.

'Oh. You have been trekking, yes?'

'We have been doing much trekking. We hope to return one day for more,' I reply.

'Yes, many people come here for our trekking,' he says, losing interest. He motions to the others to stop searching. 'Nothing to do with an expedition?' he suddenly asks.

'No, no expedition,' we reply, stuffing our gear back into the packs and ferrying it out to the rickshaw before he can change his mind. 'Phedi betola (see you again),' Ann calls.

In the street she mutters to me, 'I wonder what would happen if we admitted we were part of an expedition?'

'Maybe they'd just want your autograph,' I reply.

'No, seriously, I bet there must be a dozen other forms to fill out, or else it would cost a fortune in extra duty maybe.'

'It probably would and there probably are. But at any rate we are not part of an expedition in the official sense. Officially an expedition is a peak-climbing trip with a permit and a liaison officer; it brings radios and all sorts of sensitive security stuff, and that's bound to be why they check them so carefully. We're just a trekking party as far as that goes, even if it is for a year.'

'How far to India?' Ann asks the rickshaw wala.

'Tara chhaina (not far), memsahib,' he replies. Soon we discover that there is no electricity tonight in India either.

The Indian side of this part of the border is called Sonauli. In Kathmandu when Ann had been trying to find a route to Pithoragarh, we were confused by completely different-sounding routes suggested. Now I realise that many of the villages on one side of the border have expanded with the advent of the road till they have joined up with the villages across the border, yet each part of the new village has retained its original name.

In order to spare Indian customs the chore of sorting out all our baggage, we suggest to our rickshaw wala that he just pedals straight past the office while we go in with only one pack each this time.

'I apologise for the lack of electricity,' the Indian customs officer greets us. 'The Government is always cutting it here because India must supply a lot of electricity to Nepal. They are not making all of their own electricity there.'

'That's okay,' Ann smiles, 'we don't mind the lamp.'

'Certainly you may not mind, madam,' he replies gravely, 'but it would be better to have our electricity. This way you get a poor impression of India, because the electricity is on just across the border in Bhairawa, but here in Sonauli it is not.'

'But there was no electricity in Bhairawa tonight,' Ann stands up for her Nepali friends, 'and even in Kathmandu there were many cuts.'

'Oh no, madam, you are mistaken. When we have cuts here, they are having the electricity in Nepal, we know.'

The officer does not seem very interested in first-hand accounts of the state of the Nepali power supply. As he is clearly more comfortable with his own particular prejudice we drop the subject and he turns ponderously to the business in hand.

'Nothing to declare?' he asks.

'No,' I reply — a suddenly seemingly wealthy rickshaw wala pedalling past with a huge pile of trekking gear and dehydrated food maybe, but no, still nothing to declare. Fortunately the officer does not ask directly whether these two are our only bags, he waves us through without even bothering with a form. We catch up with our gear, change our watches back to Indian time and change our money — 145 Indian for the 278 Nepali rupees.

Ann runs ahead and finds a bus due to leave in five minutes for Gorakhpur. We are already elated at having survived, so easily, our first encounter in many months with Indian officialdom and the news of the bus sets the seal on our mood. We run along the road to Immigration, much more brightly lit, where we are questioned once again about expeditions as we fill out the forms.

'No, no. No expeditions,' we toss off casually, as they stare at our heaped rickshaw, but they let it pass and we are free to go, racing down the dark street to the bus. It is hardly bigger than a truck and too crowded inside for us after our airy ride from Kathmandu. We wrestle all our gear on to the roof, pay off the rickshaw wala with an extra big thank you for his expert guidance, and climb up after our bags.

This fertile river-land near the border is known as 'Buddha Country'. Lumbini in Nepal, only 20 kilometres from here, was the birthplace of Siddharta Gautama (who was later known as Buddha, the awakened one). Nearly 2000 years ago Siddharta, the man, wandered across these plains, seeking enlightenment and preaching the Four Noble Truths of what is now called Buddhism. He ranged far afield from his birthplace, to Varanasi, even Kathmandu some say, but Buddha returned here to die and the traditional site of his cremation is Kushinagar, five kilometres east of Gorakhpur.

The few towns we pass through are heavily barred and shuttered for night time; the countryside is dark and empty. The two weak rays from our headlamps barely pierce the darkness ahead; for hours there is nothing but highway — a single lane of tarseal leaping up and then away underneath us.

Late that night, cramped, filthy and tired, we alight outside what can only be Gorakhpur railway station. Its massive pillared colonial architecture would identify this building as a railway station anywhere in the world. The arched windows and wide stone steps are all lit up, despite the late hour. Then our halt brings with it a new sensation of heat, terrible heat, much worse than it felt in Sonauli, and mixed with it the taste of hot tarseal. Ann flops down with our baggage at the bus shelter so I volunteer to look for the place that sells train tickets.

Reports of night-time murders and abductions in those first newspapers we read in New Delhi come to my mind. There is nothing to worry about I tell myself as I walk through the dark railway grounds. I am right and absolutely nothing untoward happens, apart from my stumbling over two grumpy sleepers, so rudely awoken by my feet. The lawn of the railway station is almost invisible under sleeping forms. Dozens of people are milling around in the courtyard and there are others, whole families, stretched asleep on thin cotton mats on the floor of the foyer and waiting room. They do not look poor; perhaps they are all waiting for trains.

I find someone on duty at the booking office who advises that the next train for Kathgodam (as near as we can get to Pithoragarh apparently) leaves at 6 am. We cannot buy tickets for it now, however; we must wait until after midnight. I am not sure why and my Hindi (after nearly five months in Nepal) is not good enough to find out.

A rickshaw wala takes us to a boarding house within three minutes' walk of the station. He rattles on the padlocked wire-netting gate to wake the proprietor. Out scurries a bandy-legged old gentleman who must be well into his 80s, wearing only a loincloth. He is absolutely bald except for one thick hank of grey hair standing up from his crown. His head hardly reaches Ann's shoulder, but he sports a jaw-breaking, though toothless, smile and instant service to match. He whisks us upstairs to a three-bed room, shows us how the fans work, where the tap is for a wash, and enjoins us not to leave our baggage unguarded.

'Food?' he enquires, as if it would be no difficulty at this hour. He returns in ten minutes with a tray of bread, butter, boiled eggs, jam and tea.

'Same in the morning, madam?' he beams at Ann. We nod in delight at this royal treatment. He bats not even an eyelash when we say it has to be ready shortly after four.

With the room to ourselves I begin to feel at last the accumulated sweat, heat and dirt clamouring for attention. We fill plastic buckets from the tap in our bathroom and pour the water over each other, clothes and all. The dirty water swirls across the tiled floor and out through a drain in the corner. Ann carries a small scrubbing brush with her and uses it to attack the worst of the grime. Slightly cleaner but still tired we stretch out in our damp clothes on the cotton mattresses, with all three fans going full-bore and the lights finally out. In minutes my clothes are dry again, my throat parched.

'According to that emigration officer at Bhairawa the temperature was 35 degrees Celsius. I wonder what it is down here?'

'It must be 40 degrees easily.' It is impossible to sleep. My whole body feels feverish and I get up twice in the night to douse myself again in the tiny hotel bathroom.

At 4.15 am on the dot our faithful little man knocks on the door with a fresh round of tea and toast. He potters about at the bedside table, chatting and telling us tales of other travellers who have stayed, of the town, and of the heat. Down here on the plains, even at this hour, the pre-monsoon heat is appalling: the overhead fans beat waves of hot dry air over us as we breakfast and the slightest exertion wrings the sweat out of me, sucks at my energy. I am beginning to understand why the locals pray for the rains.

VARSHA
the rains

The rest of the journey to Pithoragarh for Ann, Corrina and Michael was just about as comfortable as that from Kathmandu. The ticket office in Gorakhpur forgot to phone through their sleeper reservations for the train to Kathgodam. Every seat in every carriage was full; they bedded down on the racks of the baggage compartment. Then they were advised that Kathgodam was not the closest train station to Pithoragarh and that they should get off at Haldwani instead. They did, to find they'd missed the daily bus to Pithoragarh. So they had to spend one last fetid night on the road. They were exceedingly glad to reach the semi-cool hills of Pithoragarh, and I was as glad to see them.

The traverse party arrived in Pithoragarh just a few days later, right on D Day, 23 June. They, and particularly SP, were raring to start the Indian section of the traverse. Instead, we had to sit about in Pithoragarh for nearly three weeks. The new Indian permit for which I had gone down to New Delhi turned out to be defective, just as the Sikkim one had been. Pete and SP went to New Delhi this time to try to get a better permit.

The IMF had written to us after Sikkim advising that a third Indian member for the expedition would be available on our re-entry to India. Corrina and Ding managed to get away for one night down in Nainital, a foothills resort close by, but Ann and Michael and I just waited at Pithoragarh — waited for the permit, waited for the promised new member, and waited for the dreaded monsoon to catch up with us.

S.K. Roy (the S stands for Shubhash, or sweet talker) arrived first. He had been dispatched from Delhi by the IMF to join us for the rest of the traverse. The introduction of this new person had a pronounced and beneficial effect on our moods — SK was a constantly cheerful and witty Bengali (who said we should call him Roy). Next Pete and SP were back with a redrawn permit. They had not been able to get any change to the Inner-line prohibition for us but, apart from that, which we had almost come to expect, we could trek where we pleased and now, at least, the District Magistrates would not have us arrested. Incidentally, the District Magistrate for Pithoragarh, Mr Joshi, made us very welcome during our enforced stay in his area. He invited us to tea one evening with his family and later arranged a volleyball game for us with the Almora regional champions. Needless to say they won.

The day after SP and Pete returned, the traverse party set off to Joshimath on the first Indian section after Nepal. Ann, Corrina, Roy, Michael and I took advantage of the break till our next resupply to trek into the Valley of Flowers, in the Chamoli foothills, and to climb up to Hem Kund Sahib at 5000 metres, the sacred pilgrimage lake of the Sikhs.

Our second rendezvous in India was in Joshimath on 17 July. Ding had an accident there, dislocating his shoulder. I had always been the 'reserve' for the traversers and it was understood that in the event of injury I would replace either Ding or Pete. Now that it had come to that juncture, however, Ding felt quite upset: he wanted Pete to wait until his shoulder had recovered but he wouldn't actually ask him for this and Pete wasn't about to offer. He had seen enough delays in the progress of the traverse already.

The doctor told us that Ding would have to rest for at least six weeks. Even discounting some part of that as medical caution things did not look good. Ding's accident would probably keep him out of action for at least one section and, if it did, then Tashi and Pete would be the only members to have completed the whole traverse. If I had put some pressure on Pete I might have forced a halt but I didn't. Maybe I was grabbing a chance too. I went as Ding's replacement in the traverse team with Pete, Tashi and Roy on the next section to Uttarkashi. Looking back to the expedition from a few years on, this is the only decision I made over which I now feel cause to be ashamed.

We left Joshimath on an overcast day, leaving Ding more dejected than I have ever seen him. It takes a lot to keep Dingle down however. A day after we left, Ding decided to defy the doctor and set out after us, with Corrina carrying their single pack. Barely two days' walk from Joshimath Pete came down with a fever and Ding and Corrina, the 'B' team traverse party, caught up with us. For three days or so we had a farcical situation with the 'A' and 'B' teams leap-frogging over each other along the track. Then Pete wanted his 'A' team to cross a high pass, the Naindi Khal (5160 metres) which Ding and Corrina finally had to admit was beyond them. Bad weather later forced the 'A' team to abandon this attempt and we were able to unite into one team at last — but not without incident. Our merger led shortly to yet another explosion between Ding and Pete. The growing friction between them had created problems for even our rest stops, and strained diplomatic talents at peace-keeping to the utmost. Pete would come and see Ann and me and give us an update on the problems of the last section. Then, Ding, a few hours later, after he'd had a chance to catch up with Corrina, would come and see me and give his version of the last section. Tashi would usually have a chat with Ann, Roy, me and Corrina, and even he was starting to open up about the problems of travelling with two people who had virtually given up the effort to get on with one another. Simple decisions like where we should have dinner during rendezvous would lead to argument between them.

In our early planning at home we had always agreed that the support party members could walk with the traverse party whenever the conditions allowed it. Later Ann and I decided that we would avoid traversing with them if we could and organise, instead, less highly charged side trips of our own, in order to reserve our emotional energies for the difficult demands of these rendezvous. In the meantime, however, for this section I was in the traverse team with Pete, Tashi and Roy, and Corrina and Ding had just caught up with us.

Now that the six of us were making our way across country as one traverse party, Pete grew increasingly restive. He complained that our pace was too slow, that the distances we travelled each day were too short, that the 'support party' was holding the traversers up. Matters came to a head, one foggy afternoon, at a rest house called Dugal Bhita. Roy, Tashi and I thought it a good place to halt but Pete wanted to keep going. Unable to get us to change our minds, he lost his temper, swore at us, and walked off into the gloom. Tashi really complained then, for the first and only time on the trip. Turning on Roy and me he said, with some justification, that this whole situation was just not good enough: such swearing always upset him but Pete's new 'take it or leave it' attitude was just too much for him. By walking off, Pete put Tashi in an impossible situation. Tashi believed that if anything happened to Pete then all of the Indian members would be blamed for it by the IMF and, as the lowest ranking (but in some respects most capable) of the group, he felt that he would be blamed the most. His job might even be in jeopardy, since he worked for a government department.

That night, after Ding and Corrina arrived, we discussed the problem and resolved that, despite the joint leadership provided for in the original expedition contract, we would now have our turn at rewriting that agreement, to allow Ding the final say whenever any controversy should arise. If Pete would not accept that, so far as we were concerned he could traverse on his own.

Two days later we caught up with Pete. Feeling that relations were too strained for Ding to deliver the message, I did it. Tashi was so mortified by the blunt way I put it to Pete that he lay on his bed, closed his eyes, and pretended to be asleep, blushing furiously. There really wasn't much that Pete could do except agree to our decision and he had the good grace to do so quietly.

From there things slowly picked up again. I have written none of this into the chapter that follows. Although it happened, it is not the dominant memory of that section of the trip for me. What endures is the magic that was part of the long monsoon trek. The discomfort has faded away behind the genuine camaraderie that did arise, a bond between all of us who went through that monsoon trek and came out into the sun again at the other end.

Before Ding and Corrina left Joshimath, they had asked Ann if she minded carrying out the support team role for that section without them. No problem: she transferred our kit (now only nine bags) quite happily without us, arriving in Uttarkashi with time to spare. While SP paid a brief visit to his family in nearby Mussoorie, Ann went trekking in the Bhandarpunch range, experiencing the same monsoon clouds that dogged our footsteps in the intervening fortnight.

7. Monsoon on the Pilgrim Trail

I arrive in Pithoragarh alone with seven kitbags that I have hauled all the way from New Delhi, the last stage on a small dark-blue Uttar Pradesh State Government bus. I find lodgings in a seedy hotel above the bus park, where I collapse, filthy, coughing and racked by attacks of Delhi-belly.

My room is small and dark, with one heavily barred window closed with wooden shutters. A bed, a low bedside table and one cane chair make up the furnishings. In the corner is the bathroom — a toilet, which is a hole in the floor, a tap, a bucket and a dipper. The room has an evil smell and costs Rs 12 a night.

I summon enough strength to strip off my travel-stained clothes and wash, then laboriously shave over the bucket. I am starting to feel halfway human again when I knock a carefully-hoarded roll of toilet paper into the bucket. Perhaps it is as well that the others have not yet arrived, but I doubt if either family or friends would recognise me — a half-naked, half-shaven, wild-haired, pathetically muttering man slowly festooning his dingy room with carefully unrolled wet toilet paper. I am too tired to go out to eat. Winding myself in my dhoti to keep off the numerous mosquitoes, I drop into a fitful sleep.

In the morning I decide 21 June is too early for Christmas decorations and roll up my toilet paper again. I dress to go out on the balcony and send the hotel boy for *chai.* Below me, the bus park is quiet and morning shoppers are buying produce from the stalls around its edge. Under my balcony, soldiers in khaki are counting ammunition boxes into a truck, watched by a crowd of porters who sit on a large rock overlooking the bus park entrance. Behind them is a public washing place, a three-sided concrete box about ten metres across, three metres high and open to the street. At each end water flows continuously out of a pipe and a small crowd is gathered around the two outlets, clad in wet dhotis or saris, soaping

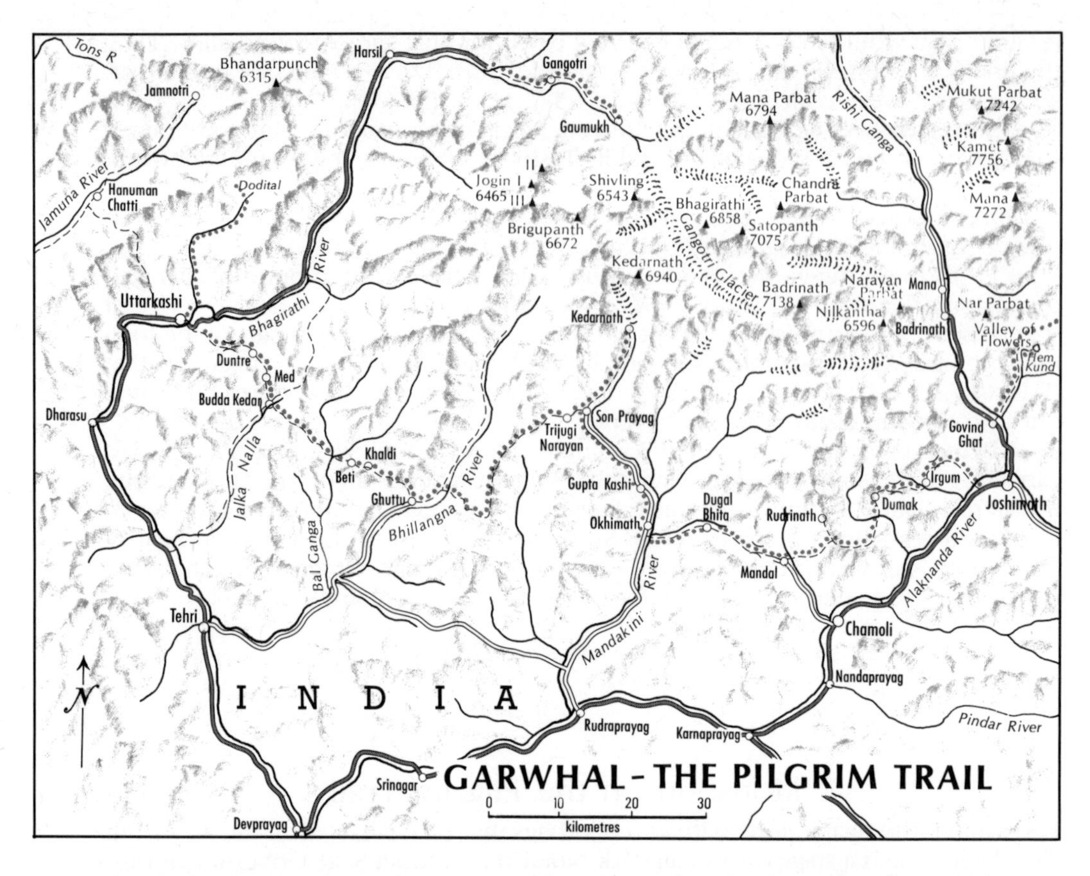

themselves under the rushing water. They keep their backs to the street, oblivious of the passers-by, another reminder to me of how well one could cope with overcrowded conditions.

At the far side of the bus park a man has set up a table to sell lottery tickets. He has a small tape machine and two loudspeakers which he runs off a car battery. His message is broadcast at full volume, over and over, and it says, 'Rajasthan State Lottery, 50 Lakh Rupees: it is in God's power to make you rich and it is in your power to test his power. Buy your lucky ticket today.' (A lakh is 100,000 so 50 lakh must be 5 million rupees.) The message stops only once, during a heavy fall of rain in the afternoon; otherwise it continues all day without pause and I fall asleep to it late that night.

In the morning the clouds are piling high in a blue sky, a promise of further rain to come. I ask the boy to fetch *chai* but he says tea is not available. 'Why?' I ask but his only response is a shrug. Today is not Sunday but I notice that the market is deserted and a strange quiet hangs over the town. I decide that if *chai* is 'not available', I shall go and seek some.

I ate yesterday in a small restaurant below the hotel. It is a simple place with two tables and some stools, the usual *dekshis* over a charcoal fire, and a drum oven to the side for heating *chapatis.* Today, however, the folding doors are secured across the front, all except the last panel where the manager stands. He waves for me to come inside, where a few people are eating by the light of a kerosene lantern although it is broad daylight outside. We settle my order and I ask the reason for the market's being so quiet, the restaurant's appearing to be closed.

'It is the police,' he tells me, 'bullies. They came with their *lathis* (metre-long batons) and beat a stall holder in the market last night. It was not right for them to do that, he had done nothing. So today is a *hartal,* a strike. The whole market is closed as a protest. Of course, exception can be made for a traveller such as yourself, we cannot let you starve.'

'Will it stop them?' I ask. He shrugs.

'Well, police are police,' he says. I nod as knowledgeably as I am able and turn to my rice and mutton curry.

Back at the hotel I find that there is a water shortage and nothing is coming from the tap. The boy asks if I want *chai* now.

'*Chai* is available?' I check.

'Yes, available now,' he says.

'Okay, two cups.' I order.

I watch him as he goes off towards the *chai wala,* noticing the large bucket that he carries. I see him fill it out of the hotel goldfish pond; the pond is a murky brown colour and contains living goldfish. Soon the boy returns with two hot glasses of tea.

'Tell me,' I ask, 'does the *chai wala*'s *pani* come from the goldfish pond?'

'Surely, sahib,' he replies, 'there is a shortage of *pani.*' I nod; the tea tastes the same.

That evening I am standing in darkness by my window when a wedding party, a *barat,* enters the street. It contains about 15 men, all garlanded with flowers, who take it in turns to carry aloft the resplendent groom. They are accompanying him to the house of his young bride and his feet must not be sullied by contact with the ground. The groom is dressed entirely in white, ready for three days of feasting and ceremonies that mark this happy occasion.

With the party comes a small band of musicians wearing bright red military coats and flat white caps. Most of the band are beating drums but three members play clarinets in ragged chorus to one man who blows a trumpet with great energy. The musicians play triumphantly while moving along the street but every 30 metres or so they pause to rest while the trumpeter plays a solo. The party stops outside my hotel, a group of figures swirling dramatically in the white light of a pressure lantern. The trumpeter dances, prances, lunges high and low, sweat glistening on his face while his gleaming trumpet splits the night. There is a snatch of conversation, laughter and a whiff of burning incense before the players move on down the street. The music floats back, haunting, beckoning. For a moment I nearly turn and slip out into the night, to follow where that trumpet weaves dreams still.

In the morning the others arrive — SP, Tashi, Pete and Ding on foot from Jumla, and Ann, Corrina and Michael by bus from Kathmandu. I am drawn once more into the day-to-day affairs of the expedition support team. This time, with the beginning of the Indian segment of our traverse, there are many delays and it is two weeks before we are ready to leave Pithoragarh. By then Roy, our third Indian member, has joined us and he proves a welcome addition. He has an immense fund of knowledge of the areas we will pass through and we will often have cause to use it.

After moving the expedition baggage to Joshimath, the next port of call for the traversers, it is time for the support team to take Michael climbing. Over *chai,* Roy, Ann, Corrina, Michael and I make plans for our climb in the Valley of Flowers. This valley was named by F.S. Smythe, the English explorer-naturalist, after two expeditions in the area in the 1930s. After weeks of rambling through rock strewn valleys and craggy passes, Smythe chanced upon this tiny valley, not far from Joshimath, just when the alpine flowers were at their peak. Smythe's visit to the valley took place during the summer, just a bit earlier in the year than ours, and with the monsoon almost begun it is a bad time of year for everything but the flowers. We go, and are lucky to find the road open, lucky to get into the Valley, lucky to get out again without being avalanched, and lucky to have had a good time.

Back in Joshimath the monsoon arrives, imperceptibly at first, with a few cloud bursts and a rainy day. Then, suddenly, it is the new reality. The temperature drops a few degrees and so does the humidity. Day and night rain drums steadily on the rooftops, patters and spatters from the guttering, drips endlessly on the verandah. There is no doubt that the monsoon has finally caught up with us; whether we blame it on bureaucratic delays or our own slow feet we are still most clearly in it. From inside the damp gloom of our hotel room we watch as cloud comes billowing in through the door and forces its way between the window bars. Water trickles and chuckles down the drains, swelling roadside puddles to veritable lakes. Down in the valley, 1000 metres below, the Alaknanda river runs high and swollen, menacing and truculent, with a roar I can hear right here in the hotel.

Michael has to leave us soon, for appointments in Bombay, and is more than a little worried by the long bus trip ahead of him. We try to reassure him, yet really feel slightly uneasy in doing so. Confined to our room by the rain and mud there has not been much else to talk of apart from monsoon disasters. The newspapers have arrived only intermittently, as the roads are washed out and then only fitfully reopened. Border Roads Task Force gangs pit their bulldozers and shovels against the annual menace. On the plains and in the hills the news is the same: bridges gone, roads cut, railway tracks washed away. Running through the stories is the constant macabre counting of bodies: a bus swallowed there, 75 dead; a train here, 300 dead. Politicians make newsworthy flights over the disaster areas in the precious helicopters, taking up space that might be used by workers or supplies.

By the time the traversers, Tashi, Ding and Pete, arrive (joined by SP for that section), Michael has gone — a wan figure squashed firmly between fellow passengers in the back of the southbound bus. We wave him goodbye, saying we'll see him back in New Zealand.

'Of course you'll make it,' Ann tries to cheer him up. 'I mean we've got to bus out of here too, you know, and our opposition in the Army expedition is bound to be saving the worst disasters for us.'

'So write to us,' we yell after him as the bus pulls out. He waves bravely at us through the back window.

We're all feeling a bit downcast at his departure and, when the expedition is invited to dinner at the local officers' mess, we gratefully accept. An attempt is made to console our unhappiest members with liberal helpings of whisky. It doesn't work and Ding tries a clowning act to enliven the party. In the process he tumbles over a bank and lands at the bottom with a dislocated shoulder and other minor injuries. His accident makes no headlines but in our small group it is enough to snap us out of our damp miseries. Once we've established that he is okay and have had him doctored up, a planning meeting brings the 'traverser relief scheme' into operation. The doctor has declared Ding's shoulder out of action for at least six weeks and I am to replace him in the traverse for that period.

It will be the first time that Ann and I have travelled separately in the expedition since Sikkim. On the last night together in Joshimath we hold each other especially close, promising to take care. We talk of how this last six months of working together, side by side each day, has strengthened the bond between us.

'Sure we've had a few screaming matches on occasions,' Ann whispers, then laughs, 'but usually only when we're really tired and hungry — when both of us are feeling low. No one could survive all we've been through and not get shitty at times. It's been neat just having you with me, an understanding person to whom I don't have to explain everything I think.' I know what she means. I get a lot of support, and thus extra strength, from Ann's company. It makes me aware of how difficult the continual separations must be for Ding and Corrina, and more aware of how lonely Pete must feel sometimes.

'You take care on those buses, you hear,' I tell Ann once again. 'Sit by the door and be ready to jump if it looks as if the road is going to go.' Ann gives me a big hug in reply. She'll be risking the monsoon roads and I the trails — I wonder which will be worse. The prospect of being killed while travelling apart from each other seems infinitely worse than dying together. I shudder at these morbid thoughts brought on by the monsoon and we fall silent, Ann lying small and warm beside me. We must have dozed off eventually for I wake in daylight and have to rush to finish my packing. Our moods are more positive in the morning and we farewell each other gaily, Ann taking a photo of the traversers as we depart.

The new traverse party — Roy, Tashi, Pete and me — leaves Joshimath in light rain, walking south along the main road towards the plains for the first few kilometres. The town has been isolated for several days by a major road block and we cross the site of the blockage quickly, picking our way between groups of road-workers, knee-deep in the mud slide with eyes watching warily upwards to where boulders are perched on the unstable hillside. We drop steeply then to the Alaknanda and cross it on an iron suspension bridge. The westbound track we now follow is not good and almost immediately we go astray in this first valley, climbing laboriously up its northern side until the track peters out in bamboo. We retrace our steps to the last junction and take the only alternative route, up mud-plastered zigzags in the rain.

A boy comes down the track towards us carrying a *doko* of apples for market. He offers one each to Roy and me before we ask. We squat together by the trailside beneath our umbrellas and the boy watches carefully as I slowly peel ever-longer concentric rings of skin away from the crisp white flesh. Roy teases me for my care, biting deeply into his own red apple to emphasise the point. He is an easy chap to get along with, as disarming as his Indian name, Shubash (sweet-talker), suggests. He is a useful companion also, like Tashi, for he knows many of the hill dialects. The young boy soon loses his shyness with us as Roy chats amiably with him.

'He comes from the village in the next valley,' Roy tells me. 'Irgum it's called. He's not had much schooling but the recruitment officers for the army will be coming through the hills soon and the boy hopes to be chosen. The army prefers to take villagers like him — they can carry heavy loads and bear discomfort.'

'Is the army a good life for him?' I ask.

'Surely. He will get food and clothing, medical treatment,' Roy looks at the boy's wide, cracked bare feet, 'shoes, even. In his village they have too many mouths to feed already.' The boy picks up his load and we thank him once more for the apples, levering on our own rucksacks as he heads off down valley for market.

It is late afternoon when Roy and I descend from the pass to Irgum where Pete and Tashi are setting up camp in the schoolroom. They are a well matched trekking pair, Pete and Tash. After five months of travel together there is a good rhythm between them, keeping up the pace and organising their campsites.

'The people are letting us sleep here,' Tashi says, 'but we must be away quickly in the morning before the children come.' He has a small fire going already and hands me the billy. 'Now, if you will find some water and peel the potatoes, Doug, I will get the brew before we cook.'

I grin at him. 'Your New Zealand English is pretty good now, Tash. When we last trekked together, in Sikkim, you made tea — now you make "a brew".'

Tashi laughs.

'Oh yes, I have learned many new expressions, some I shall try not to repeat!'

I find water easily, just up the path, where a small channel brings it out at a public watering spot, and I am soon squelching my way back along the track to the schoolroom. I lay out my bedroll before the light fades completely and change into dry clothes, padding around barefoot on the clean clay floor. The only decoration in the schoolroom is a blackboard propped on a wooden easel: it stands behind the small brazier where our fire is burning. The damp late afternoon merges imperceptibly into dusk as I sit cross-legged on the porch, peeling potatoes with my pocket knife.

In the morning it is raining still and, although we have packed, we are not yet on our way when the children arrive for school. Each child carries in a cloth shoulder bag a piece of wood for the teacher's fire and a small square slate for doing the lessons.

Once we are on our way the travel seems to be a repetition of yesterday. In a light but persistent rain we follow the track up valley, Roy and I keeping close on Tashi's and Pete's heels until the track runs out in an area of bog. We fight our way through the muck to the far side to find several tracks leading upwards. The one we take climbs steeply up a ridge and then disappears, leaving us floundering around in wet, knee-high grass on ledges above a gorge. It is so steep that on one occasion I find myself staring straight down through the murk into the tops of cedar trees below. It is no fun clambering around on ground like this, clutching an opened umbrella in one hand. The mist and cloud further accentuate the drop and we are forced to acknowledge that we must backtrack once more. Our next try is more successful. The track is just a stream bed in parts but eventually it leads out on to meadows and then a series of old but well constructed steep stone steps takes us out on to another pass, high in the same dark clouds.

We are to spend our second night at Dumak, one valley west of Irgum, and reach there by mid afternoon. The main house of the village has a large stone-paved courtyard in front of it and most of the inhabitants are outside getting some air during a short break in the rain. We prop our rucksacks against the courtyard wall and Roy and Tashi make inquiries about getting a guide to take us on the correct track to Rudrinath, the next major village on our route and possibly three days away. We have quickly tired of losing the trail each day. In the almost constant mist and cloud it is virtually impossible to navigate — even if we did have a reasonable map, which we do not, we never see any features from which we can take bearings. Our perennial guides to date, 'westward and northward', are not much use either.

The menfolk of Dumak are clustered idly about Roy and Tashi but there are two women in the courtyard also. Each of them wears one huge earring, finger thick, and so heavy that a single hole in the ear will not support it: the gold ring is threaded through two holes, one at the top and one at the bottom of the ear. The older woman has a scar where a nose-ring has been torn from her nostril. She sits patiently while the younger woman searches carefully through her hair, squeezing scalp lice and possibly ticks with sudden sharp jabs of her fingernails. In front of the doorway of the house lies a boy cretin of about 12 years old, wearing only a rough woollen top. He pays no attention to us or anything else, chewing placidly on a strip of bamboo. Twice the younger woman goes to him and wipes his bottom with a handful of grass. There are huge callouses on the boy's knees from constant crawling.

The men here are not very interested in guiding anyone anywhere. That much is evident from their faces. Tashi and Roy spend a lot of time talking and explaining our request to each new arrival. The listeners divide into two groups: those who want to know why anyone would want to go to Rudrinath at all, and those who want to know why anyone would want to go there now, in this season. Finally, with a great show of reluctance, one young man is bullied by the villagers into assisting us. After he agrees, as if to mock our navigation problems the sky clears for nearly 20 minutes and, far to the east, we see Trisul, a peak close to Joshimath, soaring to 7120 metres above pure bleached clouds. This is the last blue sky we see for a very long time.

We spend an uncomfortable night at Dumak in an upstairs room of the main house. I sleep on the floor and am plagued by fleas and Pete has a bed but is struck down with a fever. Although it is warm he is freezing and lies in his sleeping bag, zipped up tight, tossing and coughing and in the morning he feels weak enough for us to decide on a rest day. The older woman brings us tea and clucks sympathetically as she notices our scratching. She apologises for the fleas, 'They are very bad during the rains but we have no medicine to kill them so we must endure them.'

Pete and I have brought with us half a paperback volume of short stories, torn apart to save weight. During the morning I read the stories, drifting away from the monsoon into exquisitely crafted stories set in the south of France while rain drums on the thatch roof above. When the rain eases I duck out to find a place for my toilet. On the far side of the track there are clumps of tall marijuana bushes and I seek cover behind them. Marijuana is grown extensively both in Nepal and India, primarily for rope making. On the trail between the houses the villagers have laid recently-cut three-metre long stalks of marijuana plants; when cattle and other pedestrians have crushed the fibres sufficiently, the villagers will pick out the long strands and twist and weave them into rope. The English word canvas is derived from *cannabis sativa,* the botanical name for marijuana, while 'hemp' has been used as a term for rope as well as slang for marijuana.

Just on dark Ding and Corrina arrive. Ding has his shoulder strapped up and is carrying an umbrella in his one good hand; Corrina has their single pack. Ding looks a bit shaky, but determined, and they intend trying for Uttarkashi by the low route, where they are confident of obtaining food and lodging all the way. This 'low' route is the one frequented by pilgrims such as those whom we watched flocking to Kathmandu for Shivaratri in February. Many try to visit more than one holy site on their pilgrimage and a network of shelters and trails through the foothills has existed since ancient times to aid them in their journeys.

Pete still hopes that our party will be able to follow a higher route, crossing Naindi Khal pass, and for that reason we are carrying additional food, clothing and equipment. We are likely to be away from settled areas for much of the next two weeks. I admire the other pair's pluck, however. Ding is running a real risk of permanent injury if he damages his shoulder again, and it is easy enough to slip in this sort of terrain. They join us for the night since it is too late for them to press on and there are now six of us sleeping upstairs. The house is turning into a hostel for trekkers — foam mats, sleeping bags, rucksacks and drying clothes are scattered everywhere.

In the morning Pete is feeling a little better but his throat is very raw still and we, the 'traversers', decide to rest another day. Ding and Corrina set off for Rudrinath as they have to travel fairly slowly. Tashi and I take the short rope from our gear and go with them for the first half hour, to help with a stream crossing that our guide says will be difficult. In fact the crossing is straightforward for someone with two arms, but for Ding we rig up the rope as a handrail above a fallen tree and he straddles the trunk gingerly and shuffles his way across on his behind. We wish them well on the far side, then wade back across the stream to retrieve the rope and trudge back up the valley to Dumak.

As we enter the outskirts of the village we pass a small shrine where three wandering holy men, *sadhus,* squat under the roof for shelter. One asks Tashi if he has any cigarettes and we stop to share a smoke with them and talk; another has blond hair, is named Nick, and comes from Manchester.

'Indian people are not so surprised to see Westerners like myself,' Nick gently chides me for my obvious surprise. 'I have been under instruction with a guru for more than four years now,' he goes on to tell me. 'I spend half the year with him and the other half on pilgrimage, sometimes to one of the *tirths* (holy places) in the mountains, sometimes to the plains. This year I've walked the old pilgrim trail linking the temples at Badrinath, Kedarnath, Gangotri and Jamnotri. Have you come from Badrinath,' he asks, 'or been to any of the other *tirths*?' He puffs contentedly on one of Tashi's cigarettes as I briefly tell of our travels.

I describe for him the many Buddhist sites we have walked past, in Sikkim and Nepal, and the bloody sacrifices at the Hindu Kali temple in Kathmandu.

'There is nothing like that here, Doug,' he tells me, 'only peaceful ritual and worship, and the offering of *prasad* (holy food) and prayers. If you get a chance you should visit Kedarnath, if only for the scenery. It's where the god Shiva met one of his wives.'

'What is Badrinath visited for,' I ask, remembering that Ann had plans to go there before taking the expedition baggage to Uttarkashi. 'We were climbing in the Valley of Flowers near Badrinath earlier.'

He nods and says, 'It's another beautiful place, particularly when you see it on foot like this. The shrine there is in honour of Vishnu, the preserving and redeeming god. There are hundreds of shrines in these hills though and a real pilgrim, or *yatri,* would visit them all if life allowed.'

Later in our conversation Nick admits that he was as surprised to see Tashi and me as we were to see him. 'Not many people use this trail now, because of roads — pilgrims can reach the major temples much more easily by bus. On these routes there are no hotels and few *chai* shops anymore. The committees that run the smaller temples have virtually no income so the temples are decaying, the *dharamsalas* or pilgrim shelters are in poor repair, even the trails.' Nick settles back on his haunches, one hand rubbing the string of beads against his bare chest. 'Only *sadhus,* like my companions, or *sunyasi,* novices like myself, seem to use them now. You'll see for yourself — it's not like Nepal where the roads are few and the trails are busy. Only near the roads are the temples thriving here.' He smiles wryly, 'And where the crowds are great, there is little contemplation.'

'Are there other European *sunyasi* or *sadhus,* Nick?' I ask him.

'Oh yes, I know of quite a few, *sunyasi* mainly, French, German, English. Life is good to us here, people feed us as we go and we need little shelter. My *guru* is a good man too. At first I was hurt when he told me to travel for half the year, but now I see why. He does not believe in ...' Nick frowns, searching for the words.

'Cloistered virtue?' I suggest.

'Exactly,' he smiles, 'my English is getting stiff and rusty. It is a long time since I last used it.' He adjusts his loin cloth and continues, 'Yes, it's easy for me while I'm with him. Now I need to learn how to keep that same calmness by myself. Some of the other Europeans have been on this search for a long time. Their language has faded and like me they are more comfortable speaking in Hindi. Soon my English will fall away altogether, then I will be just one with all these others, a man going to God.' Tashi has finished his cigarette and we rise to leave. Nick salutes us with a steady gaze. 'Namaskar,' he says, formally.

'Namaskar, Nick,' I reply, then add softly, 'the Lord be with you.'

He smiles in recognition and responds, 'And with you also.'

Next morning we set off in Corrina's and Ding's footsteps, crossing the river past the shrine and ascending the ridge on the far side. There is an unpleasant new distraction for us on the trail: the grass and forest are alive with leeches. This is the first time I have seen them and what a horrible experience they are — small bloodsucking worms, up to 40 or 50 millimetres in length, which stand up on rocks or hang from leaves and blades of grass, waving tentacles smelling the approach of warm, fresh, flowing blood. As you pass they launch gaily into space, dropping on to your legs or shoes, and once on target they move quickly, bending their free end forward until they form a loop, then detaching the back sucker and bending forward again, taking the quickest route to your flesh. They can ooze through the nylon mesh of a sneaker or a woollen sock in an instant. Once out of sight they go quietly about their work, which is the extraction of as much of your blood as they can force into themselves. That can be a lot because they simply swell up, stretching wider and wider into a bulbous parcel. I feel no pain at all, but at our first stop I remove my socks to find nearly a dozen of the little monsters sucking away on my feet and I tear them off with appropriate expressions of distaste. They do not come away easily.

'Here,' says Tashi, passing me his cigarette, 'they don't like the heat. This will get them off.' It does but removing them is only a temporary solution, and it leaves me with a further problem. To prevent your blood clotting and thus reducing its meal, the leech releases an anticoagulant into the puncture it makes, so, even if the leech is removed, your blood keeps flowing. I think this over for a while: perhaps I should leave the leeches on; would I lose less blood? Someone should do an experiment on it. But not me, I decide.

Our pauses to remove leeches become more frequent and it is five hours before we come out on the high meadows where, our guide tells us, the ridge track leads off to Rudrinath. Up here shepherds are grazing cattle in the lush summer grass, living in small temporary huts. In one of these huts we are given fresh hot buffalo milk, the creamiest and richest milk I have ever tasted, and cups of thick whey. The shepherd in this hut is a tall Muslim, with striking red hair, a red beard and immensely strong arms; he has a walking stick half the thickness of a telegraph pole.

On the ridge top just beyond the hut we meet Corrina and Ding, returning from Rudrinath. 'It's a dead end,' Ding yells out to us. 'The track doesn't actually go through there — it just stops. If you guys go that way you'll just have to come back along here tomorrow.'

'What's the temple like?' I ask him.

'A joke, mate — all fallen down, nowhere to sleep, and one half-mad *sadhu* living under a piece of tin.' They are not pleased at their wasted effort.

We do not need much convincing to rule out Rudrinath as a side trip and soon we are all descending the steep track on the far side of the ridge, heading for Mandal, the next village on our route. It is apparent by now that this constant rain is going to mean heavy snow and even less visibility at higher altitudes. Our earlier plan for Pete's 'real' traverse team to cross Naindi Khal is quietly dropped. From this point on we travel together as a group of six, plus our guide until tonight.

The descent to Mandal turns into an utter shambles. Ding and Corrina drop behind and Tashi and Pete forge on in front. Roy and I are walking with our guide but when I make a toilet stop Roy and the guide go on, expecting me to catch them up shortly. At the bottom of the valley Pete and Tashi are waiting for me.

'Where's Roy?' I ask.

'Behind you,' they reply.

'No, in front of me.'

'Oh?'

Although we have lost Roy he at least has the guide. We find a little *chai* shop and manage to reunite Tashi with some cigarettes. Dusk sees us three walking into Mandal, with no idea where the others are. Ding and Corrina arrive well after dark but Roy is still nowhere to be seen. Where can he have got to, I wonder, with his smiling face and that shapeless old felt mountain hat with the brightly coloured pheasant's feather stuck in its brim?

In the morning we find Roy sleeping in the room next to ours above the Mandal bus station. 'Well, my guide got a little confused,' is all he will say about his adventures. The guide is paid off.

For once it is not actually raining although all the indications are that rain is not too far away on the agenda. We set off in better spirits, and slightly more cohesive order, following a track that zigzags up through leech-free forest, cutting back and forth across a good motor road. Around 10.30 am the rain begins to pelt down: we raise our umbrellas resignedly and climb through a belt of leeches on to a pass clothed in thick mist. There is a *chai* shop here, already full of *sadhus* sheltering from the rain. We sit down to remove our leeches and Tashi teaches me a handy trick. He carefully extracts a thread of cotton from my sweat-band scarf and ties a single over-hand knot in it. He takes a leech from my foot, puts it on the ground, and waits until it rears up in the air. Then he drops the loop over it and pulls the knot tight, choking the leech in the middle. He ties this leech to my pack, much to the amusement of a watching *sadhu*. 'Now,' says Tashi, 'as you go back into the forest the leech cries out to its friends and tells them, "Don't go near this man, he is a very dangerous fellow — this is the punishment he is dishing out".' Perhaps it works; for the rest of the day I see few leeches.

At a quarter to four in the afternoon we are outside a resthouse at Dugal Bhita, drenched by heavy rain. We have a choice — push on for a couple of hours in the remaining light and then camp, or stay here. No one is enthralled at the prospect of a wet night in the tents so we stay. It is a lucky choice — the *chowkidar* provides us with a meal of *dahl bhat* with a few *chapatis* and, since it is the season and we are close to the herders' meadows, fresh yoghurt.

The rooms are stale, dark and musty, and our clothes will still be damp in the morning but we can be content for the roof is good and the beds are clean and soft. There is no electricity but we are too tired to sit up anyway so by 7.30 pm we have sunk gratefully into the mattresses and dropped off to sleep.

Just on midday the next day we emerge from the forest and are able to leave the leeches behind for a time. From here to Son Prayag, halfway point on this section of our journey, we will be following the highway. I fear for my feet: my running shoes are beginning to fall to pieces, the stitching rotting away in the constant damp. The first town on the road is Okhimath and Roy and I wander around its bazaar, looking for shoes to fit me, without success. The largest size they stock is nine and I take at least 11. Perhaps I just need new feet — they look as if they too will fall apart once the shoes go. The flesh is soft and white and I have been pulling off each leech very carefully, in case I drag away large patches of skin as well.

We meet the others for a lunch of *chai* and fried *pakoras* in the Okhimath bazaar, sitting outside in a brief pause between flurries of rain. Beyond the bazaar the pre-highway footpath descends to a tall swing bridge with rusty chain-link supports strung between two stone pillars, on one of which the year '1913' is carved. Our *chai* is disturbed by a fight between a young man in his 20s and a boy of about 13. It is never clear what the fight is about but the young man seems to be disciplining the boy and beats him determinedly with a stick. The boy comes up from the ground, tears in his eyes, flailing wildly, and lands two good punches, bang, bang, before the stick drives him down again. A crowd of close to 100 gathers, but no one intervenes. Tashi can see that we are getting restive. 'Much better if you say nothing,' he cautions. 'This is a local problem and the people here will be fixing it.'

The highway, our footpath for the moment, climbs steeply to Gupta Kashi, a town at the beginning of the valley which leads to Son Prayag and then Kedarnath temple. I try, unsuccessfully again, for shoes.

There is a resthouse here but it has only one room, which Ding and Corrina share. In front is a concrete awning which will shelter Roy, Tashi and me tonight, should it rain, and we spread our gear beneath it. The awning provides cover for a lookout point which must have a good view north to the mountains in clear weather. In the last of the daylight I take out my 'speedy stitcher' and attempt to stitch the soles of my shoes back to the uppers. They are going to have to last until Uttarkashi.

The highway continues up the valley rather than up and down across country in the manner of the pilgrim trail and at first this seems a welcome change. But it is 30 tedious kilometres to Son Prayag and we simply endure the boredom of walking on the hard tarseal. It rains on and off all day long and we walk in about two centimetres of water which runs over the bitumen surface. Trying to look on the bright side, I note there are no leeches.

Son Prayag is one massive bus park. It has hundreds and hundreds of buses, thousands upon thousands of pilgrims and only four public toilets. Corrina and I look at each other. 'Had a hepatitis shot lately?' she asks me.

'I think I could do with a booster,' I reply.

We decide we have earned a rest. We will leave some of our kit here tomorrow while we make the easy overnight trip to the temple at Kedarnath.

We pick our way out of Son Prayag early, before the *chai* shops are open, moving quickly with light packs. The trail is thronged with pilgrims, dark-skinned and light, tall and short, people from the south, from furthermost Cape Comorin, from the deserts of Rajasthan. Many of the pilgrim women cover their heads with a fold of sari at our approach, hiding their faces as much from Tashi and Roy as from Ding and me. When we stop for *chai* and breakfast a group of pilgrims passes, tall men followed by porters. The porters carry a palanquin chair in which a woman reclines. She has left it late in life to make her pilgrimage; she is light and frail and only four porters are needed. The youngest of the men pauses until the porters bring the chair alongside him.

'Do you wish to take tea, mother?' he asks in an impeccable English accent.

'No,' her voice is surprisingly strong. 'Let us get on. Rain will begin soon.' She is right and the pit-pat of drops is soon heard tapping on the *chai* shop awning. When it is time for us to go we open our trusty umbrellas and trudge off into the mist. Pilgrims, homeward bound, salute us as they pass:

'Namaste, sahib, namaste, memsahib.'

'Namasteji,' Roy replies, using another respectful form of the greeting.

'Namaste,' we echo behind him. It is difficult placing your palms together in salute across your chest when one hand is gripping an umbrella handle.

Holy men meditate by the wayside, in small caves and under overhanging rocks. On their foreheads many wear the blaze of Vishnu or the trident of Shiva — signs of the gods, picked out in white and scarlet powders. 'Who knows what these men may have been in the world,' says Roy. 'Rich businessmen perhaps, or airline pilots. They come to spend the fourth stage of their life here, preparing for meeting God.'

'What do you mean by the "fourth stage"?' I ask.

Roy thinks for a moment before replying. 'Well, we Hindus see life in four stages. The first stage is that of childhood and being a student. One studies and gets ready for life. Then, in the second stage, there is life itself, as a householder: marriage, family and of course business and work.' He steps aside for a palanquin coming down the track. 'Where were we?' he asks. 'I have forgotten already. Oh, of course, the third stage, that's what the Westerners call retirement. One no longer has to work: the children support you, the old person prepares for death. Most people go through these three stages. Some, not many, go to a fourth stage, *sannyasa,* which is one of complete detachment.'

Roy points to a frail, bent old woman resting by the trail. 'In this stage an old person may leave home, family and children. She may say, "Consider me as dead," and walk away in only the clothes she wears, to beg and have nothing. If she is fortunate the people will feed her because they acquire merit by doing so. By accepting suffering, these old people can atone for deeds in their past. They may have been in business or politics and done things, even little things, that they are not proud of. Who knows?'

We pause while a porter goes by with two children seated in a *kandi,* a basket like a *doko* with a small seat inside it. The rate for the porter and *kandi* from Son Prayag to Kedarnath is Rs 140. Roy drops a few coins into the woman's bowl. 'Their work on the earth is finished and they prepare for what comes next. If they become completely detached, their soul may be released from the cycle of reincarnation.'

Tashi has followed all of this quietly. He speaks up at last. 'You know what?' he says, as Kedarnath looms up at the head of the valley.

'What?' I ask him. He grins.

'Today we have seen maybe twelve thousands of people.'

'Yes?' I nod.

'Well,' he says, 'not one pretty girl!'

'Tashi!' Corrina treads squarely on his foot.

We sleep at Kedarnath in the Modi *bhavan,* a resthouse for pilgrims that has been built and maintained by the Modi family, one of the extremely wealthy industrial families of India. On the wall is a price list for the various *pujas* that the priests will say for you if you should wish: the cheapest *puja* is Rs six; for Rs 31 there is a six-minute *puja;* and a 'special complete and permanent life *puja'* can be bought for Rs 5000.

Kedarnath temple is a long rectangular stone building with a tall hive-shaped structure towering over one end. Inside, drums are beating, while outside the *pujaris* (priests) are shuffling awe-struck pilgrims into a queue. Not far up the valley the steep rock and ice walls of the south face of Kedarnath Peak stand remote and serene. The man from the plains, placing *ghee* and flowers on a statue of a bull, believes that gods live up there. If not there, then where?

Back at Son Prayag we collect our gear from the hotel keeper. The way to Uttarkashi lies straight up the valley side from the road, where the rain comes down in curtains through the trees. Each of us wants to travel quickly now for we are sick of this rain, sick of the leeches, and sick of the sound of running water.

Trijugi Narayan is where we stop for the night. There is a temple here, reminiscent in design of the temple of Kedarnath and very old. It has sunk so far into the earth that a three-metre-high rock wall has been constructed around it, up to the level of the surrounding ground. A fire is said to have burnt here endlessly for three ages (*tri jugi*), since the marriage of Shiva to Parvati, the wife he wooed at Kedarnath.

A *pujari* takes Pete and me to see the fire, motioning to us to leave our shoes at the edge of the rock wall before splashing barefoot into the damp mossy square. We see the sacred fire burning on the far side of the inner portal. The *pujari* turns from us to attend to his prayers, lighting small wicks in *ghee* bowls and sticks of incense. He chimes a tiny bell continuously in his left hand as he sings and passes a tray of lamps back and forth before black stone images of Shiva and his new wife, Parvati. Replacing the lamps before the pair, the *pujari* then swings incense back and forth in the same way. There are echoes in the darkness, a sound of bells over voices, song and prayer. Then a piece of wood crackles in the fire; flames flare up, driving back the darkness, and the light picks out the eyes of older images behind Shiva, row upon row of nameless and silent gods.

The *dharamsala* behind the temple is a large two-storeyed building in stone. We are virtually the only occupants although there are some 30 rooms. These rooms are windowless and we camp on the verandah instead, where all six sleeping bags can be spread under the ample roof. We cook on our own stove too, having been able to buy some rice from a villager. Our excess clothes are draped over the balcony and hung off window bars behind us. Nothing is dry now; my walking clothes are drenched and my spare clothes are damp. There is some slight comfort in changing from one to the other, but not much.

Two hundred metres away the world ends in clouds. I sit and watch as the light fades from grey to greyer, from daylight into night, and soon I cannot tell what is field, what forest. In the village below a radio is playing on fading batteries; a bell tolls at the temple. Later there is the flip-flop of rubber thongs as a young boy pads along the balcony with a lantern and an umbrella, off on some errand in the night.

Next morning the man who sold us the rice brings us tea and *puris* with boiled potatoes, early as promised. This is the first time on this whole section that I have eaten something other than tea and biscuits for two meals in a row. Everywhere else there seem to have been food shortages: the householders do not cook an early or midday meal and most of the villages are too small to support a 'restaurant'. We ask if there is spare food at each *chai* shop we come to, but the answer has always been the same: '*Chai* shops sell *chai,* restaurants sell food'; where there are no restaurants there is little food for us. When we have eaten our fill of this man's *puris* and paid our bill, he presses a bag of apples on us as a present. My stomach can hardly credit what is happening to it and continues to rumble in gratitude long after we have left the *dharamsala.*

The next ridge we climb is crowned by a deserted village. We wait sombrely for an hour in the doorway of a shattered, dripping hut for Ding and Corrina who took a wrong turning. There were meadows here once but now dock and other weeds stand waist high, inside the huts as well as outside. Was there disease in the village, I wonder, or was it abandoned for some simpler, more commercial reason, such as the decrease in pilgrim traffic causing the failure of a *chai* shop? There is no one left to ask.

When Ding and Corrina arrive, we set off again and for two and a half hours we wend our way along the steadily narrowing ridge. The track is well defined but exposed to rain and a slowly rising wind. I feel like I've been looking out at the world from under this umbrella, water dripping from its ribs, for a very long time now. I disturb a sluggish snake on the path, two metres long and 50 millimetres thick, with a beautiful glistening pattern of golden diamonds on its back.

'Is this one dangerous, Tashi?' I ask.

'Oh, no,' he says, prodding it with his umbrella, 'this fellow is all right.' I am far from convinced and step gingerly past it.

About 100 metres further on Tashi suddenly grabs me by the arm and, screaming 'Look out!', jumps high off the path. I follow suit only to find, when I return to earth, that I have been the victim of a practical joke. Tashi thinks it is a more humorous snake-scare than I do, and we continue along the ridge with periodic outbursts of Tibetan cackles coming from just behind me.

Apart from the deserted village we see only two huts during the whole day. In the first we shelter to cook up the remains of our rice. The second, a shepherd's hut which we reach at 7 pm, is still five kilometres short of the next village, Ghuttu, but the shepherd and his daughter who are living here for the summer graciously invite us in to share the shelter of their matting roof against the rain. I curl up next to two goats who are obviously waiting anxiously, like us, for the monsoon to end.

In the morning we make a quick hot drink and decide not to eat until Ghuttu. The track soon disappears and we stumble through a maze of irrigation ditches between fields. These bring us down to a stream and then, an hour later, back to the track. The surface of the track is crumbling and has been undercut by running water, just about as bad as the ditches.

Ghuttu, like any village we have sought by name, has grown in my imagination to quite a substantial town. It turns out to be a very small collection of buildings at the end of a new road. No cooked food can be obtained and we share a meagre breakfast of biscuits that have waited too long for a buyer. As is usually the case in roadend towns, the locals make a pretence of knowing nothing about the trails and protest that the best way to our destination is to catch a bus. After all, they reason, if you can afford the bus who in their right mind would walk?

Beyond Ghuttu we plod 1100 metres up the far side of the valley, past piles of plastic irrigation pipes to the junction of two ridges. The track is better here and leads down a long gentle spur. The rain stops, the cloud rolls back, and I walk in the sun again at last. It is so long since I have felt its warmth on my skin that I make detours off the track wherever a tree cuts off the sun's rays.

Roy and I pause to watch men splitting bamboo. Taking thick, soft waterlogged stems which have been stored in a dammed ditch they cut a notch at one end, brace the stem, and draw a sharp bar ten metres through its length. Pop, they have two halves. Pop, quarters. Stacked to the side is the finished product, long thin strips for walls and matting. Roy asks the men for directions, approaching the topic gradually for sometimes the hill people are shy or even suspicious. Roy waits a little, to listen to the bamboo workers' talking and identify the dialect they are speaking, and he then breaks the ice by singing a snatch of some local song, a love song by the sound of it, to put them at their ease. Only then does he call out and ask about the road to Budda Kedar.

'Oh, sahib,' the older man smiles, 'Budda Kedar is too far for you to reach today. But about one hour is Khaldi and another hour again is Beti.'

'Down the ridge?' Roy asks.

'Yes, sahib, just follow this way,' he indicates the route below us.

'Which is the best place for sleeping?' Roy asks. The older man smiles again.

'There are no hotels, sahib. Beti is a small place and Khaldi is smaller. There is one shop at Beti, near the school, but Khaldi has nothing.'

So it proves. Khaldi is a depressing place, shady and dripping wet in thick forest. We push on for Beti, making the most of the clearing sky. I even put away my umbrella, slinging it from my pack; what pleasure that gives me. Beti is an airy spot on the end of a ridge with a fine view across to the far side of the valley where terraced fields are sown in grain. The people give us their schoolroom to sleep in and we hobble about in the last rays of the sun, drying gear on the grass and trying to dry out our bodies as well. The damp has caused problems for all of us with our feet. Gaping cracks have opened between my toes; Tashi's and Corrina's are worse.

'How far now?' Corrina rolls her eyes at me in mock despair. We check the

Corrina at lunch in the persistent monsoon rain, Tipra valley in the Garwhal.

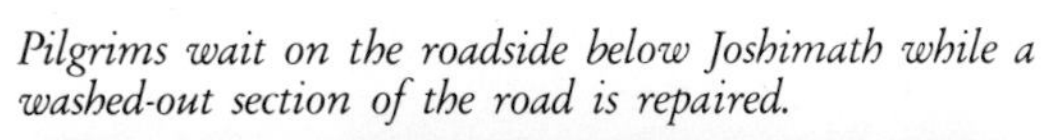

Pilgrims wait on the roadside below Joshimath while a washed-out section of the road is repaired.

Kedernath temple, high in the mountains of Garwhal.

Tashi takes a kandi-wala for a ride.

Ding and Corrina completed the monsoon trail section on foot despite Ding's dislocated shoulder.

There are many different ways of making a pilgrimage.

Our trail 'drops steadily through beautiful dark green pine trees to Budda Kedar, where two rivers meet'.

In monsoon clouds, workers clear the path to Hem Kund, a Sikh pilgrimage site.

A mixture of messages at Badrinath.

map on the schoolroom wall: there are two major river systems left to cross before Uttarkashi.

'We'll make it,' we assure each other.

Today is 15 August, India's Independence Day. Late in the evening a group of young schoolboys go about the village with a lantern, chanting slogans about Gandhi and Independence. Perhaps they take us for Englishmen — in any event they come and chant outside the schoolhouse until Roy goes out and asks them to move along and chant somewhere else as we are trying to sleep. Some of the boys take offence and rocks are thrown on our roof and one comes flying in through the bars on the window. We close the shutters and more rocks come down on the roof. Roy is not perturbed. He is a very aristocratic chap but somewhere along the way he has managed to pick up some decidedly cunning ways of the world. He goes outside and calmly throws rocks on to the roofs of the houses nearby; he blames it on the boys and the outraged residents, who know them all by name, send them off home very quickly.

'That was good work, Roy,' I say from my sleeping bag. He organises his bed by the light of the last candle.

'Not really, Doug,' he replies, 'these are simple village folk. They are very direct so that was not very difficult. Now,' he says, eyes sparkling, 'take my mother — there is another kettle of fish altogether. She is always trying to trick me into meeting young girls to marry.' He shakes his head in reluctant admiration, 'She is very subtle. I have to keep on my toes. Well, good night everyone,' he says, blowing out the candle.

In the night a quiet thief reaches in between the window bars and takes my sweat-stained shirt from where it hangs over the shutter. Fortunately, I had removed my wad of grubby rupees from the pocket before going to bed. Now I must wear one of my climbing singlets, a warm garment and uncomfortably clean compared with the rest of my clothes and body, all unwashed for more than 10 damp and active days. I wish the thief had stolen my rather more unsavoury shorts instead.

Our track from Beti continues along the broad ridge, through fields, and then drops steeply through beautiful dark green pine trees to Budda Kedar, where two rivers meet. We go straight through the village, across the bridge and up the valley on the far side, past wide fields of rice, towards Med. The rain begins again, steady and heavy. Huge fat drops drum on to my umbrella; the spray comes straight through the fabric. Everywhere the villagers say that the monsoon is due to end soon. Perhaps this is its final fling because it seems to provoke a corresponding frenzy amongst the leeches; when the rain stops they will have to lie dormant for another year and they seem to be preparing themselves for this by feverishly devouring what may be their last meal for months. As we approach Med the track is narrow and overgrown and we have to push our way through leaves and branches. There are leeches on my arms, my legs, my umbrella.

'My umbrella — is nothing sacred?' Ding's falsetto comment is just too close to the bone to raise a smile from the rest of us. We stop frequently to remove the leeches and this makes the going slow and wearing. My socks are matted with blood and every time I take them off I find two sorts of leech: the newcomers, which are attached and sucking; and the older ones, which tumble out as a swollen ball of blood and drop to the ground. Occasionally I stoop to bursting them with a rock; it is a bit futile so late, but satisfying.

Med is tiny, two or three scattered houses, but we manage to find *chai* at a farmhouse which has a few provisions for sale. Outside the door sodden, bedraggled chickens pick at a rotting heap of dung and scraps. A boy brings the *chai* and I watch carefully to see if he has his thumb in the greasy cups. On the trail outside the farmhouse we had to step carefully around a mound of human faeces containing a white intestinal worm as thick as my little finger. Intestinal worms are a common health problem: each village takes its water from rivers and streams that carry the suspended and dissolved effluent of the villages above, and thus an infection in one village is passed on down the line. We restrict our drinking to boiled tea but even this is not complete protection. We regularly dose ourselves with worm-pills, just in case.

A *sadhu* comes into the farmhouse, has a good look at each of us, and then goes up to Roy. 'Raksha Bandhan, sahib,' he says. Roy immediately extends his right arm to the man, baring his wrist. The *sadhu* ties a coloured cord around Roy's wrist and Roy gives him a few coins. Tashi notes our surprise and explains that it is the custom, on this day every year, for brothers and sisters to swear their support for each other.

'If I was at home,' he continues, as the *sadhu* ties a wrist cord on him also, 'my sister would be doing this, not the *sadhu,* and I would wear the cord as a symbol of her wish that I lead a long life and come to no harm.'

'What about your sister then?' Corrina asks.

'She wears one too — I tie it on for her and promise that I will always look after her.'

We each volunteer our wrists in turn.

There is a resthouse in the next village, Duntre, but the *chowkidar* is afraid he may get into trouble if he lets us use it. Although the *dharamsalas* are open to everyone, through the generosity of private benefactors, the few resthouses we have passed have been built by various government departments and are maintained for the use of departmental staff travelling on business. We are welcome to use the resthouses (as the staff seldom visit) for a nominal fee, provided we first obtain the relevant 'chitty' from the department concerned. The problem is that the departments are usually in New Delhi, hundreds of kilometres away, and when we were there and able to obtain such chitties it was impossible to predict the exact dates of our stays in the resthouses. At previous resthouses we have relied on Roy's considerable persuasive powers to bring around the *chowkidars* but, tonight, only that magical piece of paper will do, and we sleep once more on someone's verandah.

The food is some recompense. Late in the evening we cram into a tiny *chai* shop in the bazaar where they have rice and *dahl,* potatoes and *chapatis* ready for us. They have a battered transistor radio also, which I am allowed to tune to the BBC world service. Suddenly the words 'New Zealand' come crackling through the static. We all crowd around the set. The South Africans are in New Zealand playing rugby. New Zealand has won the first of a three-match international series, 13-9. There have been 200 anti-apartheid protestors arrested, and much violence. Things must be very bad at home. Our thoughts are a long way from India tonight.

We have a slow start in the morning or, rather, we pack up early and then the *chai* shop offers us fresh eggs for breakfast. What is more it is not raining. We sit outside the shop and write our diaries. I take off my shoes and try to dry my feet in the sun. I look around at our little group. Ding is shirtless, trussed up in his shoulder bandage and as thin as a poker. Pete, Tashi, Roy and I are all much of a muchness, sweaty, grimy, our legs a patchwork of scars and leech-bite scabs. Corrina's long dhoti hides the damage on her legs. Not one of us looks worth passing the time of day with.

'Thank goodness the last pass is coming up,' Roy speaks for all of us. 'This is not very delightful, this monsoon trekking. It is just endurance.'

When we do get moving our way lies along the highway and we have to stop while a gang from the Border Roads Task Force blasts rock from a blocked section.

After the echoes of the explosion have died away we are permitted to cross the landslip to the start of the mule trail or *pugdandi* which leads to Uttarkashi.

The *pugdandi* curls away into a plantation of conifers. Sap is being tapped from these trees and each one bears oozing scars in its bark and little tins beneath to collect the liquid. A woodpecker is there also, tapping away for reasons of its own. We sidle along the edge of a gully, not far above a tinkling stream. Then the track drops to the water where a natural pool has formed.

'Well, I guess we're about to re-enter civilisation,' Pete says, turning to me, 'what do you say we stop here and wash?'

I need no urging. Pete rummages through his rucksack for our one remaining sliver of soap. I strip off and dive into the pool, leaning back in the water, delighting in the cool clean rush of it. I seem to be in a small well, a shaft sunk among the tall trunks, sunlight streaming down from the gap high above. We soap ourselves vigorously, rubbing away grime and blood. Afterwards we dry in the sun, steeling ourselves to don our sordid clothing one last time.

Where it rejoins the highway, the *pugdandi* brings us out on a low pass. There is a *chai wala* here, with his little shop set up under a canvas awning, and we stop in its shade. Tall cumulo-nimbus clouds pile up to the south but the day remains fine and dry. Perhaps the monsoon really is finished at last. Two porters pass, hill-folk of Garwhal, each with a small wooden spindle dangling by a thread of wool from one hand. They carry carded fleece looped around one wrist and, almost unconsciously, they spin the fleece into thread as they walk, the spindles twisting down to just above the ground then magically rising up toward their wrists again.

Peter and I are here alone, the others are spread out somewhere behind us. I order tea. Instead of using the customary term 'bhai' or 'young brother' to address the *chai wala,* I call him 'bai sahib' which means something akin to 'head boy' or 'chief waiter'. The *chai wala* grins broadly, the chief waiter of a staff of one, and brings us the tea.

'Where are you going, sahib?' he asks.

'Uttarkashi,' I reply. 'How far is it?'

'By road it is 24 kilometres, but by the *pugdandi* maybe six kilometres.'

'And which way is the *pugdandi* from here?'

'It lies there, through the trees,' the *chai wala* points down the valley. We nod. 'And where are you coming from, sahib?'

'We are coming from Joshimath.'

'Joshimath? By walking?'

'Surely. It is 13 days now.'

'Thirteen days. Has it been raining, sahib?' Pete and I exchange glances.

'Oh, yes,' I say, nodding, 'there has been some rain falling.'

SHARADA
autumn

We were all at Uttarkashi by 16 August. The monsoon really had ended and our spirits lifted accordingly. Ding, however, was worn out. The strain of picking his way one-armed along the steep muddy trail had taken its toll. To give his shoulder a chance to mend we postponed the traverse party's departure for one week. Taking advantage of the break the rest of us took off in all directions.

Tashi had received a telegram saying his mother was ill and he flew half way across the continent to Darjeeling, to be with her. Then Roy had bad news as well; his father had suffered a stroke. As the oldest son remaining in India Roy had heavy family responsibilities so he flew immediately to Calcutta. SP went home too, to Mussoorie. Home was a bit far for the rest of us, so Ding and Corrina rested up at the HMI in Uttarkashi and Pete, Ann and I took off for the hills. We trekked up valley to Gangotri, where the international climbing camp with Doug Scott had been held successfully without us.

Gangotri is one of the holiest places in Hinduism. A Shiva temple here is the lodestone for devout pilgrims and above the temple we scrambled up to the foot of a glacier where the waters of the most sacred river Ganga issue from the ice. The river's source is called Gaumukh, the Cow's Mouth. It was a peaceful place and it did all three of us good. Pete seemed more relaxed now, away from Ding. He and Ann got on well and the journey up into the real mountains again was refreshing for all three of us after the heat and damp of the lowland monsoon rain-forest. It was hard to turn back, south to the traverse route, but Ding had organised a special dinner at Uttarkashi's Nehru Institute of Mountaineering for Corrina's birthday and we didn't want to miss out on that.

Back in Uttarkashi everyone seemed to have benefited from the break. Tashi's mother's health had improved so he had returned, and Roy also was able to rejoin us from Calcutta. On the next traverse section to Manali, SP accompanied Tashi, Ding and Pete. Roy, Corrina, Ann and I accompanied the baggage from Uttarkashi to Manali, where there was a third Mountaineering Institute in which we could stay.

With two weeks to spare before the traversers were due, Ann and I went climbing to celebrate my twenty-ninth birthday. We left Manali on 2 September. Corrina, full of health and confidence after her successful monsoon trek, went south into the foothills towards Kulu, where the apple harvest was in full swing. The orchards were a tangle of poles and ropes holding the laden branches of fruit aloft. The narrow sealed roads of the Kulu-Manali valley were choked with large trucks, piled high with boxes of the juicy harvest, red and crisp. The nights grew cooler.

8. Gangstang

The journey from Uttarkashi to Manali is 36 hours of virtually continuous bus travel that leaves us absolutely shattered. We sleep through the next day and night.

Manali is an alpine village, peaceful and calm. Clear blue skies stretch above

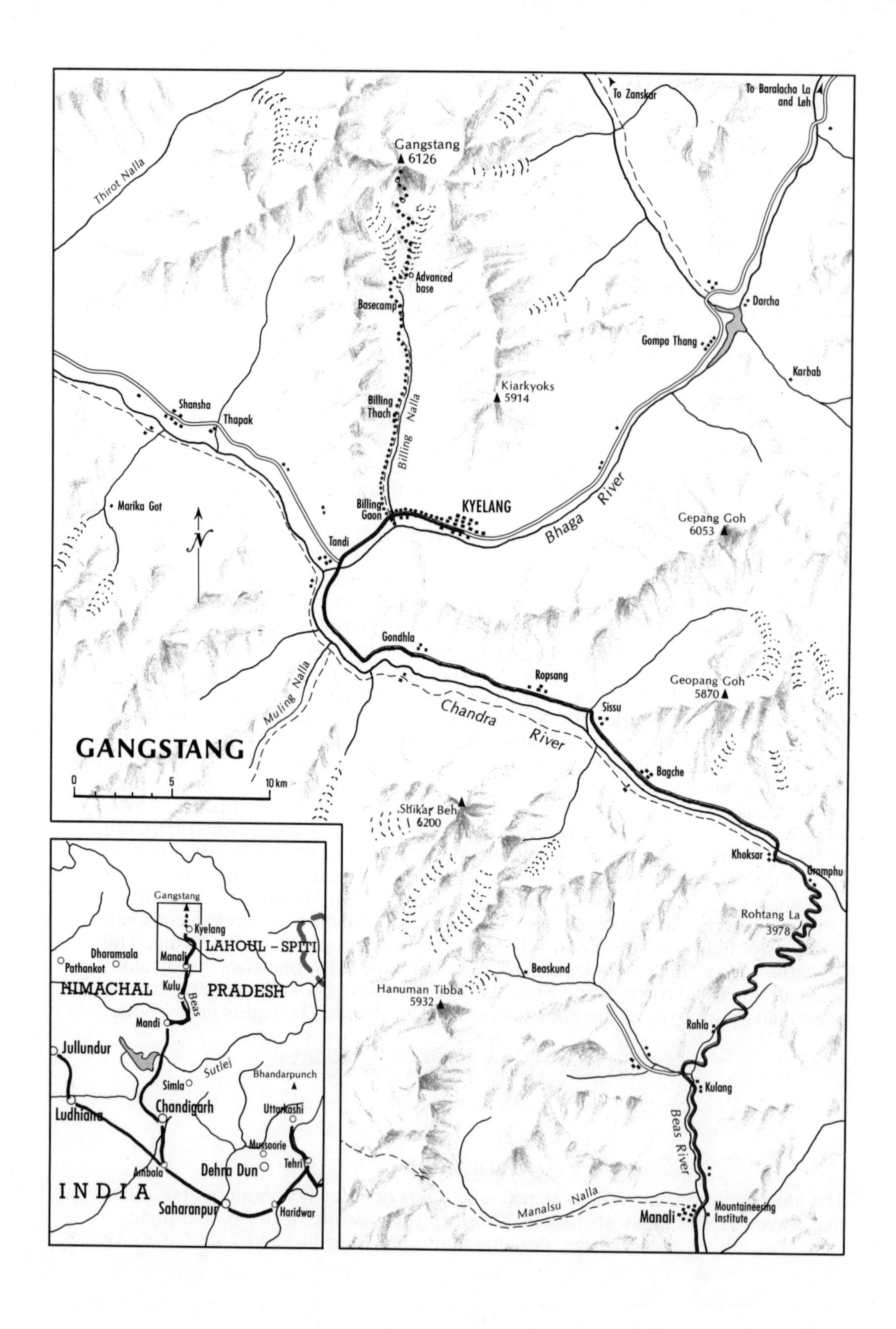
GANGSTANG
Gangstang
6126
Advanced base
Basecamp
Billing Thach
Billing Nalla
Billing Gaon
KYELANG
Kiarkyoks
5914
Thirot Nalla
To Zanskar
To Baralacha La and Leh
Darcha
Gompa Thang
Karbab
Shansha
Thapak
Marika Got
N
Tandi
Bhaga River
Gepang Goh
6053
Gondhla
Ropsang
Muling Nalla
Chandra River
Sissu
Geopang Goh
5870
Bagche
Shikar Beh
6200
Khoksar
Gramphu
Rohtang La
3978
Beaskund
Hanuman Tibba
5932
Rahla
Kulang
Beas River
Manalsu Nalla
Manali
Mountaineering Institute
0
5
10 km
Gangstang
Kyelang
Manali
LAHOUL - SPITI
Dharamsala
Pathankot
HIMACHAL
PRADESH
Kulu
Beas
Mandi
Jullundur
Sutlej
Bhandarpunch
Simla
Chandigarh
Ludhiana
Uttarkashi
Mussoorie
Tehri
Ambala
Dehra Dun
INDIA
Saharanpur
Haridwar

the autumn coolness of an orchard-filled valley. Dense pine forests and shining blue-tinged fir trees cling to the upper slopes and tall stately larches grow down by the Beas river. To the north of the town a snow-covered, saw-toothed ridge appears to block the head of the valley. Most of the houses are set back in apple orchards or groves of walnut, oak and elm trees. The homes have a country-house air — tall, elegant, two-storeyed buildings with many windows and spacious verandahs running around both levels.

Across the river is the Mountaineering Institute, where we find a rare treasure in India: trekking maps of the area. They are short on detailed information, such as contour lines, but we buy a set of three anyway. At least they have the village and river names marked and give the heights for a few of the surrounding peaks. We meet the director of the Institute, Mr Harnam Singh, a distinguished-looking gentleman in his late forties.

'Ah,' he says, 'I see you have purchased the trekking maps. I hope you enjoy using them.'

'We certainly plan to,' Ann replies. 'It's such a change to be able to buy a map at all, and these are quite adequate for trekking. The villages are shown and the tracks.' She smiles. 'So are a few peaks.'

'Oh, yes, there are a number of peaks in the area that are not difficult. Are you thinking of climbing?'

'Perhaps,' I reply, somewhat guardedly, knowing that permission is required to enter most of the mountain areas. But then I realise I have warmed to Mr Harnam Singh, his attitude is friendly and enthusiastic. 'Well,' I add, deciding to be open with him, 'I think we will try a peak. We have some of our equipment with us.'

'Good,' he replies. 'I would come with you but I am not doing this new "alpine-style" of climbing without porters and big camps. If I was young, perhaps, but not now. Of course I still do climb, I am a leader.' He looks around, checks that there are no instructors listening, and continues with a wide grin, 'But my legs, you know, they are not leaders. So, porter opens route, I come behind with flags for photographs.'

Browsing over the map we light upon a glaciated area north of Kyelang, the administrative capital of the Lahoul region, which lies just over the saw-toothed ridge above Manali. The map marks one peak, Gangstang (6126 metres), as significantly higher than the others, but it is difficult to gauge the scale of the area without contour lines.

'How long do you think we've got?' I ask Ann.

'It depends, hon — a bus comes through daily for Kyelang but we'd need to buy extra food first. We could leave the day after tomorrow. Let's see,' she checks the date of our next resupply, 'allowing a day for the bus back, that leaves ten days to try to get to the peak. We might be pushing it?' It is framed as a question but I can tell from her voice that she has already decided. We are going.

We unpack our ice axes, rope and harnesses and try to decide how much ice equipment as opposed to rock gear we will need. A guess is the best we can do: going by the height of Gangstang, we decide that the climb will be mainly on ice — crampons and ice hammers, overboots, storm clothing and sunglasses join the pile. For meals we can use a few of the freeze dried meals we brought from New Zealand, very easy to prepare when high altitude reduces the boiling temperature of water. We also buy an impressive mound of supplies from the general store in Manali bazaar: chocolate, sweets and biscuits for high energy snacks; tinned cheese, milk powder and cornflakes which are the only 'solid' foods we can find for breakfast and lunch.

Kerosene is available for our stove but we are a bit worried that the additives or impurities in it might affect the stove once we're in the thinner air of high altitude. After inquiry we buy it anyway: we are told the only alternative, petrol, is likely to be watered down with kerosene!

I want to buy one of the heavy homespun jackets or vests that we see the local shepherds wearing; they look thick enough to be at least showerproof. There are some for sale in a plain wooden building sporting the sign 'Gandhi Shop'. Inside, large printed wall posters advocate a return to homespun and woven articles of clothing for 'warmth, utility and cheapness'. Unfortunately I am much taller than the usual Manali shepherd; I cannot even find a vest to fit. Instead we buy a woollen shawl each, handwoven with the intricate chequered border for which the Kulu-Manali shawls are renowned. Strident tartans in bright yellows and reds are also common patterns. The young male shop employee shows Ann how the local women tie it: the shawl is woven long enough to wrap around the body once and over the shoulder to the front again, like a shortened woollen sari, and the Manali women fasten these folds at the shoulder with a large and usually ornate silver brooch.

Our last tourist purchase is a selection of Manali hats, one for me and extras for friends at home. These homespun, woollen pillbox caps, with upturned brims of velvet or bold-coloured weaving decorated with gold braid, are a necessity for the Manali menfolk in winter for they often shave their heads leaving only a single lock of hair at the crown. I am shy of wearing my hat here, however, where they come from, and save it for colder weather elsewhere.

We delay our departure for a day, at Harnam Singh's invitation, to attend a seminar held to honour the twentieth anniversary of the founding of his Institute of Mountaineering and Allied Sports at Manali. The guest speaker will be no less than the Dalai Lama (Ocean of Wisdom), the spiritual leader of Tibetan Buddhism. In 'self imposed' exile from Tibet since 1959 (after an unsuccessful attempt to resist Tibet's increasing domination by China), the Dalai Lama has been joined in India by thousands of Tibetan refugees, whom we often see employed as roadworkers throughout the hill regions. These refugees (and tourists) flock to Manali for the annual rites at which the Dalai Lama officiates. He is venerated by his followers as the fourteenth reincarnation of Chenrezig, a being who has waived his right of entry to Nirvana until all his followers have attained that same blessed right. The crowds do not gather today, however, for this mountaineering seminar has not been widely publicised.

The proceedings have reached a rather dull stage, in hot mid-afternoon, when a flurry of officials marks the arrival of the Dalai Lama. Ushered directly to the podium, he is a slim man of middle-height, shaven-headed, bespectacled and dressed in the Buddhist monk's robes of maroon and saffron, right shoulder bare. Three rather burlier monks and a tall, senior Indian policeman in a heavy khaki overcoat arrange themselves about him. Seated cross-legged on the platform the Dalai Lama addresses us calmly and in a pleasant voice for about 20 minutes, in Tibetan. When he finishes, he says to the audience in English, 'If you have any questions, I will sit here and answer them.'

There are some questions, most of them relating to the operation of the refugee camps at Dharamsala, the Dalai Lama's abode in India. Then one gentleman wishes to know why yoga is not recognised as a science, to which the Dalai Lama replies simply that he does not know. With only a minute further to go, the last question is:

'What is your personal conception of God?' The Dalai Lama chuckles.

'Well,' he says, 'various religions have various conceptions of God. As for me, I am a follower of an obscure Buddhist philosophy.' He shrugs eloquently, 'That's all,' and smiles. The audience smiles with him — he radiates an infectious good humour.

To travel north to Kyelang we must cross the Rohtang La (3978 metres), by bus. This I am looking forward to — the experience of travelling to such an altitude without any effort, crossing the main divide of the Himalaya without lifting a finger (let alone a foot) for a change. Our bus begins its journey one hour down valley at Kulu, so of course it will already be full when it reaches here.

The bus is late. As we stand about we take *chai* from a shop near the bus station; we have several glasses of tea but do not pay for them — the custom is to settle up for everything at the end. A crowded bus swings into the depot: it has the correct numerals stencilled across its front so we makc for it. Ann passes up our three rucksacks of supplies and equipment, I stow them amongst the produce on the roof and then we struggle aboard.

Ann finds a seat and I am resigning myself to standing when three people squash up a little further to add me to their three-person seat. I gratefully accept the proferred room and manage to gain a couple of inches of resting space, hooking one foot around the base of the seat in front and bracing myself with the other leg in the aisle.

We are off, rattling across the loose wooden planks of the Beas bridge and turning left on to the Manali-Leh 'highway'. This is one of the highest roads in the world, and cartoon-style road signs along the way proudly proclaim it as the product of India's paramilitary road building forces. India's previous single road link with Ladakh, from Jammu-Kashmir, passes too close to the line of control with Pakistan to make it a secure road link and, at great expense, this road has been built through a series of barren mountain areas in Lahoul, Spiti and Ladakh. Its highest point is the nearly 5000 metre high Baralacha La, a pass south-east of Leh, Ladakh's capital.

As the crow flies, the Rohtang La leading to Kyelang is hardly 10 kilometres from Manali. However our bus must travel nearly six times that distance, zigzagging back and forth across the hillside to gain height. No adjustments are made to the engine to compensate for the reduced amount of oxygen at this altitude, and the bus wheezes and backfires increasingly; it is showing the same kinds of problems we can expect from our stove if it turns out not to like burning impure kerosene at high altitude.

From the Rohtang La we enter Lahoul. The Lahoul district is in Himachal Pradesh State which is part of India. The Lahouli people, however, are predominantly Buddhist and the land is, geologically, on the fringe of the Tibetan plateau. This plateau is by no means flat: the horizon to the north presents row after row of barren, steeply eroded valleys and rock peaks, a striking and vivid contrast to the prosperous green slopes of Kulu-Manali, only a stone's throw behind us. The cause of this sudden change is the high mountain divide we have just crossed. The monsoon winds sweep in from the south-east and drop their precious rain on the southern slopes of these hills before rising over them. Lahoul, Spiti, Ladakh, Tibet, all the northern lands are in the rainshadow of the Himalaya: virtually no rain falls here in any season. But yet, I am told, after parching hot summers the land is blanketed for nearly half the year in deep snow. Spring-melt and glacial streams provide the only source of water and therefore extensive irrigation is necessary.

On the wide slopes of the pass itself some growth remains from the summer rains that reach this far: blue poppies and grasses, waving in the cool breeze. From this height we look straight across the Chandra river, 1000 metres below, to the next range of mountains, a crumbling vista of black rock summits and rock-pinnacled ridges. We scan these crests in some dismay, seeing no sign of the snow and ice peak that we imagine Gangstang to be.

Winter is approaching and groups of semi-nomadic shepherds, mainly Ghaddi men who travel north without their families, have begun their annual migration home to the warmer southern valleys and the plains. We overtake them with their flocks on both sides of the pass. The goats and sheep have many young with them; occasionally a herder can be seen carrying a newborn lamb or kid, carefully bundled in woollen cloth. There are traders also: on the long descent to the Chandra we stop twice, once on a corner barely three metres wide, to allow the passage of heavily laden mule trains bound for Manali. Later I see two yaks, the first since Nepal.

Just above the river, at a tiny military depot called Khoksar, we have time for a late lunch of spiced meat and rice while our passports are checked. The highway north of Kyelang is closed to foreigners and Indian civilians, so the military have to ensure that we return this way after our attempt to climb Gangstang. Our personal details must be entered in the register at the military depot. My profession, lawyer, involves a hilarious exercise in diplomacy as Ann wonders how many times she can correct the officer's attempts at spelling it before he throws her into jail in frustration. As we wait, I suddenly realise that we did not pay the Manali bus station *chai wala* for his tea. Here, as elsewhere in the mountains, many traders trust in the honesty of their customers; they have neither the time nor inclination to watch everyone for payment. I make a mental note to pay on our return.

After Khoksar comes a long hot afternoon in the bus. At least we both now have a seat. Mud-walled buildings, with the flat roofs that are the certain indicator of a dry climate, merge into tawny hillsides; some are dwarfed by the mounds of hay that have been stacked on the roofs for winter stock-feed. Contour-hugging irrigation ditches are etched into the steeper slopes and, below them, intense patches of green stand out.

'Top grade potatoes,' volunteers the man next to Ann, 'exported to Gujarat and Bombay, even as far as Calcutta. We grow only potatoes here.' Ann expresses polite surprise and he waxes most lyrical. 'These fields were nothing but stones,' he continues. 'See the walls? The walls are made of the stones and each one of them has been picked by hand. Look,' he says, pointing through the window, 'see the ditches?' We both look again at the carefully constructed conduits that descend so gradually in precisely graded lines over the hillside opposite. 'Yes,' we both reply.

'Those ditches are going up into the valleys to the stream. Sometimes for many kilometres.' We nod and smile our admiration at such an engineering feat, all done by manual labour. I decide to ask our companion if he knows what the mule trains were carrying from here over the pass.

'Wool,' he answers and then, glancing around him, he whispers, 'from Tibet.' Is he joking? I am not sure. By foot, Tibet's border lies at least a fortnight's travel away to the north; why would the traders carry wool from that distance, to an area that has its own sheep and goats? The man does not seem to be joking; perhaps the traders use this route in order to be able to see the Dalai Lama too.

As part of an afforestation programme for the region, tree cuttings have been planted at two-metre intervals along the roadside. Poplars and willows are the most common. The young trees need protection from browsing goats and the local people have found an effective means of providing this: they remove the tops and bottoms from old tin cans and slide the resulting cylinders down over the trunks of the saplings. Eight or ten tins give protection high enough to discourage the goats. The tins do not need to be removed: by the time the trees are strong and tall enough to withstand browsing, the tins have almost rusted away.

Our bus turns north-east up the Bhaga river from the Chandra and we reach Kyelang just on dark. The tourist resthouse has only one double room left, which they offer us at the 'cheap' rate of Rs 20 each. There is a catch — access to the communal resthouse toilet can only be gained through this double room and the other guests must be allowed to walk through during the night. We settle for two spaces in a large canvas marquee outside, for Rs three altogether.

The resthouse manager, who seems to be the only staff member present, installs camp-beds for us and tells us what is available for dinner — omelette and chips! We order triple helpings of tea, chips and garlic omelettes, to 'build up our strength' for the days ahead.

Over dinner we explain to him that we would like to do some exploring (without mentioning Gangstang), and ask if he can recommend a porter to help us for the first day. The food we bought in Manali was so bulky that we have had to bring three packs. We figure, however, that we should be able to find a suitable site for a base camp within a day's march of here, and be able to approach Gangstang on our own alpine-style from there. He promises to arrange us a porter for the morning.

'Dal Bahadur is the porter's name,' he tells us.

Our third rucksack nearly dwarfs young Dal Bahadur, who is only slightly taller than Ann. He tells us that he is from Surkhet, in Nepal, and has been here only two months. From his willingness to accompany us, just for a day's work, I get the impression that he has not had much work since he arrived.

Ann, Dal Bahadur and I backtrack a few kilometres along the main road to the Billing Nalla, the stream flowing from Gangstang if our map reading is accurate. A new concrete bridge crosses the stream and a sign tells us we have reached 3120 metres above sea level. We turn off the road to follow the stream, climbing steadily up a trail on the true right side of the Billing valley. The ground is dry, bare except for rocks, and we walk in a cloud of dust of our own making.

Dal Bahadur is having some problems with his load. The pack he carries is probably only about 15 kg, less than the standard porter weight, so it is lighter than ours but it slows him down regardless. I am puzzled by this, as porters are generally better able to carry heavy loads than we are, but when we ask Dal Bahadur he does not say that anything is bothering him. We stop twice to move some of the food from his pack into ours; he protests but eventually agrees, and still is not able to keep up with us.

As we slowly gain height, we can look down across the river to an irrigated area where the last of the wheat harvest is in progress. Haphazard terraces on the steep hillside are a beautiful pattern of sheaves of green and yellow stalks, laid out on a carpet of golden stubble. A group of stooped, black-clad figures cut the growing wheat with sickles, while others tie the bundles and carry them back up the hill to an open courtyard for threshing.

There are two villages marked on our map on this side of the Billing Nalla. We had hoped to be able to lunch at the second of them and travel a few hours further up valley to establish a base camp within sight of Gangstang. However, we do not reach the first settlement, a makeshift collection of tarpaulin-roofed huts, until 2 pm and the residents are puzzled by our destination.

'This track,' they say, 'it does not go anywhere; it ends in mountains.' When we merely look pleased at this news, they press further. 'Bharap, bahut bharap (much ice),' they warn, but the mention of ice still does not dismay us. An old man then demands our attention: he walks to a nearby boulder and skulks behind it, hunching his shoulders, grunting, and pawing at his chest.

'Bharap admi, bharap admi,' he says and the others echo him.

'What's admi?' I ask Ann. She does not know; we look to Dal Bahadur for help but his English is not up to the translation and he looks bemused by the whole thing. I wonder if it is a word from the local language, since Hindi is not the tongue of Lahoul-Spiti, and then it suddenly becomes clear.

'Snow man!' Ann guesses it. 'I think they mean yetis live there.' Dal nods seriously at the word yeti.

'Oh,' I reply, 'jolly good. Yetis, eh? How marvellous. We didn't see any in Sikkim or Nepal — I thought we were going to miss out altogether.'

Billing Thach is an hour further up valley, the residents tell us, when we cannot be dissuaded from proceeding. It takes us nearly two hours, with Dal Bahadur travelling very slowly indeed. We decide we had better stay at the *thach* (summer settlement) tonight, which will give us a whole day to push further up valley for a base camp tomorrow. We ask Dal if he would like another day's work. He would. He has his bedding with him, rolled up on top of his load.

The summer village is built on the sunny side of a low knoll and it is hard to tell where the hill ends and the dwellings begin — stone huts are built one on top of the next over the surface of the knoll, the floor of one hut resting partly on the earthen roof of another. At the very top, in an empty, stone-walled stock pen the width of the village, a shepherd stands, watching our approach. We ask if we may sleep somewhere in the village; he looks a bit doubtful about it, mutters something and then disappears into one of the houses. He returns nearly ten minutes later, looking just as doubtful about us, but leads us to one of the lower huts and waves us inside.

The door of the hut is made of three heavy planks hinged and padlocked to a stout, recessed, wooden frame. 'Yeti protection?' I murmur. The doorway is low, even Ann has to bend to enter, and there is only one gap in the outside wall for a window. This has been filled with small rocks and twigs to keep out the winter snows. There is no furniture inside, all is stone or dirt. In the hearth are the still warm ashes of a fire. According to Tibetan custom the last fire before leaving home is always of juniper and the smell of it hangs in the air; the owners of our hut must have retreated for the winter to the main village, down past the bridge where the Billing Nalla crosses the main road.

Through the wall behind us we can hear a faint murmur of conversation and the distinct shlock, shlock, shlock of a butter churn. I boil water for a brew of hot chocolate before tea and Dal Bahadur squats down in the doorway, munching one of our crisp Manali apples that Ann has given him, watching attentively as we potter about. We have hardly laid out our sleeping bags before we receive a visit from three high-spirited women of about Ann's age, coming ostensibly to milk a yak-beast that has appeared outside our door. The faces of these women intrigue me for they look neither Indian nor Tibetan, although each of them wears the coral and turquoise necklaces of Tibetan (and Sherpa) folk. Their dresses are of heavy wool, pleated to about knee-length and two are dark maroon in colour, the other brown. Underneath these dresses they wear loose cotton trousers that are dun-coloured like the earth and narrow towards the ankle.

After waving hello through the doorway one of the women says something to her companions, presumably about us, that has them in fits of laughter. Ann chats with them, asking if they are sisters. She receives a long, involved reply in Hindi, covering all kinds of relationships from third cousins to 'just friends' and recounted with much hilarity. Two of the women, called Dechin Chomo and Angmo Debbi, actually are sisters. They all sit down in the doorway with Dal and ask us about our families. Ann describes our brothers and sisters to them: how old they are, what country they live in, what they work at, how many children they have. When our chocolate is ready, Dechin gives us some fresh yak milk to add to it — what a luxury! — and they promise to return later with a little yoghurt for our dinner. Dal wants none of these milk products, however, eating only some of the curried vegetables and *chapatis* that he has brought up with him from Kyelang.

Later Dal borrows Ann's pen and copies the word 'Simond' from the faded label on one of our ice axes on to a spare sheet of paper that Ann has given him from the back of her diary. He explains that he has only just finished school and that he wants to keep learning as much as he can. When Ann asks him how old he is, we are both shocked to discover that he is only 12. There are many children in his family and they all must work for a living, he tells us. We feel like slave-drivers, having asked a 12 year old to carry a load for us, but Dal insists that he would like to continue tomorrow, that he needs the experience and his family needs the money.

I am feeling ill when I wake, dogged by diarrhoea from a stomach infection I picked up in Manali. Ann cooks the breakfast for us and as the stove has less pressure than it should she dismantles it for a thorough clean. We both hope that this is not a sign of the impure kerosene affecting it, for unless the stove works properly we will not be able to travel far from this lower valley. Luckily it works well when reassembled. Rats ate the last of Dal's *chapatis* in the night so he shares our hot milk and cornflakes, picking hesitantly at what for him is a novel mixture before putting half of it aside as we leave.

The shepherds have taken their flocks up the valley well before us this morning and the dust of the trail is patterned by hundreds of hoof-prints. The steep rocky sides of the valley cut off any view of the terrain ahead; I have yet to see any sign of snow.

About an hour above Billing Thach Dal suddenly drops to the ground behind us, moaning softly, and Ann asks him if our food has made him sick. No, it is his head, evidently paining him badly, and he now tells us that he could not sleep much last night because of it. He retches sporadically and looks weak. Ann and I are both feeling fit but then we have been walking at this altitude for much of the last few months; Dal, by contrast, has been eking out the time in Kyelang without much to eat and with little exercise while he waited for work. He now has altitude sickness and any more time spent at this height (about 4150 metres) will only spell more trouble for him; he must go down. Ann explains this to him and he cries out aloud in protest, obviously alarmed. I assure him that we are not angry, that we will pay him for his work today and that he has done a very hard job, but his sobs continue. Gradually he does quieten down but he is still upset at any suggestion that he go back. I insist and he just lies on the ground, moaning piteously again and clutching his forehead. His eyes are swollen almost shut from crying and it is clear that he cannot go down by himself. Ann suggests that she take him down as far as Billing Thach and check along the way whether there is a shepherd who would help us by carrying Dal's pack from here on, at least far enough for us to camp within sight of the glacier. She takes Dal by the hand, talking to him reassuringly, and they set off down the valley together. I start to feel that our 10 precious days for climbing are rapidly slipping away.

I watch them go for a while and then look at the three packs that I am left with — mine, Ann's and the porter's load. I take one of them and carry on up the valley for 10 or 15 minutes, until the other packs are just specks in the distance, and then I drop the first pack and walk back to collect the next. I play a little mental game to keep myself amused in my task. During the first shuttle I decide on the order in which the packs should be carried: I will carry the heaviest one first on each stretch, so that each successive walk over the same terrain will be slightly easier. I convince myself that I am getting a small reward when I carry the third and lightest pack although the difference in weights of the three is only a matter of four or five kilograms. In this way I pass an amusing couple of hours, shuttling packs up the valley, in and out of gullies. I gain height steadily and as I do the views open out behind me to the south. Directly down the valley are the sharp rocky peaks to the west of Manali: Shikar Beh (6200 metres) and Hanuman Tibba (5932 metres).

It is early afternoon before I spot two unladen figures coming quickly up the valley and I flop down against the packs to wait for them.

Ann has a tough-looking shepherd with her. He is at least three times older than Dal and picks up his load with a grin that conveys the immediate impression that he can carry loads a lot bigger than this one, all day and all night too. I immediately wish that I had put back into his pack some of the things that we took out of it to help Dal Bahadur.

'How did you get on with Dal?' I ask, handing Ann some biscuits to eat as we walk.

'Okay,' she replies. 'By the time we got to Billing Thach he'd cheered up a bit. I found Angmo Debbi and tried to explain the problem to her. She said that her grandmother was going down to the lower tent-camp and could take Dal with her. All the shepherds were away though, rounding up their flocks for the move down to Billing Gaon at the road. I just had to wait and see if anyone came up the valley from below.'

Ann nudges me in the ribs, trying to look contrite, 'Angmo and her sister gave me a cup of tea. I did think of you, briefly, out here in the sun toiling away before I said yes.' I manage to smile ruefully and she continues. 'It turned out that Dechin and Angmo both spoke some English, and they gave me the local equivalents of some of our Hindi words. And guess what I did,' she finishes triumphantly. I cannot guess. 'I went down to their kenda heap with them.'

'Uh huh,' I reply, feeling pretty sure that an explanation must follow.

'They'd collected all the yak and sheep and goat droppings from round about in their *dokos* and heaped them up on a big flat boulder. Next thing I know, Angmo's got a great big stick and she's bashing the pile of droppings — WHAM! WHAM! WHAM! Bits of dung were splattering around but it didn't smell too bad.' Ann looks at me to see if I believe her. 'When it was soft, we patted it into kenda, those flat round dung-cakes used for fuel that you see drying in the sun outside houses sometimes.'

'We?' I ask.

'Yeah, I gave them a hand, and it really didn't smell.' I have to laugh then and Ann finishes her story. 'Dechin and Angmo called me their "honorary sister" after that, and we joked about whether it was because they'd tricked us last night, pretending they knew no English, or because I went down and gave them a hand in their "poo-patch". I thanked them for the yak milk last night and they really laughed at that. Dechin pointed out that "yak" is the name for the male animal — it was "nak" milk we were drinking. Then this shepherd appeared from the tent-camp and Angmo told him our story and he said he had seen Dal Bahadur heading slowly back down to Kyelang. He's agreed to help us for this afternoon but he says we've probably got another eight hours' walking to go before the glacier. We'll have to shuttle loads over that part on our own because both the summer settlements are moving out of the valley tomorrow.'

A huge cloud of dust heralds the descent of the village's flock of long-haired sheep and goats. It flows around us and our shepherd exchanges a few words with the herders; they predict snow to low levels in the next two or three days. The Billing valley points almost due north and loses the sunlight early so our shepherd tells us that he must turn back by 3 pm at the latest to ensure his safe return.

Ann and I follow him along narrow goat trails through moss-covered, rounded boulders of ancient moraines, and in and out of sheer, eroded gullies. Our muscles are tensed with the strain of keeping a precarious footing. A few short grasses and herbs grow in the shade, a prostrate variety of pink daisy and more of the hooded blue poppies. We scramble over occasional ridges of larger rocks and, suddenly, just on 3 pm, we round yet another corner to see Gangstang. There is no doubt: it is the first snow peak we have seen for miles around, and it towers over the head of the valley. The south-west ridge, angling up from a saddle between Gangstang and a low peak to the left of it, looks like a possible route, snow and ice all the way. Hallelujah! Even our companion seems infected by our enthusiasm and he says that he knows of a good campsite nearby. Sure enough, in less than 10 minutes he leads us to a tiny grassy meadow, only five metres away from the river.

The shepherd does not linger and, as we pay him for his help, he warns us seriously of the very cold nights and reminds us of the herders' weather prediction. 'Snow is coming,' he repeats, 'snow is coming.' He wishes us the best of good fortune and sets off down the valley; only then do I realise that we did not even know his name.

A litter of cognac bottles, old tins and plastic suggests that this campsite has been used by larger expeditions before us. I wonder if they too were going to Gangstang. I bury their rubbish while Ann gets the stove going for a drink. As we ascended we stopped beside most streams to drink but, after the recent example of Dal's altitude sickness, we decide that we had better drink more, just to be on the safe side. Some say that as much as 10 litres of liquid per day are necessary for adequate acclimatisation: because of the reduced amount of oxygen in the atmosphere, our blood thickens as it manufactures more red blood cells to carry oxygen and if we don't keep up our fluid intake and if we ignore the early warning signs of altitude sickness, it is possible that we could suffer blood clots (thrombosis) or a sudden release of fluid in our lungs or brain cavities (pulmonary or cerebral oedema) as our bodies strain to cope with altitude.

I unroll our tiny blue tent. The two roof-supports unfold and the tent pops into shape; we throw in packs and sleeping bags to weigh down the floor, before tying the guy-ropes over nearby rocks. The stove continues to burn well, boiling water in about 10 minutes. Fragrant steam from a stew of beef casserole and noodles soon wafts through our campsite. The glacier below Gangstang is still out of sight but we plan to carry loads up the valley tomorrow, looking for the best approach, and hopefully leave our loads at the glacier snout. We can ferry the last loads there the next day, giving us a chance to get a longer look at our possible route on the mountain and a better chance to acclimatise. Ann prepares a soup after dinner to increase our liquid intake. It is a 'Snap' brand soup, made in India, and the outside of the packet shows a plump chicken in a tureen. Our brew, however, tastes like old socks and leaves what feel like rocks in the bottom of my mug — definitely an acquired taste.

A stoat bounds across the moonlit clearing, silvery grey with white underside, long and lean. The stoat's agile body ripples, snakelike, as it roves, sniffing and turning in search of prey. Its pointed head bristles with sharp teeth. I wonder whether the herders' weather prediction will prove accurate, whether the snow will fall. There are only a few clouds visible, scudding across the inky depths of the night.

The stream that enters the river near our campsite freezes overnight. Since our plan is for a fairly easy day today we postpone our departure until 9 am, when the sun has reached our tent, and prepare to carry a few of our heavier items of equipment and food in our rucksacks. On setting off our first task is to cross the now unfrozen stream. Ann is not particularly worried by cold and crosses straightaway, barefoot, pretty sure that there is no way of crossing and keeping her boots dry at the same time. I am more optimistic and make two unsuccessful attempts at crossing in my boots before having to bow to the inevitable. Ann takes photos of me as I cross, cursing my boots that I have slung by the laces around my neck and which box me in the ears at every step.

A series of small clouded tarns in the rubble at a bend in the river marks the point from which we have to climb for easier travel. We scramble up steep scree slopes to an old lateral moraine trough about 100 metres above the river. I can now see the exposed terminal face of a glacier that plunges down from the rock peaks opposite us on the the true left of the valley. The huge ice cliffs of the glacier, their surfaces rock-studded and spattered with grey mud, are not a welcome sight. We remain on the true right side. Further on I find a clump of everlasting daisies, a plant that is common near our home in New Zealand. Its straw-coloured flower heads are tattered and dry. Edelweiss flourishes here as well, poking its furry blossom out of the gaps between boulders. A flock of choughs flutters in noisy company above us. Beyond them is only blue sky.

The trough ends suddenly where a landslide has scoured the slope. We will be able to see more of Gangstang from the far side and decide to cross rather than lose height. I leap from boulder to boulder over the sharp-edged, unstable mass of debris, every sense alert for the warning graunch of rock pivoting beneath me. Tiny stones whirr down through the air from the shattered rockface above. I notice that the layers in the rockface have been folded in great rust-coloured swirls, shattered by immense pressure in some bygone age, and then hastily look down again to watch my feet.

We dump our packs in relief at the far side, sit down to eat a few biscuits and gaze at Gangstang. Much of the intervening ground is hidden by the ridges cutting into this valley, but I can see a large snow field above them that appears to lead to the saddle between the peaks. From there the summit ridge looks only another 300 metres higher, the angle of it steepening markedly towards the top. If only we knew what lay between us and that snow field. A bank of low cloud passes over our valley from the west, the temperature drops, and the whole prospect is suddenly rendered grey and forbidding. Who knows what we may find on the unknown intermediate ground, or when we are stranded high on that ridge, affected by altitude perhaps, far from anyone who has the slightest idea of our whereabouts? Have we enough time, only five days left, to reach the peak and return?

How quickly a small change in temperature can have an effect; with the reappearance of the sun, our doubts evaporate. If it is too difficult we will come down again. Simple. In the meantime we can see a feasible route back through the lower moraine to base camp that will save us the hard climb on to this ridge. We bound down the moraine wall to the foot of the white ice of the Gangstang glacier. There is a broad area of dry glacial sand in the lee of a large rock which will do for advanced base and shelter our gear. We stuff both our loads into one pack and tuck it into a corner between two boulders before turning back, unladen, through the moraine again. This lower section is much easier than the route we came up by, consisting of bands of firm flat alluvial gravel between ridges and dotted with beautiful tarns.

At base camp we stretch out on our sleeping mats in the sun, dozing in each other's arms. A foraging *pika,* a small furry rodent looking like a cross between a mouse and a rabbit, hops cautiously across the grass toward us. It comes up inquisitively to within a metre of where we lie and we watch enthralled as it nibbles delicately at stalks of grass, nose and jaws wrinkling and twitching in fastidious perpetual motion. I reach carefully for the telephoto lens for my camera, but our little visitor whisks away between the rocks. It waits motionless for some minutes before returning, a small fist-sized bundle of soft fur, with bright, watchful eyes. I try again to take a photograph but again it whisks away before I can, and so it goes every time I raise the camera.

Apprehension returns with the morning. My stomach is upset again but I force

Buddhist chortens, with prayer flag wires, frame the view of Golab Kangri (left) and Kangla Chang peaks, south of Leh in Ladakh.

Harvesters in the Billing Nalla valley leave a tidy pattern of sheaved wheat behind them.

The evening sun highlights the rock peaks of the lower Baltoro glacier, Pakistan. Paiju (6602m) is on left, Uli Biaho (5965m) centre left, Grand Cathedral group (5866m) centre in shade, Greater Trango (6280m) with the sun on it behind the Cathedrals, and Trango Tower (6250m), the 'nameless tower', the rightmost rock spire in front of the sunlit snow peaks in the right background.

Doug (front) and Pete stop on the Baltoro glacier for a photo session.

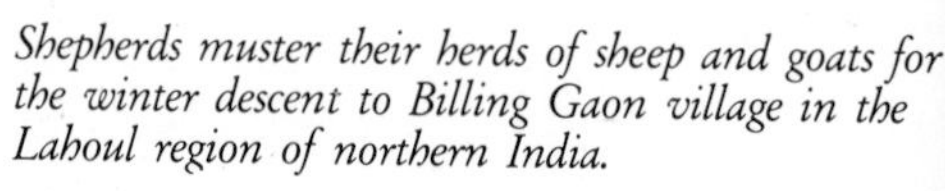

Shepherds muster their herds of sheep and goats for the winter descent to Billing Gaon village in the Lahoul region of northern India.

Lahoul-Spiti folk wear heavy homespun woollen robes in summer and winter alike. Silver braid and traditional turquoise and coral necklaces brighten the garb of this pair at Kulu.

The Royal Palace at Leh is joined to the Leh gompa on the ridge above by long strings of prayer flags.

Kenda cakes drying in the sun.

Nuri, who joined our expedition in Pakistan as liaison officer, leads Ann and Doug on the trail north from Dassu village to the Braldu gorge.
(Peter Hillary)

The train journey to Pakistan provides a break for Pete from his usual trekking activity.

down breakfast. Against all odds, cornflakes and milk and hot tomato soup make me feel a bit better. We leave a small dump of excess equipment and food hidden in the rocks for our return, then scatter the last of our crumbs for the *pika.* Despite heavier loads it takes only three and a half hours by the low route to get to yesterday's gear dump. I carry our small plastic jerry can of kerosene in my hand as there is no room for anything more in our packs. The outside of Ann's is hung with the tent and stove and our assortment of snow stakes and ice screws.

As we unpack, a chill wind springs up, whipping the glacial sand into dervishes. We hastily construct a low rock wall around the tent and use ice axes as well as stones to anchor the guys in the sand. The wind brings cloud and then flurries of snow that force us inside. Our tent is shaped like a two-metre long chrysalis, just wider than our two sets of shoulders at the entrance and narrowing to a point at the other end where we bundle our packs, the rope, storm gear and spare clothing, anything that might be lost if left outside overnight. Crampons and ice screws are slung over the snow stakes and ice axes that anchor our tent: they are not going to blow away.

It is a cosy fit inside the tent when we are asleep; awake, it is rather less congenial. Our arrangement of the entrance has to strike a delicate balance between necessary activities like cooking and food sorting, writing and mending. I lie propped up on one elbow, trying to stitch more securely the tape wrist-loops on to my mittens. It is difficult in this position but if I were to kneel my head would hit the roof. Ann cooks another of the 'Snap' soups with dinner, this time 'vegetable flavour'. It tastes most of all like mothballs. That does it. Whether we need liquids or not, we are not going to carry mothball-flavoured soup sachets up a mountain. I remove them from the pile of food that Ann has sorted for tomorrow's meal.

'Have you no sense of taste, woman,' I grumble.

In the evening I lie awake for hours, staring up through the open door of the tent at the wheeling stars, tracing the swift passage of satellites. There are lots of satellites cruising over the Himalaya and some of them are for peaceful purposes, no doubt, such as weather forecasting or telecommunications, but often, late in the evening or early in the morning, I imagine that the cold unwinking eyes of the world's military establishments stare down at me from those beautiful moving beacons of light.

The following morning I feel nauseous again after breakfast. Ordinarily, when anything like the dreaded 'Delhi belly' affects one of us we just stop eating and try to drink a lot. If we have to eat, plain boiled rice and green bananas are acceptable, but these are obviously not available here. At this altitude we need extra energy just to keep warm let alone do any work. High-fat dairy products make up the bulk of our supplies and these only inflame my stomach problem. If I eat what we have I get weak, but if I do not eat I will get even weaker. Diarrhoea depletes the bodily fluids and reduces the effectiveness of all the drinks we have been consuming in order to acclimatise. Already I have a headache and my urine colour is darker than usual, both indicating that I am not acclimatising well. I decide to swallow some antibiotics and see what happens.

We are starting to run out of time for our climb and must not be late for the rendezvous in Manali, but there is no question of turning back yet. With four days remaining, we decide to combine our reconnaissance of Gangstang with an attempt to climb it. We make up two loads: cooking gear, tent, and half the food in one; the other half of our three days' food and a small pile of climbing gear in the other. They weigh hardly 20 kg but they feel like more at this altitude. I decide to leave our big camera behind and we each take a smaller one, instead, with plenty of film. The remaining gear and food to get us back down valley we stow in our third pack, between the boulders of our advanced base.

This is it, nothing to stay for now.

We don overboots and crampons, rope and harness, at about 4900 metres where rock meets ice. It takes only a short while to fall back into the rhythm of glacier travel, pleasant in weak sunlight. Most of the crevasses are narrow enough to jump, saving us time-consuming zigzags in search of crossing points. A pure stream of meltwater runs along the surface of the ice and we stop to fill our waterbottles. Ahead the ground is more broken where the glacial ice tumbles around a ridge of loose reddish rock. I move out to the right where the ice is less shattered and make a short traverse across a steep ice slope. My pack threatens my balance and I check each step carefully as I go. Ann follows. We climb to the top of the ice slope and, much to our surprise, find ourselves in the bottom of a huge ice bowl, not even hinted at from below. About a kilometre ahead and to the right, huge ice cliffs and seracs cut off further progress. To our left, the earlier rib of red rock continues.

'There must be a lot of ice above us to feed these seracs,' Ann calls out. I grunt in reply, wondering briefly if the snow field above will be the one we saw on our carry from base camp two days ago, the one that leads to the saddle below Gangstang. There is no indication from our surroundings as cloud has obscured much of the western horizon and the peak of Gangstang has been out of sight since we mounted the glacier.

We have a late lunch at the foot of the rock rib then coil most of our rope, leaving about 10 metres between us so that we can move together as we climb. The slightly gritty rock is still warm from this morning's sun and we get the bonus of a bird's eye view down to the glacier system west of ours. Crevasses and slump holes glimmer a translucent blue-green against its rock-dusted surface. The rock rib provides easy travel and we soon unrope. The rib takes us up past the seracs at the head of the first ice bowl and then comes to an end, at the edge of a second ice field. It is the one that feeds the glacier we were on earlier, but it does not appear to lead to Gangstang. Our view is once again confined by ice cliffs on the horizon immediately ahead of us.

'Whaddya reckon?' It's my turn to query this time. 'This doesn't look like the snow field we saw — there's no sign of Gangstang.'

By mid afternoon, when thick cloud piles in and forces us to make our first camp, we are only halfway across the ice field. We pitch the tent on a strip of ice about three metres wide, with two parallel crevasses on either side. Despite the apparent danger posed by crevasses, our position is quite safe (the prospect of sudden cracks opening up in the glacier between these crevasses is remote), and not far away is a trickle of meltwater, so we need not spend hours melting ice for our brews. I cook tonight — sweet and sour pork, hot chocolate, camomile tea, and more chocolate. The warm base of the stove slowly sinks down into the melting ice. From the glacier beneath us there sounds an intermittent far-off rumble and, all around our tent, snow is falling. This is yeti weather.

In the morning our water supply is frozen and the snow still falls. But inside the tent we are warm and dry, fully clothed inside our sleeping bags with our boots tucked in as pillows — if we left them out of our sleeping bags they would quickly freeze. My headache is gone and I take my pulse: at rest it is down to 54, normal for me when I'm fit, so there is room for optimism again. If only this snow has not set in for good. We are packed anyway, ready to go; when the snow stops, just after our second breakfast brew, we have only to shake the tent clean of snow and ice and roll it up. We tramp across the rest of the second ice field and crampon quickly up the most stable looking section of the ice wall, separating us from what we assume must be the approach to the saddle next to Gangstang. Two hundred metres of climbing brings us over the lip, to find ourselves locked into yet another ice field. The rock ridge has reappeared on our left and offers faster travel.

'This mountain's beginning to repeat itself,' mutters Ann as we cross to the ridge. We scramble along it for an hour or so and, when the rock becomes too unstable, Ann leads through to a low ice ridge on our left where we emerge at last in sight of Gangstang. But what a discovery — the main summit looks hardly closer than it did from our base camp. Gangstang must be at least 500 metres higher than the other peaks around and we have badly underestimated the distance to it. At least one more ice fall must still lie between us and the elusive saddle.

Out to our right is the lip of what we hope will be the last ice plateau to be crossed and jumbled rubbish, torn plastic and rusted tins mark the position of an old expedition campsite. Glacial advancement has left these remnants teetering on the crown of an uplifted ice serac, ready to plunge over and downward into a cool green crevasse below. It begins snowing again but there is still about 20 metres of visibility so we press on. At the lip of the third ice field we catch just a glimpse of a crescent of rock peaks in the murk to our left before being driven back by biting gusts of wind, sharp and snowladen. In the lee of the ridge we pull on storm clothing, plop our packs down and sit side by side, our backs to the driving snow, hoping for a clearance.

I open a packet of biscuits and a tin of cheese and we pass them back and forth, cutting thick slices of cheese without removing gloves or overmitts. There is not much to say. We have been through this before. Either it will get better or it will get worse, or it might just remain the same. Talking about the possibilities will not help. Two hours pass, the temperature drops steadily and it begins to grow dark.

'We'll have to camp,' Ann says.

'Yes, blast it,' I reply. We stamp out a flat space in the fresh snow. Ann hacks at the gnarled clumps of ice beneath with her axe while I fumble to untangle the cords of our tent in the searching wind. For each corner guy rope I hammer in a snow stake and ice screw for anchors as well as the usual ice axe. Ann finishes first and immediately dives into the tent, trying to tear off parka and overtrousers in the same motion as untying her crampons. I follow quickly behind. We bitch at each other about who is bringing the most snow into the tent.

Our forced camp is at 5800 metres, too high and too cold now for meltwater. The recent snowfall has already been tossed about by the wind and mixed with the old surface layers of ice that are filthy with glacial dust but this is our only source of liquid. Ann's little peppermint-tea strainer that she takes everywhere with her proves useful at last: I line it with toilet paper, and we filter our laboriously melted drinking water through it. Half an hour's work produces an odd tasting lukewarm drink which still leaves a very noticeable mud residue in the bottom of the cup. About five centimetres of snow an hour fall on the tent roof and, by reaching carefully along the side of the tent, I am able to scrape up some clean snow which speeds up the drink preparation a little. Even so, it takes another hour to get enough water to add to our dehydrated stew mix for dinner. My turn to cook again and the meal takes half an hour to prepare because of the low temperature at which water boils at this altitude. When it is ready I have only enough appetite to pick at it, leaving the rest for Ann.

All of this activity has to be accomplished in the mouth of our poky little two person tent. The door is zipped firmly closed and Ann must give me fair notice before she can even turn over.

Just as night falls there is a slight clearance in the cloud and we hurry outside for a look. The rigmarole necessary for exit would be hilarious if it were not so tedious: wriggle a hand out of the sleeping bag, undo the snap-release cord that keeps the hood snug against the face, lever out an arm and unzip as little as possible of the sleeping bag. Shuffle hips out of bag, turn over without squashing partner and get up on to knees without knocking the roof (which would encourage condensation), or standing on any snowgoggles or suncream that might be in the way. Grope towards the tent entrance, scrabble around for boots, check that they are your own and that you have them the right way around. Open the tent door without letting any snow fall in, reach one boot out into the snow and stand in it, hastily following with the next boot for balance. We both go through this procedure and stand outside, trying to make out the terrain between us and the saddle. It looks as if we could cross over on the right hand side at the north-eastern edge of the ice field. There is a badly broken area just below the saddle but we will not know if that is passable until we get there.

'If it's fine tomorrow, we'll make it,' Ann says. 'It's the weather that's held us up — we only managed three hours' travel yesterday.'

'Have we got enough food left? We've been two days from advance base.' I take a last look at Gangstang before the cloud returns. Ann laughs and turns to me, 'At the rate you've been eating Doug, it's unlikely we'll run short.'

I have to go out for toilet trips twice in the night and lie awake, slowly warming up again, after each interlude. It is nearly 5 am when I have to go outside for the third time. I begin the slow process of extricating myself but suddenly realise that there is an awful urgency about this occasion. I move faster but to no avail. I am still lacking one boot when, with a terrible sinking feeling and a strangled groan, I realise that I am too late. It is not pleasant out there in the predawn darkness with my ski-pants down around my ankles, trying to clean myself up by feel. Snow is still falling steadily and large quantities of it accumulate in my trousers; when I finally pull them up, clumps of resistant snow promise a slow cold melt from within. In the snow I can clean up my hands but a faint albeit identifiable odour still hangs about my trousers.

When inside at last, I draw the hood of my sleeping bag tight around my neck and lie there, weak and humiliated, feeling decidedly sorry for myself. Ann sleeps soundly on, snug in her sleeping bag. I struggle to resist the almost overpowering urge to wake her up, savagely, and tell her how lucky she is.

Snowfall keeps us in our tent until 9.30 am. Then the sky clears and the sun is hot. Ann leads off, both of us tied into our web of rope and harness. Deep cold powder snow clings to her crampons and every third step is followed by a brusque kick against her ice axe to knock off the accumulating snow. She probes with her axe before each advance, checking for a safe route ahead. We belay for the jump across a wide crevasse, nerves and muscles taut for an insecure landing on the far side. The hot sun mocks our slow progress, cracking our lips with its fierce heat. This is textbook glacier country and we are forced into textbook glacier travel — relatively safe, but slow and tedious.

Three hours later finds us just below the saddle, buffeted by wind streaming over the low peak to our left. I lead up a long ramp of ice that narrows as we gain height. It ends in a wide bergschrund, nearly three metres across, that cuts us off from the summit ridge. To both sides lie gaping slump holes, too huge for the new snow to fill them, so we backtrack and Ann tries a lower ramp through the ice fall, but this one too comes back to the bergschrund.

There is one other possibility. We could circle back, strike off north-westward towards the low peak, cross that and approach the saddle from the far side. It will take a lot longer. Out come a packet of gingernut biscuits and our waterbottles and we debate the odds. We are at about 5950 metres, hardly 50 metres below the low peak, and if we go this other way we will not get higher than the saddle again today. We would have to camp there and hope for clear weather in the early hours of tomorrow in order to be able to attempt Gangstang's south-west ridge. The ridge itself looks a breeze. We decide to try the new route and lose a lot of precious height, retracing our steps to the plateau; losing as well as the three hours of energy spent trying the first, abortive route to the saddle.

We circle around, heading for the skyline on the northern rim of the plateau. The wind is growing in strength and dogs our progress through tall sastrugi, where the wind has whipped up the snow and moulded it into frozen waves, knee to waist high, catching at our rope, feet and axes. Step, prod, step, prod. Up towards the rim of the plateau we climb, checking the whiteness ahead under a baking blue sky. Ann hates the heat and longs for the shelter of clouds for a change. She gets her wish before long, the cloud pouring in once more from the west with flurries of snow. It is her turn to lead again as we share the strain of searching out a route. Step by step we rise, slowly, steadily, carefully, until the prod of her axe uncovers the black hole of another crevasse. Not the biggest we have seen, but big enough; just one more step and she could have been down, falling with the shards of ice that tinkle their way into the darkness below her. The ground on the far side of the crevasse rises steeply.

'This one's too far to jump,' she yells back at me, her words nearly lost in the wind. 'I'll try further along.' I just nod, too tired to move up to her. Ann tries both ways, left and right, pushing through the waves of sastrugi for 20 metres or so before turning to the crevasse again. Each time she is faced by that same cavernous drop. We are close to the edge of the plateau; there is nowhere else to go.

She comes back to where I take in the rope, hunched amongst the sastrugi, and we look at each other. I point to the crevasse, 'If you go into that, hon, I'm going to have trouble helping you out.' We both smile, the decision already made, snow pattering on our anoraks. We hug each other awkwardly, enmeshed in coils of rope, and turn our backs on the driving snow.

The shepherds were right. It snows continuously as we fight our way down valley.

The traverse party arrived in Manali on 15 September, a few days after Ann and I returned from Gangstang. Pete and Tashi were fit and ready to go but Ding's health had deteriorated further. He was running a fever, his shoulder was still weak, and he thought he might have suffered a hernia. Relations between Ding and Pete were bad again too. It didn't seem as though things could get worse. That was Ding's opinion, at least, because he decided that this last Indian traverse section was not going to go ahead without Corrina in the party.

Corrina had fully recovered from her earlier stomach troubles; no problems had cropped up on her trek south of Manali and she was keen to go. Support team members' accompanying the traverse team had been envisaged in the expedition agreement and Ann and I had nothing against her joining them, as she had for the monsoon trek. Pete, however, insisted that Corrina would slow them down. Ding denied this: she could walk as fast as he was able to at present and was going whether Pete liked it or not. Tashi and Roy didn't have anything to say about it. SP, on the other hand, was more than a little influenced by the worst point in Pete's argument — having a woman in the party would ruin the apparently magnificent achievements of the traverse expedition. A few timely threats of philosophical debate on the topic from Ann and Corrina soon silenced this line of argument and so the traverse team for the last Indian section was eventually finalised.

After a week's rest the traverse team set off for Leh, with Tashi, Pete and Ding joined by Corrina. The support team left in its usual tangle of travel arrangements. I went to New Delhi to talk with the Pakistan Embassy about our next objective — the Karakoram mountains in Pakistan, the western-most outliers of the Himalayan range. In Delhi I dumped excess equipment at the IMF and then joined up with Roy who had left from Manali for the Calcutta nursing clinic where his father remained ill. We bussed together to Srinagar. Ann, meanwhile, had bussed to Srinagar directly from Manali, taking a couple of days off by the lakeside while on her way to Leh with the last of the expedition baggage. A further two-day bus journey brought us to our last Indian resupply at Leh, the capital of Ladakh, where we met SP once more.

The traverse team also arrived by bus. In the sparsely populated Zanskar area north of Manali the rather meagre route directions they obtained from villagers led them astray. They were highly annoyed to reach the Kashmir-Ladakh highway a full three days' march past their destination of Leh and then have to backtrack along the road. It had been a thirsty, dusty, weary section, a trying end to the joint section of our Indian traverse.

Our team of the last eight months had to separate again here, but this time it was to be along the line of nationalities. Only the Indian members had permission to go inside the Inner-line to the Karakoram La (5671 metres), a high pass near the line of control and a disputed border between India and Pakistan. The five New Zealanders were forbidden to go north of Leh. In our minds the Indian Defence Ministry thus remained firm in its commitment to our competitors, the Indian Army expedition. That expedition was months behind us, only now approaching the western border of Nepal according to a recent newspaper account. Their slow progress, we thought, must be due to an excessive attachment to comfortable travel.

Whatever the reason, if the other expedition that started first could no longer beat us, the Indian Defence Ministry was going to ensure that they at least would be able to go into areas that we could not.

We booked five seats on a jet back to New Delhi and spent our last two days in Leh, farewelling our three Indian team mates. Our time in Delhi was rather less emotional. We hurriedly sorted out bits and pieces of equipment and food, and packed for our last traverse section, leaving by train for Pakistan on 16 October.

Our original plan for Pakistan had been for a traverse of the Hispar and Biafo glaciers, leading into one long trek up the Baltoro glacier to K2, the second highest mountain in the world. Our time had nearly run out, however. It was well into autumn and we could not achieve all these objectives before winter. We'd learnt some sense. We all agreed that the most we could attempt was the route up the Baltoro glacier to Concordia at the foot of K2. We would be lucky if the winter snow held off long enough even for that.

9. Pakistan and the Karakoram

On our way to catch the 'Frontier Mail' from Old Delhi station, we pass a fair where there is a huge sign, 'Man sits with poisonous snakes in glass cage'. We have no time to stop this evening, not for that, nor the other attraction, 'Waxworks models of Indian freedom fighters martyred by the British'.

The night grows cold. Autumn has faded towards winter and the night sky is clear of the summer's dust. Travel through India has taken months longer than we expected and it is possible that the lower valleys of the Karakoram may already be closed by snow. I sit for a long time by the train window, hands clasped about my ankles on the seat, chin on knees, watching the dark north-western plains slip away, feeling the swift passage of a sliver of moon. Its light glints clear and cold on the trapped irrigation waters.

We prepare for sleep, five worn-out travellers. The carriage light switch is broken and will not turn off. Twice we call for the guard and grudgingly he comes. Perhaps he knows the problem, for without hesitation he thrusts his finger into the wire-tangled interior of the switch and jiggles it about until the light dies.

At Amritsar in the morning, still in the Indian half of the Punjab, we are transferred into a run-down train for the last few kilometres to the border crossing at Anil. Armed soldiers are posted at 100-metre intervals along the railroad tracks. Not, as it turns out, because of the Indo-Pakistan conflict, but in an effort to counter the campaign of civil disobedience mounted by some Punjab Sikhs for Sikh independence. Railway tracks have been uprooted, buses ambushed, buildings damaged, and the central government has mobilised the army in response.

One of the national banks has an agency at the station where I have my Indian rupees changed for Pakistani, and then we shoulder our packs and walk the length of the platform into Pakistan. The uniforms are different but the countryside is still the same. On this side they call on one god and back there they call on many; if either side is right their god has shown them no particular favour. The sparrows and mynas hop in the same poor dust and the carrion birds wheel in the one undivided sky, feeding on either side at will.

The Pakistani customs officials are very thorough, searching through the bags of every passenger. It is a couple of hours before we reach the head of the queue.

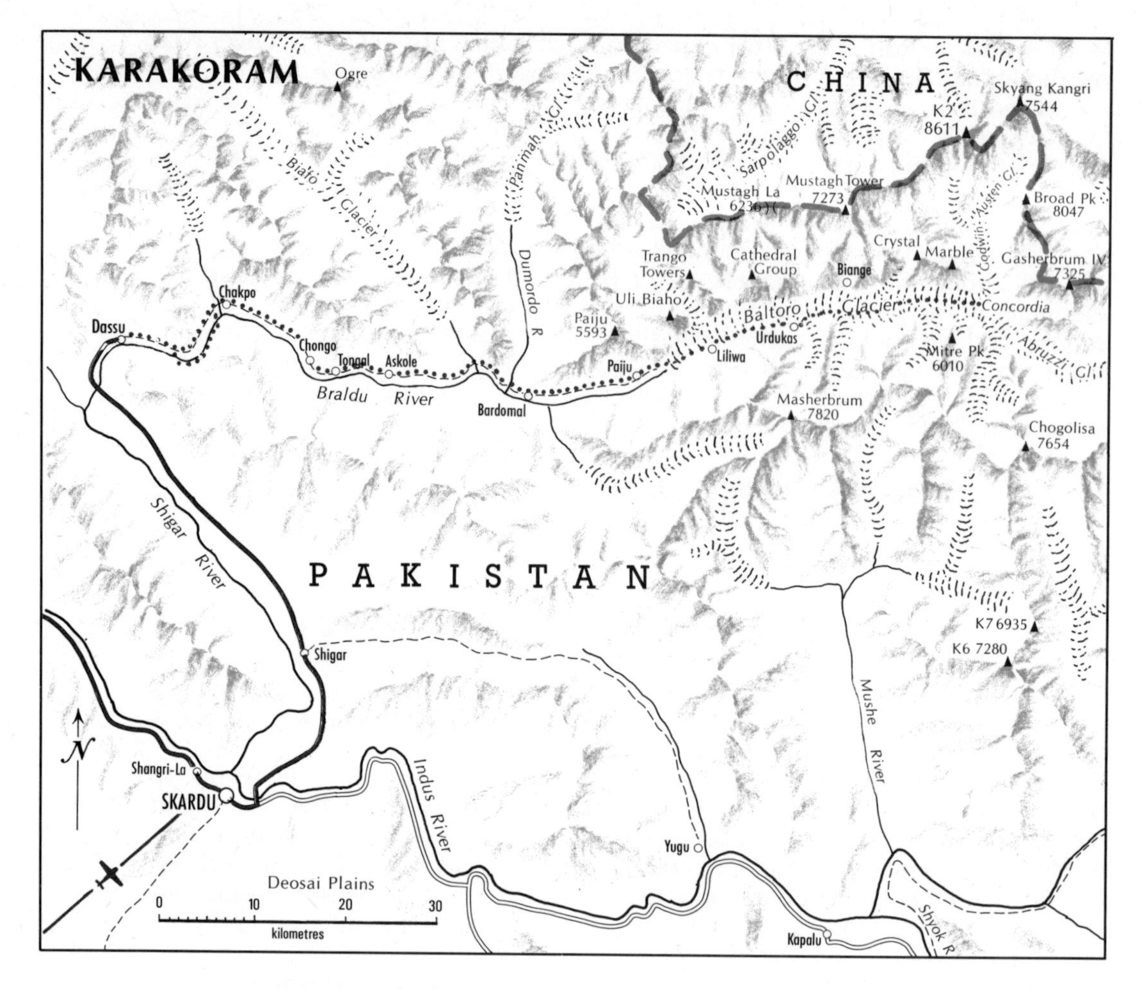

'How much money do you have?' they ask me.

'Rs 1100,' I reply.

'Too much,' they say and divide the money amongst the five of us. Having us all equally rich (or poor) seems to satisfy the currency regulations and we are waved through to board the Pakistani train for Lahore.

At Lahore, capital of the Pakistani province of Punjab, we buy rail tickets for Rawalpindi. This is not difficult but there is no reservation system for seats. The Quetta Express pulls in from the south and we board, our preliminary search turning up only one free seat in a 'Ladies Only' carriage. A second try produces a nearly empty first-class compartment and we take that over, letting down the sleeper-seats and dozing in comfort.

We reach Rawalpindi late at night and a new mini-van taxi whisks us to the Shalimar Hotel, a glitteringly modern establishment which looks fiendishly expensive.

Next morning we go in search of more modest accommodation. We are directed to 'Mrs Davies' Rest House' and feel instantly that we have found the right place: a slightly ramshackle mansion with a fading touch of its former glory, it sits with long shaded verandahs in amongst trees, back from the road. We take a suite for five.

This is the 'base camp' before the base camp. The dining room is festooned with flags and pennants, posters and photographs, from Karakoram mountaineering expeditions spanning the last three decades. Many bear endorsements of Mrs Davies' wonderful cooking. Dinner is served beneath still fans that await the heat of next summer. Ancient, dignified waiters creak slowly in and out of the kitchen, bearing plates of soup, veal, steamed potatoes and boiled cabbage. Between courses I enquire after the health of Mrs Davies. The waiter places one hand on his heart and replies, sadly, 'Mrs Davies passed on in 1957, sir. Her son is the manager now. His health is good — Inshallah.' Inshallah means 'Allah be willing'.

Rawalpindi is the old capital of Pakistan, only recently supplanted by the neighbouring and newly built city of Islamabad. Mini-buses ply the 10 kilometres to the new capital from a depot behind Mrs Davies'. They depart every five minutes and there is seldom a queue. After a short drive along the motorway we are dropped at the Ministry of Tourism in Islamabad, to present our credentials. Our reception is courteous and efficient, in keeping with the trim and impressive appearance of the new city. Yes, they have received all our letters during the year; yes, they got our last message about travel from Delhi; yes, the liaison officer is ready to come with us and he will meet us tonight at our hotel. And yes, they did expect us some months ago. Were we delayed? Yes.

We return to Rawalpindi very pleased — there seem to be no problems as far as our permit is concerned, a welcome change after India. There we finally concluded that you had no problems with permits provided you refrained from actually applying for one.

Rawalpindi's streets seem clean and prosperous, and there are no beggars that I can see, and few women. The men about the town are dressed in the loose *kurta pyjami,* full pleated trousers under a matching knee-length shirt. Light blue, cream and grey-brown are the favoured colours. Often a rich velvet jerkin, deep blue or scarlet and trimmed lavishly with gold braid, is worn over the top. The clothing shops, of which there are many, have a selection of these jerkins on racks above head-height outside their doors. The sunlight glinting off the gilt and the warm colours of the velvet emphasise the feeling of space created by the wide tree-lined avenues.

There are numerous imported vehicles on the roads, although the traditional horse-drawn *tongas,* light wooden buggies with two seats facing forward and two back, are also in use. Sometimes we see women riding in these, shrouded figures in the full veil of the Islamic *burkha* who watch the world through gauze-covered peep-holes in the heavy material. But more often the few women we meet about town wear a loosely draped scarf to cover their heads, wrapping it once below the chin rather than completely hiding the face.

In a narrow side street of the Raja bazaar we chance upon a row of money-changers with their low wooden stalls set up on the pavement outside shops. Each stall has a heavy sheet of glass clamped over the top of securely pinned banknotes of various currencies. Since we arrived in Pakistan the banks have refused to change our remaining Indian rupees. I ask one of the money-changers if he will change them for us.

'Certainly, sir,' he replies and quotes the official exchange rate I received in India. We rush back in a taxi to Mrs Davies' and return with all the Indian rupees we have between us. A small crowd gathers as we squat on the footpath counting the two piles of notes — blue-grey Indian 100s for the red Pakistani.

'What are they doing?' one of the onlookers asks the money-changer, unable to see what currency we are exchanging.

'They have Indian money,' he replies, using 'Hindustan' to describe India.

'Ah, Hindustan, Hindustan,' the name is repeated by several in the crowd. 'Are they going to Hindustan or coming from that place?'

'I do not know,' replies the money-changer, 'but they are exchanging Indian rupees for ours, so perhaps they have come from that place.'

'Surely we have,' says Ann. 'We came from India only a few days ago.' The crowd is surprised by her joining in the conversation, as is the money-changer.

'But madam is speaking very good Urdu,' he tells her.

Ann is puzzled by this and shakes her head, regretfully telling them that she speaks only some Hindi and Nepali. 'We'll only be a month in Pakistan. It's hardly time to learn Urdu, unfortunately.'

'But you are speaking Urdu now, madam, that is what we are speaking and you understand us clearly.'

'But,' says Ann, 'in Hindustan they call this language Hindi; there's no mention of its being Urdu too.' Are you sure? her look implies.

'Oh, madam, surely they are not calling this language Hindi,' says the money-changer sorrowfully. 'Urdu is a very ancient language. It is most unreasonable of them.'

'Well,' Ann replies, 'that is what's happened. But it's a blessing for me because I thought I was learning only one language and now I find I've learnt two!' The money-changer laughs at this and repeats it for the benefit of those onlookers who may not have heard. We pocket our thick wad of rupees under their approving gaze.

'Allah be with you,' says the money-changer as we go.

Back at Mrs Davies' our liaison officer has already arrived. He is Major Muhammad Matlub-ul-Hasan Nuri, an officer in the Infantry and an instructor at the Pakistan School of Mountain Warfare. He has been on several expeditions before but these were of the 'old school' fixed-camp variety, with lots of porters, cooks and the attendant rigmarole. On one of these expeditions he went up the Baltoro glacier to Concordia, our destination, and he has first-hand knowledge of the difficulties of the journey: from Rawalpindi there is a Pakistan International Airlines (PIA) flight to Skardu, a sector that is frequently closed owing to inclement weather; a jeep needs to be arranged from Skardu, to take us to the roadend at Dassu; and then there is a three-day trek through the gorge of the Braldu river to Askole, the last village; a further three-day trek above that, to the Baltoro glacier; and then four days' travel on the glacier itself to Concordia.

Concordia is not a peak. It is the glacial amphitheatre at the head of the Baltoro and the first place from which K2 can be clearly seen. Our objective is not to climb K2; it is to set our eyes, rather than our feet, upon the second highest mountain in the world. Some people dispute that the Karakoram is even a part of the Himalaya. We have no wish to join in that debate — the expedition set itself the task of walking across the roof of the world, from Kangchenjunga to K2. We have travelled a long way since we began in Sikkim but the task is not finished without seeing K2. Our plan is a light-weight race against the approaching winter, without porters or other encumbrances. Each of us will carry his or her own personal equipment and a share of the party gear and food. This way we hope to be able to cover the ground quickly, pushing as far up the Baltoro glacier as we possibly can, hopefully all the way to Concordia. The plan is a reasonable one, we feel, based on our experience this year.

Nuri listens carefully to our account of our plans and then pauses, thinking before he replies. He is quite tall and slim, has an open, youthful face and looks very fit; I would guess that he is in his early thirties. We await his reaction with some apprehension. There are strict rules in our permit governing the treatment, rationing and equipment of liaison officers: Nuri is entitled to a cook and porter just for himself, as well as rations which maintain his accustomed diet. But, if we are obliged to take a cook or porter for him, we will then be bound to their strict 'porter days', unable to progress more than the porters' set daily distances between camps. That would be far too slow, almost guaranteeing that we do not reach Concordia before the snow. We cannot go without Nuri though, for that would constitute a much graver breach of our permit. In those circumstances we would be promptly, and no doubt roughly, recalled by the authorities before we got much past Islamabad. Does he trust us enough, after this brief meeting, to risk doing it our way?

'I'll try it,' Nuri says firmly, 'but I cannot promise that I will be able to carry as much as you.' We smile in relief, knowing we now have a chance of success. Ding assures him that as long as he is willing to carry his personal equipment we will carry all the rest.

A final briefing is necessary at the Tourism Ministry but only Nuri and Ding need attend. Pete, Ann and I try to get seats for tomorrow's flight. It is lucky that we saw the money-changer's stall when we did — today is Thursday with businesses only open for a half-day in the morning and tomorrow is the official day of rest when businesses are closed all day. It is difficult keeping track of which day is a holiday: India's day of rest was Sunday, Nepal's Saturday, and now in Pakistan it's Friday.

The route to Skardu lies north at first from Rawalpindi, over foothills and then increasingly higher mountain ranges, following the gorge carved out by the Indus river on its long passage to the sea. The plane that flies this route is a twin-engined 727 Fokker Friendship which has a flight ceiling of around 6500 metres. Near Gilgit, where the air route and the upper Indus valley turn eastward around Nanga Parbat (8125 metres), the plane must cross a subsidiary ridge close to 6000 metres high. The river valleys are too narrow to turn a Friendship in, most of the surrounding peaks are above its altitude ceiling and there is no radar, so the flight is dependent on clear, settled weather for visual navigation. There is very little margin for error.

We are fortunate. The weather is fine and they will fly but there are only two seats available so Ann and I go. Pete comes to see us off and we chat with a couple of the other passengers until the flight is announced.

'Good luck,' Pete calls as we leave. 'See you in Skardu.'

Ann and I have both cameras ready for photographs of Nanga Parbat, but the plane flies so close, the mountain is so wide and the top so high above us, that it is impossible to get one photo of the whole of it. The stewardess comes with a message from the pilot inviting us into the cockpit. He and the uniformed co-pilot beckon us forward, asking if we managed to get a good photograph.

'No luck at all,' Ann admits ruefully.

'Hold on tight, then,' says the pilot and he banks the Friendship into a steep curve around towards the mountain. He keeps it there long enough for us to take several photos each. We thank him.

'Oh, it is nothing,' replies the pilot, glancing back briefly from the dials of the cockpit. 'PIA likes to look after its passengers and, in any case, the Brigadier asked us to let you get some photographs.' We look at him questioningly.

'The Brigadier?' Ann asks.

'The gentleman that got on the plane with you,' the co-pilot explains. 'Mr Aslam Khan. He's a very famous soldier, retired now, but an important man in Skardu.'

'I had no idea,' Ann replies. 'I hope we see him later, we'll have to thank him too!'

The pilot turns to us again. 'You are welcome to stay in the cockpit if you wish; there is much more if you want good photographs.'

Framed by the cockpit windows, range upon range of mountains roll away to the north, a jumble of snow-capped peaks seemingly without end. Only those highest or most striking have yet been named, let alone climbed. Rakaposhi (7788 metres) in the Hunza Kingdom slides away behind us; to the north-west the Karakoram runs into the Russian Pamirs and the Himalaya stretches out to the south-east. Central to all this chaos of impressive peaks is one that stands paramount, a huge triangular mound of granite, soaring above the rest. The pilot observes us photographing it.

'Yes, K2,' he says proudly. 'The second highest mountain in the world. You're lucky to see it so clearly — it is on the Pakistan border with China, easily 100 kilometres from here.'

'Shall we go back to our seats now?' I ask, when the pilot lines up his final approach at Skardu.

'No need,' he replies. 'You get a better view in front with us — aren't the poplars beautiful there by that lake? There's very good trout fishing too.'

'Is there?' I respond abstractedly, trying to wedge myself behind his seat as the end of the runway slips under the nose of the plane and the paint-lines on the tarmac stream by. We touch down gently and the plane taxies up to the terminal. Ann and I extricate ourselves from behind the pilot's seat.

'We like to do this for tourists,' he tells us, escorting us to the door. 'After all, you have come a long way to see our country.'

Out in the sun again, by the airport building, we renew our acquaintance with the Brigadier and thank him for speaking to the pilot.

'It was nothing, truly nothing,' he responds warmly and then, on learning that the others of our expedition are not due until tomorrow, asks if we would like to stay with him for the night. 'I am building a resort for tourists at a small lake just a few kilometres from here. The rooms are not completely finished yet but, as mountaineers, I am sure you will be able to endure sleeping in them. My jeep can bring you back tomorrow to meet your friends.'

'There — you see,' says the Brigadier. His resort is a beautiful oasis in the dry mountain desert that makes up the valley of Skardu. A clear lake, 300 metres wide and fringed with graceful poplars and willows, reflects the blue of the sky. A steep and rocky hillside rises from the opposite shore, lending an air of remoteness to the setting.

'I am calling it Shangri-La,' the Brigadier tells us, 'after the novel where the aircraft crashed in an unknown valley north of the Himalaya. Come, I will show you why.' He leads us to the paved walkway around the lake edge. Just back from the shore sits an old DC3 aircraft, with 'Orient Skyliner' emblazoned along its side.

'Orient Airways is the name of the airline which became PIA, the people who flew us today,' he explains. 'Many years ago this aircraft made a forced landing on the river flat just a few miles from Skardu. It was too costly for the Airways to repair or remove it so they stripped the engines and any valuable equipment and abandoned the shell. When I began building the resort I thought of it and had it carried here.

A flight of stone steps has been built to the rear door of the DC3. The exterior of the plane looks like any other aircraft but the interior has been skilfully converted into a luxurious, centrally heated chalet. There are also self-contained bungalows built at intervals around the lake shore. No two are identical but all have polished stone floors, modern amenities, and beautiful teak furniture carved especially for the resort.

'It's certainly not spartan, Brigadier,' Ann laughs. 'I can endure this without any problem.'

A screen of Lombardy poplars, as well as apricot, apple and cherry trees, runs between the bungalows and the paved walk along the lake side. Jutting out into the lake at the far end is a light and airy building. Its roof has been constructed in the pagoda style, curved eave rising above curved eave.

'That is our restaurant and bar,' explains the Brigadier. 'We offer many outdoor activities, fishing, horse riding, hiking, but we must also cater for those who enjoy the social life.'

In the evening the Brigadier invites us to his home. Over dinner Ann mentions what the pilot told us, about the Brigadier's having been a famous soldier, and asks if he would tell us how this came about.

'He should not have told you,' the Brigadier replies modestly. 'I think of those days as well past. Mind you, my son flies for PIA too, and those young chaps are all good friends. I suppose I could satisfy your curiosity then, since you are my guests.' He looks down for a moment before beginning. 'In the world war of 1939-45 I was in the Indian Army. We were all one. But only two years later, when Independence came, the army was split and then there was war between India and Pakistan. Terrible things were done and, to make it worse, we were fighting our old comrades. It was very sad, you must understand,' he turns to us for concurrence. 'All of this area in the north-west was disputed territory. India claimed it but of course the people were all Muslim as I am. I was a colonel then, posted here for the winter with virtually no troops. Because of this I worked with the Baltis, the local people, as much as I could. They knew the country well and could move quickly. Before long our small force had the Indians bottled up in the towns and forts and we could move as we pleased through the countryside. Through their skill we took all of this area, the towns too, and held it. You said you had been to Leh?' he asks. We nod.

'Well, my men crossed the entire Deosai plain, over 3000 metres high. They did this in mid winter, each man with only his rifle and two blankets. They got to within five kilometres of the Indian stronghold in Leh and we very nearly took that also.' He smiles on completing the tale. 'So, now you know the story. It was a long time ago and I pray it will not happen again. War is extremely unpleasant. Oh, bai!' the Brigadier calls for the bearer who has been serving our meal. 'Bring the photograph.'

The bearer hands him a mounted photograph which the Brigadier holds facing him for a moment before turning it towards Ann and me. 'This sort of thing is more enjoyable.' The photo shows the Brigadier in a rowing boat on a lake, possibly the lake outside. He is a powerfully built man but he is obviously straining to hold aloft a huge trout. 'Eighteen and a half pounds,' he tells us, 'that's a better foe.'

'A brown trout?' I ask. His face lights up.

'Oh, definitely a brown. They live to a great age, staying deep in the water, cautious and cunning. If they are hooked though, oh, they fight.' He shakes his head in emphasis, 'They fight so hard!'

Two days later, while the sun is still rising from behind the peaks, an overloaded jeep weaves its unsteady way down the dusty main street of Skardu. Our six-person expedition heads east out of town, following the Indus into the Karakoram mountains. The road becomes noticeably rougher when we turn north-west to follow the Shigar tributary. The bridges over the dry *nallas* are creaking, wooden-sheathed structures which sway alarmingly, and the dirt track is only wide enough for one vehicle. Everywhere there is sand, blowing before the wind. Only three percent of Pakistan's original forest cover remains.

Four of us are crammed with the packs in the open back of the jeep and are soon covered in thick, gritty layers of dust. Exhaust fumes percolate through the floorboards. By general consensus we stop the jeep for *chai* in a small roadside village, where there is at least some shade under the spreading apricot trees. A crowd of men gathers to watch us. We watch them too but perhaps not quite as obviously. They each wear a flat woollen cap with a rolled padded brim, and a woollen shawl wrapped tight against the wind. Their faces are burnt dark by the sun.

'These Baltistan people are Shia Moslems,' Nuri explains to me. 'They follow Ayatullah Khomeini and believe that he is a very holy man. In Skardu they have recently changed the name of the main street to Khomini Avenue.' Our driver is a Shiite also and Nuri has conversed with him, 'He was telling me earlier that the Ayatullah has mastered the religion and knows if it is right to kill or not. Neither he nor the villagers believe they can question what the Ayatullah does.'

'What do you think?' I ask Nuri.

'Well, you know I am a Muslim too since I cannot help but wake you up in the night when I go to pray, but I am in a different part of Islam to these fellows. I should say nothing about that while we are here though.' He thanks the boy who comes to collect our cups. 'By and large these are very gentle people.'

We reach the village of Dassu in the early afternoon. The road stops here and we leave the jeep. It is three days' walk to Askole, the last village, and since we don't have to hire porters we simply shoulder our packs and start walking. There is one trail and it leads directly up the Braldu river valley. The villagers of Dassu ask Nuri where we are going.

'To the mountains?' they exclaim, shaking their heads. 'But it is winter there. These people must be crazy.'

The harvest is completed, all the fields are bare and a few scattered stalks by the threshing pole are the only evidence of the activity. The Dassu folk have brought in their food stocks and are battening down for the winter. There will be snow soon, no doubt, something to add to the meagre rainfall which sustains life here. The annual precipitation is around 100 millimetres a year, most of which falls as snow. The surroundings clearly reflect the critical state of the water supply: each village of flat-roofed houses is set near a stream, and only in the small plots around the villages is the earth watered and temporarily stabilised. When we step beyond the irrigated fields the ground is baked as hard as iron, and the scattered vegetation consists of isolated thorn bushes, occasional tussock-like grasses and a few lichens.

A couple of hours from Dassu the sandy, boulder-strewn river flats we have followed come to an end in a blank wall of rock which rises straight out of the wild rapids of the Braldu. On our side of the river valley the wall climbs sheer for 600 metres. One hundred metres back downstream a single wire cable spans the rapids. There are three Baltis, farmers, watching us from the other side of the cable-way and one crosses the river to us, suspended in a small cage from the cable. He greets Nuri, 'Salaam, sahib.'

'Salaam,' Nuri replies, touching the backs of his right fingers to his forehead in the Islamic salute.

'The trail turns off, sahib, about a kilometre back, and goes very high to cross these bluffs,' the farmer points up into the cliffs above us. 'It is not a good track so it is no wonder that you missed the turn off — there is another trail across the river that is just as good.'

'Is there a charge for crossing the cable?' Nuri asks him.

'Oh yes, sahib. Rs 20 each.' Nuri smiles, as we all do.

'A kilometre is only a little distance for us,' Nuri says, 'but thank you for your help.' We are old hands at this bargaining game now, and Nuri is also adept as we discover. The six of us turn cheerfully downstream, waving goodbye to the farmer.

'All right, sahib,' he calls after us, 'twenty rupees the lot.'

The cage is fun. He loads us, one by one, and we race down the cable at great speed, swaying to and fro in the cage at the cable's low point just above the rushing water. The farmer's two companions haul us laboriously up the other side, hand over hand on the drag rope. I am the last to cross and by the time I am over the others are numbed to the bone by the wind. It is near dark and we decide to camp. Not far upriver is a partly-roofed shelter built against a rock. It is surrounded by willows and only 30 metres from the water. We make camp here, Corrina and Ding in the rock shelter while Nuri, Peter, Ann and I stretch the tent fly between two willows. Once our sleeping mats and bags are laid out our beds are ready. Pete and I fetch the water, Nuri goes with Corrina and Ann to gather sticks for our fire, and Ding prepares the stew. In a little more than a quarter of an hour we are all squatting around the crackling fire, waiting for dinner to cook. The whole operation is conducted with a minimum of discussion and considerable economy of effort. Nuri is impressed.

'This is very simple,' he says.

'Oh, yes,' Pete replies for us, only half joking, 'the secret is not to be too comfortable.' There is not much chance of that for Nuri. He is a trifle weary from this first day's march but cheerfully borrows Ann's alarm-watch to ensure that he will not miss his night-time prayers.

Pete is up at 5.30 am to put the brew on. Nothing need be done till it boils so I lie in my sleeping bag, gradually easing awake. It will be several hours before the sun strikes the valley floor. An hour later I am stamping around in the cold waiting for the others to finish stuffing gear into their packs. We make a last check of the ground where we have slept, for anything overlooked, and depart. We follow a faint trail through the boulders by the riverside and within ten minutes we are bluffed again. A sheer rock face, the twin of the one we crossed the river to avoid, rises straight out of the Braldu. Its summit is at least 400 metres above us. We clamber around it for a while but decide that exposed rock climbing, with loads, on messy bluffs above a river, is not the most sensible thing we could do. Resigned, we straggle back towards the campsite and soon come across what must be the right track. A broad, well-cut stairway leads determinedly up the side of the bluff.

The crest reveals a sudden dramatic contrast in scenery: the track loses itself in a network of smooth tilled fields, neat rock walls and tidily-pruned apricot trees. We wander upwards, from terrace to terrace, but the track does not reappear. At length we reach a village that has been built on the edge of an alluvial fan, making use of the rich deposited silts of an alpine stream to grow the crops to support the villagers.

The first person we meet is a dwarf but then his fellow villagers come to marvel at us, and we discover not one of them stands taller than Ann's shoulder. One or two have goitrous growths on their necks, a sign of lack of iodine in their diet. They speak an obscure dialect which baffles even Nuri, but it needs no translation for them to realise that we must have lost the track. After some discussion amongst themselves they appoint a guide, who leads us through the maze of fields to the distant edge of the fan. From this vantage point the Braldu assumes a more gentle guise, snaking between the rugged rock walls of the canyon. Other ridges drop steeply into the valley and I can see only as far as the next big riverbend where a patch of green indicates another tributary and another village.

'Chakpo,' says our guide, 'Chakpo.' It takes a moment to realise that he is telling us the name of the village. He points out a faint goat track down the edge of the ridge and indicates that we should cross back to the other side of the river at Chakpo.

The Chakpo bridge is two logs, laid side by side between rocks five metres apart in the Braldu. Back on the western side of the river again we spend a frustrating afternoon, trying to follow a trail that continually disappears, leading us up into steep flood-washed *nallas,* then along sliding scree slopes and slipfaces that threaten to drop us into the Braldu, singly or together. Descending to the river to avoid a deep *nalla,* we end up tripping over huge riverside boulders, still encased in ice from the night-time cold. At one point we have to edge sideways behind tottering mud pinnacles, taller than us, that provide the only footholds on a greasy and otherwise sheer bank.

'I didn't believe it this morning,' I hear Ann say behind me to Ding.

'Believe what?' he replies.

'I thought it was just local pride that made those farmers tell such lies about the track on their side of the river. Now I see that it was absolutely true ...'

'Both tracks are abominable, right?' Ding finishes the sentence for her.

We stumble upon an area of hot pools at about 4 pm. Chemicals from the mineral water have daubed the hillside in white, pink and ochre streaks which, with the accompanying trim of icicles and mud, lend the scene a surreal appearance. We decide to stop but soak only briefly, knowing that the short hours of daylight will necessitate an early camp. There has been no suitable site since Chakpo. Ann just dabbles her feet at the edge of our pool, willing to give up the pleasure of a hot pool to save herself the discomfort of donning the same old trekking clothes over a damp body. To save weight we carry only a tiny hand-towel between us.

The shadows lengthen as we push on along the steep river gorge, searching with growing urgency for a flat space to camp. We are finally forced by darkness to stop on a sloping patch of grass between boulders. Ding and I flounder down to the river, dropping over banks of collapsing clay in the dark, and try to clamber back up without spilling the water. There are no sticks here and we have to cook on the primus, eating into the small stock of kerosene we have brought with us for travel on the glacier.

The weather has been very settled since we left Rawalpindi, but bitterly cold. There was no cloud again last night and it is so dry that there was no dew. Rather than waste time and fuel on a breakfast brew, we set off in hope of a rapid exit from the gorge. Ann and Pete go ahead along the river bank, seeing the valley open out before them. Just 15 metres from what looks to be the final corner in the gorge, the river shelf they have been following drops away, undercut by the icy deep water of the Braldu. Virtually in hands' reach of the end they have to turn back. I see them retracing their steps towards me and we backtrack together; half an hour down the valley we find the point where we should have turned off.

The trail climbs for nearly an hour over increasingly exposed crumbling rockfaces, back and forth in the sunlight until at last it breaks free over the crest of the ridge. The descent is a hundred times safer. It falls gradually in long gentle loops following ledges in solid rock, nothing like what we have just ascended. We reach the next village of Chongo at 10 am, four hours after we set out.

'It is on the main route up valley, so we are on the right track. I did wonder,' Ann mutters.

Beyond Chongo a family is threshing the last of their harvest. We stop for our breakfast nearby. The family has yoked five *gae* (yak-cattle cross) together in a row, tethering the end one to a central threshing pole. A young girl drives the *gae* forward in a tight circle, around and around the pole. Their hooves crush the grain from the wheat stalks and, behind them, a young boy forks the broken mixture into the air. The wind carries clouds of chaff down the valley and leaves the heavier grain behind. I photograph the three at work. There is no objection and the young girl does not cover her face from the camera.

The trail passes through a cluster of square wooden frames, about 10 centimetres high and 70 centimetres across, set upright in the ground.

'Do you know what these are?' Ann asks Nuri.

'They are graves,' he tells her. 'The people are buried upright.' This reminds

The autumn sun is not hot enough to melt these icicles formed in the night-time freeze of the Braldu valley.

Corrina and Ding, one day's travel east of Concordia. Gasherbrum IV (7925m) is the highest peak on the horizon.

Threshing time in the cold higher valleys of northern Pakistan. The grain is trampled by five gae, harnessed to a central threshing pole.

Ann and Pete clear out the bivvy cave at Urdukas on the Baltoro glacier.

Doug sways precariously above the Braldu river as he waits for us to haul him up to the riverbank.

K2 (8611m), second highest mountain in the world, viewed from the plane cockpit on the route to Skardu.

Neatly terraced fields provide a contrast to the extensive erosion on steeper slopes above the Braldu gorge.

Graves by the trail past the threshing yard at Chongo village.

Doug on the Baltoro glacier.

Ann of our earlier discussion about religion during the drive to Dassu and she asks Nuri if he would mind telling us more about his sect.

'We are only a very small part of Islam,' he says, 'called the Ahmadiyyah. We believe that everyone should have as much schooling as possible, including women. My sisters were educated up to university level, as I was. So was my wife, she is a teacher.' He stops for a moment, deciding whether he wants to say more. I look back down the curve of the valley past the cemetery, down to the bare grey earth with the small patch of gold that is the harvesters of Chongo. Then Nuri continues about his faith. 'We are outnumbered in our attitude to our women, for example, but we still persevere with encouragement for them. In our sect the religion is followed closely. That is why you see me doing my prayers during the night. But the members are encouraged to participate fully in the life of the world also. My parents urged me, and my sisters, to learn debating and to compete in many sports. The sect does a lot of missionary work too, especially in India and Africa.'

'There was an article in *India Today* about that, I think,' Ann remarks. 'It mentioned something about resentment in southern India because of recent conversions to Islam.'

'That's right,' I add. 'If the article was correct, Andra Pradesh state is passing a law making it illegal for a person to convert from one religion to another.'

Nuri laughs. 'That will be hard to enforce,' he says. 'There will always be conversion by Hindus who want to leave the caste system.'

'That seemed to be a factor,' I tell him. 'The magazine quoted an upper caste man from a village in which all of the sweepers had converted to Islam. The man said, "Now, if one of the sweepers is walking past and I tell him to do something, he just ignores me." They must have been like slaves before.'

'Yes, the caste system can be like that,' Nuri agrees. 'God did not give people their intelligence so that they should be born and die as sweepers, generation after generation.' He smiles. 'You understand this anyway as Christians. You know, as a Muslim I feel much more at ease with you Christians than I do with Hindus, for you and I each believe in a single God.' He pauses. 'Of course, it is a great heresy in Islam to divide God and give him partners — that is what we cannot accept about your beliefs.'

Our early starts are somewhat incompatible with a balanced food intake. Yesterday our stomachs protested as we reached late afternoon with only a few biscuits between us and the previous night's stew. Today we are determined to have a good meal around midday, when it is at least warm enough to sit around. Between Chongo and Tongal a mill-race cuts across the track and we stop for lunch, with water close by. A hollowed log has been used as a diversion pipe between the race and the mill, and long icicles droop from the log, hanging 40 and 50 centimetres toward the ground. The midday heat does not last long enough to melt them.

Ann walks up for a closer look and the miller gives her permission to take a photograph of the flour-dusted interior of the mill, lit by shafts of hazy sunlight from the many cracks in the roof. Three children sit quietly on their haunches in the doorway, waiting for the miller to finish work. He scoops the flour, brass *mana* by brass *mana,* into a cured goatskin that has been specially stitched to hold exactly a maund (about 40 kg). For each maund he grinds the miller charges Rs 100, although he tells Ann that he is often paid in kind. One of the children scampers off home to Chongo and returns, before our stew is cooked, with a dozen eggs nestled carefully in a fold of his ragged garment. He offers them to us for Rs 15 and we buy them all.

There are more hot springs, close to Askole. We soak up the warmth of the sun and water combined, and I try to bring my diary up to date. I have to do this during the day because the evenings are so cold now that the ink in my ballpoint freezes and will not write.

Askole is the last permanently inhabited village on the Braldu. All the expeditions stop here on their way to the Baltoro and the *lambardar* or headman of the village is now well known to the climbers of many countries. Haji Medi is his name (Haji is the respectful title accorded to those Muslims who have completed a pilgrimage to Mecca) and on arrival in Askole we are shown immediately to his house. It is a long mud-roofed structure, like the other village houses, with walls of poplar and stone caulked with straw and mud. The village mosque is the only building constructed entirely from wood. Haji Medi orders a room cleared for us of its stored goatskins and rugs and we are ushered inside for tea and hard-boiled eggs. Nuri begins negotiations about a meal for tonight. We can have one chicken or 1 kg of mutton for Rs 50. In the end we have neither — the Haji produces some dried ibex. Conservation principles cannot bring a dead ibex back to life and I bow to the inevitable. I justify my acceptance by reasoning that it is more likely to be the leg of an unfortunate mountain goat or a *shapu,* the Asian mountain sheep, than the increasingly rare ibex, but I keep this opinion to myself.

Strange men may not enter the kitchen (because they would see the women of the household), so Ann and Corrina take an unscheduled turn at the cooking. We are sitting reading by the smoky light of a kerosene lantern in the Haji's spare room when Ann and Corrina return.

'Here it is, folks,' says Ann, plopping the huge pressure cooker of stew on the folding camp-table. The table promptly folds up, dropping the stew to the floor and plunging the room into darkness. There is a definite hush followed by a few muttered comments as we begin to adjust our eager anticipation of food to the awful possibility that the stew is spread across the less than hygienic floor. At last someone finds a match. Blessed relief, the pressure cooker lid has remained in place and, what is more, the lantern is unbroken. 'Ibex' is a strong, tasty meat and we make short work of it.

Around 5 am the village is roused by the call to prayer. We listen to the padding of feet and the soft murmuring of voices as the faithful pass by on the track.

Later we talk with Haji Medi about the possibility of taking a local person with us as a guide, to speed our travel for the three days to Paiju at the foot of the Baltoro glacier. We have no need for a porter, since there is nothing surplus, or even heavy, in our packs — sleeping bags, warm clothing, cameras and film, a few plastic bags of chocolate and lemon-flavoured drink powders, boiled lollies, tea, milk powder, and enough dehydrated meal sachets left for eight dinners. This food is likely to run out on the way back, as Concordia is reputed to be a 13-day round-trip from here, but we bank on travelling fast enough to survive.

We have trouble finding anyone to come with us. They say there will be too much snow; they want new clothing given them, boots, and vast amounts of money. In the end we decide we can do better without a guide. We buy 36 eggs and as many fried *chapatis* as they can make us, and drink copious quantities of tea as they prepare them. This new store of food is divided amongst us.

Fresh snow has fallen on the peaks on the south side of the valley. They get little sun and it lies there all day, menacing us with the threat of more winter snow to come. In the lower villages the residents would draw a line with their hands at about knee-level to indicate the likely depth of snow on the glacier; as we have ascended through the villages, so also has risen the predicted depth of snow. Here in Askole the line is drawn thigh deep.

Beyond Askole the trail wanders erratically over the terminal moraine where the Biafo glacier flows into the Braldu valley from the north. While crossing the moraine I twist my ankle slightly. Walking on it becomes painful and I tighten my other boot a little to compensate. The result is a shin badly bruised by the tongue of my tight boot. Maybe it was not such a good idea to wear boots: the others have stuck with their light shoes. By the time we are off the moraine I am moving with a definite limp. Ann and Nuri stay behind with me and Ann takes a couple of items from my pack, without much struggle on my part. Nuri watches this, with some astonishment, and apologises to Ann for not being able to carry them himself.

'You are very strong for a girl,' he tells her. 'You are already carrying more than I without Doug's things too.'

Ann scoffs mildly at this, answering him with a twinkle in her eyes, 'But women are as capable as men, Nuri; look at those Braldu women working long hours in the fields and carrying heavy loads.'

'If I could, I would spare them the hardship too,' Nuri assures her.

'Well, this really isn't a hardship for me, Nuri, honestly — look at all the talking we do as we go, the learning we're going through, and I choose to do the walking. I love it!'

'You know,' Nuri replies, seriously, 'that is what people in our society find so very intriguing about the West. Not just that the women are so free to do as they wish, but even the men. It is very unusual for our young people to live away from home, as you do, and make decisions for themselves. No one would take a job unless their parents approved — often the parents decide the career the young person follows, and then the parents choose the marriage partner. My mother and father were upset at my being so keen on an army career, but in the end they relented enough for me to try it. Now that they see the satisfaction it gives me they are reluctant to press me further in the meantime.'

'Would parents not wish their children to take up a sport like trekking, then?' Ann asks.

'Many of them would not. As well as the hardships there are dangers. What if the young person were killed? Who would look after the parents in old age? These are very practical concerns here.'

The Dumordo river drains the Panmah glacier into the Braldu. The main braid is only about 10 metres across and looks fordable. Nuri tells us that there is a bridge that the porters reconstruct after the spring floods, a couple of kilometres upstream. That is too far. Ann, Peter and I link arms with Nuri and ford the river in a rush, stumbling a little on the slippery boulders. The water rises thigh deep but we surge on, nearly breathless with the unbelievable cold. On reaching the far side my body is shaken by great judders of uncontrollable shivering and I bundle on all the rest of my clothes, but the shivering takes an hour to subside.

Light snow falls in the late afternoon and it looks as if we are due for a change in the weather. We hunt for Bardomal, reputedly a cave which is the second porter halt from Askole. As we go we forage for wood in the scattered scrub on the river edge. A leafless briar rose has huge rosehips on it and Ann picks a few to try in our tea. Nuri points out another thorn bush with edible berries, and the ubiquitous sage-brush that grows on the steeper slopes. Along the way we spy many small caves high up in the riverbank but pass these by, hoping for something a little easier to reach. Ding, Corrina and I are in front when we come round a corner and confront a small herd of ibex browsing for food. There are about eight of them, as surprised as we are. They turn to trot briskly up steep sloping slabs above the river, well out of camera range.

Just beyond is the large cave of Bardomal, where Braldu floods have hollowed out the base of a rib of rock. The water has carved out little niches and platforms in the rockside and we lay our sleeping bags separately this evening; one here, one there, like pale blue parcels filed in the rockface. The sloping roof of the cave is blackened by the smoke of countless fires.

There is little wind tonight and no mistaking the deep chill that grips these valleys when the sun is off them. We eat quickly and clamber into our sleeping bags, retreating from the cold. The fire cannot warm us so we let it die, conserving the remaining wood for the morning. The last of the smoke curls slowly out from under the overhanging roof and spirals up into the night.

At around 5.15 am I slip reluctantly out of my sleeping bag to cook the breakfast. Retrieving my boots from the hood of my sleeping bag I discover that the soaking they got in the Dumordo has frozen them solid. I stumble about the cave fumbling for a stub of candle, and crack my head firmly on the roof. There are subdued mutters to be heard as I turn to coax a few sticks into flame. Breakfast is biscuits and hot chocolate and does not delay us long; it is warmer on the move. We hide the few twigs of wood that are left, for our return, and are soon moving up the riverbed in frozen shade, hands stuffed deep in pockets.

My limp worsens through the morning and drags at my energy. On the moraine yesterday I must have strained something in my heel for that is tender now and increasingly bruised by my frozen boots. Ann takes a look at it and diagnoses tendonitis, probably just because medication for tendonitis is the only real medicine she carries now. I take her word for it and swallow a couple of anti-inflammatory pills with water when the trail next meets the river.

The valley widens here and the track climbs up and over shingle fans, some as much as a kilometre wide. The streams that formed them are dry now, awaiting the melting snows of the next spring. From the top of such a fan we get our first view of the snout of the Baltoro glacier: ugly ice hummocks, grey, rock-spattered, huge. There is a more reassuring glimpse, closer to hand, of the half dozen trees of Paiju, the third of the regular porter stops.

'This is much faster progress than I am used to,' Nuri says. 'You know that, but it's not nearly as bad as I expected. I'm finding it almost as easy as when I travelled with porters and had all the comforts.' I have to grin at this.

'We're keen on the comforts too, Nuri, don't you worry, but it feels like all the luxuries are at home now, and we're wanting to get back to them. This is amazing country but I'd hate to be caught here till spring.'

Nuri mulls over this for a while, and then asks if he could ask me something more personal. 'We enjoy talking with each other, don't we?' Nuri observes. We agree.

'Well,' he continues rather hesitantly, 'one thing I have noticed is that you five New Zealanders, you have been travelling together for ten months now and you are not very talkative. This is a very silent party I think.' I smile, knowing what he means. This morning is a prime example: we are spread out over a kilometre or more, small dots of figures making their way at their own pace. We move in ones and twos as the inclination takes us, but seldom in a group of more than three.

'We know each other too well I think, Nuri, after living so closely together for most of the year. We're all tired.' Nuri laughs at this. 'No, it's true,' I continue, 'we have the common objective still of reaching Concordia, but the general commitment to making the expedition a success of friendship as well seems to have lessened a bit. For the moment, we are a bit too familiar with each other's failings, and it's difficult to retain sight of the good points.'

We are trying — he can see that. To be on the safe side, topics of conversation with too much potential for disagreement are delicately skirted. We talk civilly of logistics for the journey, the news (if we have heard any), the weather, things we see. Our dreams of the future we tend to keep to ourselves now. Most often it is our own thoughts that keep us company, that warm us along the way. I have found myself mentally reliving the past, going over it again and again. Now, as the year draws to a close, I feel myself increasingly unburdened, as if my past has all been analysed, classified and understood. This last trek, if it is a triumph of anything, is a triumph of endurance; we are going to Concordia, only to turn right round and come back again. What matters most to us, now, is getting home in one piece: the journey itself is enough of a risk at this time of year.

A bright splash of colour lines the stream at Paiju: a glow of yellow and gold poplars in the sunlight. Pete has forged ahead this morning and a curl of smoke beneath the trees holds promise of lunch.

From Paiju there is nothing but the maze of the glacier, a nasty storm-tossed surface of boilerplate ice overlaid with loose rock. It angles north-east and then east away from us, two kilometres wide and nearly 70 kilometres long to the head of it at Concordia. Travel on the glacier is not easy and definitely not fast. Ann and I walk together, taking it in turns to find the route. This really means making a route — skirting the steep faces of slump holes, winding along the rim of sharp ice ridges, picking a convoluted path from one vantage point to the next. Then Pete takes over from us, pushing on out of sight, building cairns here and there to mark his route. We are angling towards the true left of the glacier, stopping occasionally just to stare at the changing faces of emerging peaks. Masherbrum (7821 metres) is a graceful snow-tipped cone to the south-east. The Trango group presides over the northern horizon: tall, incredibly steep spires of rock, with puffy cloud at their base accentuating their sheer walls. What beautiful rock they must be made of to stand so tall.

Later, cloud comes sweeping down the glacier muffling all sound and the clatter of rock underfoot resounds hollowly. As the cloud steals the last of the sun's warmth the noise of meltwater dies away too and the evening freeze begins. I scan the moraine wall anxiously, searching for a track to lead us up to the shoulder above, to Liliwa camp. We find it a little after 4 pm, by which time the sun is well below the peaks.

Successive waves of porters have built roofless rock shelters here on a scrap of flat moraine. Their expeditions have carpeted the ground with litter — cans, bottles, film containers and paper. We get to know it well as we scavenge the area for anything worth burning, keeping an eye out for anything worth eating too. We rig the fly over a shelter big enough for four and Corrina and Ding use the tent.

'Coming down to get water with me?' Ann asks, clutching the billy and our collection of water bottles. It is 200 metres back down the moraine wall to the nearest water and we have to break a thin layer of ice to scoop it out. Up valley all but the bottom third of Gasherbrum IV (7925 metres) is hidden in thick scudding cloud.

When I wake in the morning my feet are very cold. We have only five of the especially warm Fairydown 'Polar quality' sleeping bags for this section of the trip, and six people. I was to continue to use my lightweight bag with Ding's lightweight goretex-covered bag as an outer but, unfortunately, the second lightweight bag has been left behind in the store of equipment at Mrs Davies'. I have only my own lightweight sleeping bag plus my spare clothing to wear at night. Moreover, when we stuffed my bag with extra down in Kathmandu, we managed to attack only the baffles between shoulders and shins; the technical problems of putting more down in the baffles around the feet and hood areas seemed too difficult at the time. Now I wish I had spent more time on it. Each day on the glacier I feel slightly weaker: on the reduced food intake we have I find I am losing large amounts of energy just trying to keep warm each night.

Before we leave Liliwa I climb up to the base of a cliff to take a photo of our desolate campsite. I return by a different route, crossing a patch of snow. A double line of paw prints stands out in the smooth white surface, with the faint suggestion of a scuffed mark between: an alpine fox in heavy winter fur perhaps, tail dragging, although heaven knows what it could live on up here now. Since we left Paiju I have seen no wildlife, just two black crows, billing and cooing on a rock not far from us as we crossed the glacier. They seemed not at all disturbed by our passage.

It remains overcast all day as we trudge along the gravelly trough below the southern moraine wall of the glacier. Nuri recalls that the trip from Liliwa to Urdukas, the next porter halt, takes about five hours: five hours pass and still the glacier flows on past us. A subsidiary glacier, and then another, surge in from a side valley to the south; we pick our way over the sprawling white ice of their influx, grateful for the change they offer from the increasingly difficult lateral moraine. Then the trough disappears in a giant's toss of boulders. The newly fallen snow promises even more treacherous footing as we have to leap from one boulder to the next. The peaks that feed these glaciers remain remote, swathed in cloud, with only the occasional distant rumble of rockfall hinting at their presence.

We reach Urdukas after a stage of over six hours. The map marks the next porter halt as about the same distance again. The daylight does not last long enough to allow for two six hour treks so we decide, somewhat reluctantly, to stop here.

Urdukas was a campsite long before mountaineers found reason to visit. The old trade route over the Mustagh La (5420 metres) to China ascended the Baltoro as far as this.

'We Muslims were great travellers,' Nuri tells us. 'The full name for our language is "zaban-i-urdu", meaning "camp language". The name came from the great Royal Camp of the Moghuls in Delhi from where the Moghuls once ruled India, but we travelled much further afield than that. To China was not too hard for our people.'

The trade route is closed now, by geographical as much as political changes, but Urdukas is still in use. The site is a cluster of rock bivvies: overhung caves and shelters, perched on a steep hillside. It must be beautiful in summer, lush and green with vegetation, but now the shrubs are all leafless and the grass withered and brown under the snow. There is no water and no wood and, by mid-afternoon, it is already too cold for me to be able to write in my diary. The view is the only consolation. We are 300 metres above the glacier and I look down on the scalloped patterns made by line after line of shattered ice marching westward in a huge shallow crescent, cold white ice topped with rock. Just on dusk the sun emerges, briefly showering the peaks with light. Opposite us is the Grand Cathedral group (5866 metres), named for its Gothic-shaped towers. They spike the sky in one intense golden pyramid, as does Paiju peak (6602 metres) from this aspect.

In the night I hear the tiny rustle of a rat or *pika* trying to get into our food. I am too tired and too cold to get up and shoo it away. Later, ibex or goats pick their way through shale beneath our camp but Ding's cough alerts them and there is a faint drum of hooves before I drift back to sleep.

When dawn comes we are all slow to rise, our camp gripped by a fierce cold. My feet feel like blocks of ice and I force them into my frozen boots: my boots have never really dried out after the soaking they received on the river-crossing three days back. Each night they freeze solid and each morning they have to be reluctantly warmed back into a useful shape. I am getting the hang of it though — the secret is to open them as wide as possible at night; that way I can at least get my feet into them in the morning. If they freeze shut in a compressed shape it is almost impossible to force them open. Once my feet are inside the boots I try to crush the stiff icy leather down close to my feet to lace the boots up. They are not 'on' in any real sense of the word, but if I clump around in them carefully for half an hour or so the heat given off by my feet softens the leather enough to lace them tight at last. Of course while the boots soak up the heat from my feet, my feet soak up the cold from the boots, so this is not the most pleasant way to travel. Walking for the best part of the day with freezing feet somewhat dampens one's enthusiasm. At least Ann's tendonitis pills are doing something for me — I feel no pain from my heel.

When we do strike camp it is only to descend the moraine to the nearest patch of sunlight on the glacier, to warm up to operating temperature again. There are three more porter days of travel between Urdukas and Concordia but the rest of the porter campsites are on the northern rim of the Baltoro. It seems too far out of our way to cross to the other side.

Ding checks how much food each of us is carrying. We have enough for four days including the small cache of food we left at Urdukas this morning.

'Two from here to Concordia, two to get all the way back to Askole. We didn't wear running shoes for nothing, Pete!' Ding turns to me. 'You're pretty quiet, what do you think?'

'Oh, I agree, I agree,' I reply. 'I'm sure we'll make it but, tell me, which do you think is heavier — exposed or unexposed film?'

'What on earth has that got to do with it?' he asks.

'Not much, but if we're going to have to move fast I wonder if I ought to shoot off all this film I'm carrying.'

We make reasonable progress after a hurried lunch. The icy surface in the centre of the glacier offers easier going than the jumbled lateral moraine, but the distance to Concordia seems not much less. We use Gasherbrum IV at the head of the valley as our guide: when we can see the base of Gasherbrum we will be looking at Concordia.

Darkness forces us to camp and we carefully construct two parallel rock walls, higher at the middle than the ends, and string the tent fly over them as a roof. The layer of fresh snow underfoot has to be scooped off the ice to prepare our sleeping space and, underneath that, there are numerous sharp rocks held firmly in the glacier's grip. Not everyone is worried by them: some of us have already given up much hope of 'a good night's sleep', and do not think that such a tooth-studded surface will make much difference; others chip industriously at their patch of ice, removing each rock at the expense of much energy.

It is Ding's turn to cook tonight. He fiddles with the stove, cursing inventively, but the washer on the pump keeps inverting, making it impossible to maintain pressure in the fuel tank, and the flame dies away again and again. His fingers are freezing. Later we work out there is another problem too — the cold is causing the impurities in the kerosene to solidify. We eat half-cooked stew and go without a drink. Even if we were not eking out our food, we would still be down to only one reasonably-sized meal per day: food can be properly cooked only at midday, and even then it is 'weather permitting'. It snows during the night and I wake to find the fly bowed down towards me by snow accumulated in its centre. I get my arms out of my pit to steady myself, then gently push my feet high up against the underside of the fly, shaking the snow off the edge.

The cloud clears to reveal the growing size of the major peaks. Gasherbrum IV and Broad Peak (8047 metres) loom close ahead of us and Masherbrum is now receding behind us to the south-east.

'We can't be far off Concordia now,' Pete suggests at lunchtime, as we peer around through our cameras.

'No,' says Nuri, 'maybe an hour and a half.'

Nuri's hour and a half lengthens into four hours as we trudge on up the glacier, crunching through the drifts of fresh snow that lie precariously on the glistening ice. Out to our left a series of ridges off Crystal Peak (6236 metres) and Marble Peak (6125 metres) run into the northern lateral moraine wall of the glacier. Each ridge seems to promise a view round the corner and up the Godwin-Austen glacier to K2, but for hour after weary hour the promises raise false hopes, and each ridge is succeeded by a further one. We stumble on through the deepening snow, desperate to make it to Concordia today.

Daylight is beginning to fade when we finally turn the corner at a quarter to five. There is our view of K2. Only a very little lower than Everest, it stands more apart from the surrounding mountains, a huge upthrust pyramid of granite, tipped and lined with snow. That is all.

There are handshakes and hugs. The sun sets before we finish making our hurried camp, sinking deep into the snow. It's my turn to cook: I lie as far into my sleeping bag as I can while struggling with the primus. The pump washer is causing problems again and three times I slip off my mittens to strip the parts down and reassemble them. In the end it is just too cold. I have managed to melt half a billy of water and announce finally: 'There isn't going to be anything to eat. All I can manage is a drink.' There is no complaint as I hand around cups of lukewarm chocolate.

That was on the first day of November, 1981. It takes four more days to retrace our steps to Askole, one of them in a wild snowstorm. We are on half-rations for the first two days and run out of food on the third. Just on nightfall on the first day I fall through a layer of ice on the glacier, waist deep into a stream below. My trousers freeze solid and I carry them strapped to my pack like a plank of wood. My boots are the main casualty — this is one dunking too many, the stitching finally parts when the boots freeze that night and I complete the walk with both boot soles flapping.

We arrive at Askole hungry, footsore and dirty. Before we leave the next morning the six of us have eaten our way through 70 eggs, 107 fried *chapatis,* 100 cups of tea, two kg more of the 'ibex', seven kg of potatoes, plus some miscellaneous *masala* (spices), salt and onions. There is great hilarity as we work out the bill in the morning and the Haji is impressed with our capacity.

'Can this be correct?' he asks one of his boys, when he looks at the figures.

'Oh, yes, sahib,' the boy replies. 'These people were very hungry last night.' The Haji shakes his head: it is a big bill for such a small party.

'Where are you going now?' the Haji asks me.

I smile. 'Home,' I reply.

Epilogue

In 1887, Francis Younghusband decided to attempt a journey from Peking to India, a distance of 5500 kilometres. He crossed the Gobi desert, Chinese Turkestan and Yarkand. He had a choice of two passes by which to enter India — the Karakoram Pass, which is straightforward, and the Mustagh Pass. The latter had been crossed once, 30 years before, but only from the far side.

Younghusband chose the Mustagh Pass and came down the Baltoro glacier through Askole (which he thought a dirty place) and Skardu to Srinagar. The first Englishman he had seen for seven months greeted him after the fashion of the Victorians: 'Don't you think,' he said, 'you should have a wash?'

We needed one too. We had worked long and hard and were happy. Nuri was not complaining either. This was toughening him up, he said, ready for his next expedition to Nanga Parbat.

Nuri and Ann struck up a warm, close relationship during the month we spent together. Early on in the section Nuri had spoken confidentially to Ann and me one evening.

'I wonder, Ann,' he asked, 'did you ever live here in Pakistan before?'

'No,' she smiled, 'this is my first time in the East at all, Nuri.'

'You have not even been to school here?' he pressed. She shook her head.

'This is very odd,' Nuri explained. 'You see, when I was young my parents sent me to a school that was very progressive for a Muslim family, and there were many foreign students there also. There was one young girl, in particular, with blonde hair and the sweetest smile. I was hardly seven years old but I remember her distinctly. She would smile at me across the room and I could not help but smile back.' He smiled then, and looked at us both. 'I thought you were her, Ann,' he said. 'I was sure of it, because no one else could have such a smile as that. We were like secret brother and sister. I feel like you two have that feeling as well.' We did. Nuri's nature made that easy. He had chosen to trust the five of us, as had Tashi, SP and Roy, but Nuri had come with us alone and had had no gradual introduction to our ways. He had pitched in to the full extent of his abilities, given up his few rights and privileges and accompanied us cheerfully. It was hard — even minor troubles such as blisters, hunger and tiredness are difficult to hide when travelling together. We felt protective towards him, Ann often making sure he had enough warm clothes or offering him a few extra of her dried fruits and nuts at rest stops. Yet it wasn't as if he needed that help, and his quick sense of humour made light of many of the rough spots on our trip. His name, Nuri, means 'light' and 'enlightened'.

I have some of his letters now before me — his joy when he heard we planned to marry, his special memories of Ann and his wishes for our future happiness. A later letter has a curious insignia at the top, a stylised mountain, and the words 'Among the Cool Glories of Unfolding Dawns We Ascend 26,600'.' 'Pray for me please, dear friends,' Nuri wrote. 'We have had a good summer of climbing and I am ready now for Nanga Parbat.'

Nuri is still on that mountain. An avalanche killed him there. His wife and young son survive him; so also do his mother and father. They were always worried by his involvement with these 'savage' mountain places; but refrained from using their power to forbid him to go. Nuri spoke of his parents with unfailing love and respect.

He can't come back this time and we all feel the loss.

God has spared the rest of us, dealt kindly even with our hopes. SP is back with the Indo-Tibetan border police and has been promoted, the equivalent of a colonel. Roy has also been promoted, seconded to be vice-principal of the Himalayan Mountaineering Institute, in Darjeeling, where this trip began. Tashi is still there too, instructing again with the same reliability which stood the traverse party in such good stead for all those long months.

Ding and Corrina married in April 1982, just a week before Ann and I. They live now on the south shores of Lake Taupo, from where Corrina organises and leads trekking parties back over some of our old routes in the Himalaya and Ding co-ordinates an adventure tourism company. Together with friends they have established a youth development programme aimed at reducing youth crime and youth unemployment in New Zealand. Their first child, a beautiful daughter called Ariaan, was born at Easter 1985.

Pete lives on a small farm near Hanging Rock, in Australia, with a good friend of ours and we have visited them often. He has organised other expeditions since the traverse, particularly those to Makalu, Lhotse and Everest mentioned earlier, and has recently returned from an attempt on Rimo (7409 metres), a peak near the Karakoram La, the pass north of Leh that we were forbidden to visit during the traverse expedition. Pete and Ding have both attempted Everest, on different routes and different expeditions. Neither expedition reached the top.

When Ann and I returned to New Zealand, at the end of 1981, I left the National Park Service and returned once more to practising law. Ann finished her law degree and taught law at Victoria University in Wellington for two years before starting practice as a barrister in 1986. These changes in our lifestyle have not made the writing of this book any easier. Ding's and Pete's book of the expedition was published in November 1982, and Ann and I resolved not to read it until ours was finished. We kept to our promise.

We have read their book now, with the benefit of several years' hindsight, and I wonder if the friction between Ding and Pete doesn't partially obscure the magnitude of their achievement. The traverse was, without doubt, a very long and serious undertaking; few parties could have stood up well to the stress of the enforced intimacy it created. The American mountaineer Arlene Blum, when visiting New Zealand in 1984, said that she and Hugh Swift had had many a falling-out on their later traverse. Only the Indian Army team failed to mention conflict when reporting their achievement, having finally completed their traverse in May 1982. Perhaps the rather more rigid hierarchical structure of their personal relationships had a little to do with this. I wonder.

But the achievement of that first traverse can never be undone. It was for that reason we have tried hard to keep the friction out of this book. It crops up between the chapters, but we did not wish it to obscure the Himalaya itself, or its peoples, or even ourselves — for these were truly magic days for us, days when we were fit and healthy and had a wonderful challenge to meet, in a wonderful place, among extraordinary people. We thank them.

Ann and Doug
Wellington, 1987

Glossary

achaar	chutney
aloo	potato
baisahib	headwaiter
barat	wedding party
bhai	younger brother
bhanjyang	pass
bhavan	resthouse
bidi	locally made cigarette
burkha	opaque, full-length veil worn by some Muslim women
chai	tea
chai wala	tea vendor
chapati	flat discs of unleavened bread, kneaded then baked, often cooked on hot embers
char	four
charas	hashish
charpoy	woodframed bed without a mattress. Rope is woven across the frame.
chatti	rough-fired unglazed pottery cup without a handle
chauk	public area or courtyard
chautara	stone platform built up as a resting spot, often around the trunks of pipal and banyan trees due to the shelter of their thick leafy foliage. The platform is usually in two levels, the lowest at an easy height for porters to leave their loads and don them again.
chillum	pipe used for smoking
chiya	Nepalese tea, brewed together with milk, sugar and occasionally spices
chorten	Nepali term for a stupa
chowkider	guard or caretaker
chu	river
dacoit	bandit
dahi	yoghurt
dahl	pulses, e.g. lentils
dahl bhat	cooked meal of lentils and rice
dajiu	older brother
dekshi	large aluminium pot with flattened upper rim
dharamsala	resthouse open to members of the public and often built in pilgrimage areas
didi	older sister
doko	woven basket used for load-carrying
dudh	milk
gae	yak-cattle cross
gompa	Buddhist monastery

harijan	in India's caste system the harijans are the outcasts, the lowest of the social hierarchy. Their name is often given in English as 'untouchables' for any contact with them by a non-harijan is considered deeply defiling to the higher caste person and requires ritual cleansing to remove the impurity.
hartal	labour strike
ingi	long sleeveless woollen robe worn by Sherpa women
jelebi	deep-fried Indian sweet
kandi	woven seat used by porters to carry people
kukri	traditional Nepali knife, long and curved
kurta	long loose shirt worn over trousers
lambardar	village leader
lassi	whipped yoghurt drink, often salted
lathi	wooden baton
lingam	sacred phallic representation of the Hindu god, Shiva
maidan	flat grassy park area
mana	rice and cereals, milk and sugar are measured out with this brass container which holds nearly half a litre. Fruit and vegetables are weighed against a pau, approximately 250 grams.
mani	Buddhist prayer carved into rock surfaces
marg	street
masala	spices
masala dosa	large pancakes made with potato, rolled and stuffed with spicy vegetables
nalla	river
paisa	Indian currency is divided into rupya and paisa. There are 100 paisa to a rupya.
pakora	vegetable slices deep-fried in batter
pan	chewing mixture, often containing spices and lime with tobacco or betel nut
pani	water
phul	egg
pika	'mouse-eared rabbit', bigger than a mouse, smaller than a rabbit, a bit like both but more like a rabbit
prasad	holy offerings, often food
pugdandi	mule trail
puja	prayers
pujari	priest
puri	deep-fried chapati-like bread, so light that it puffs with air when cooked
pyjami	loose trousers
rigi	potato
rupya	rupee. In 1981 the Indian rupee was worth about US11*, approx. NZ14*. The Nepalese rupee was worth 25% less than the Indian one.
saag	green vegetable
samosa	savoury vegetable parcels wrapped in pastry and deep-fried
sannyasa	fourth and last stage of life for a Hindu person
sastrugi	wind-formed pinnacles of snow and ice
shapu	Asian mountain sheep
sirdar	organiser

stupa	Buddhist monument
sunyasi	acolyte
tabla	traditional hand drum topped with hide
terai	fertile plains south of the Himalayan ranges
thach	summer village
tikka	vermilion powder worn on the forehead by Hindus
tirth	holy site for Hindus
tole	street square
tonga	horse-drawn carriage
topi	flat-topped brimless hat often worn by Nepali men
tsampa	barley, roasted and then ground
tumpline	rope used by porters as the support for a load
yatri	pilgrim
yeti	abominable snowman, perhaps legendary
yinyang	a tantric symbol representing the balance of forces in the universe

Acknowledgements

Expedition sponsors:

Supplier	*Product*
Air India	Airfares between Australia and India
Alliance Freezing Co.	Freeze-dried foods
Australian Outdoor magazine	Publicity & t-shirts
Bristol-Myers	Sustagen & Sustalyte drink powder
Damart-Thermawear (UK)	Polypropylene underwear
Arthur Ellis & Co.	Liteweight & Polar sleeping bags
Hallmark International	Chrysalis tents, packs & one-piece climbing suits
Howe & Bainbridge (USA)	Klimate tent fabric
Kodak	Photographic film, mainly Kodachrome 25 & 64 asa film
La Prade (France)	Ice-axes
Montres Rolex (Switzerland)	Rolex watches
Mountain Safety Research (USA)	M.S.R. stoves
Norsewear	Woollen jerseys and socks
M. O'Brien Ltd	Adidas TRX running shoes
Olympus (Japan)	OM1, OM2 and Xa2 cameras; 28mm, 50mm macro, 75-150mm zoom & 300mm lenses
Redwing International (USA)	San Marco 'Taiga' climbing boots
Roche	Aquasun sunscreens
Roy Turner	Elite climbing ropes
Wilderness Products	Fibrepile jackets & salopettes

Maps (prior to expedition):	Ian Stirling, Angela Newton, Mal Clarbrough, Ian Parker, Howard Symmes, Bruno Zahner
Medical:	Drs Gavin & Bev O'Keefe
Dental:	C. E. Robins, BDS; P. McDonald, oral surgeon
Diplomatic assistance: NZ	Brian St J. Gore; Staff of Ministry of Foreign Affairs, Wellington
India	Peter & Phyl Cox; Staff of New Zealand High Commision, New Delhi; Mr Muhammad Ali, Embassy of Pakistan
Pakistan	Messrs Awan & Fiaz, Ministry of Tourism & Culture, Islamabad
Assistance in India:	Shri Harish Sarin; Capt. Mohan Kohli; Col. L. P. Sharma; Mr Harnam Singh; Mr Motwani & staff of Indian Mountaineering Foundation
Assistance in Nepal:	Liz Hawley; Bobby Chettri
Mail system:	Jessica Wilson and Fergus Barrowman
Diary typing:	Robyn Wilson
Word processing:	Jax Edkins; Nicky Dickson; Josie McDermott
Cartography:	Chris Edkins; (original of sketch map on p.7 by Graeme Dingle)
Photo collections made available:	Corrina & Graeme Dingle; Peter Hillary; Hedgehog House; Jos Lang; Michael Okkerse; Jane Pearson & Marti Heine

Proofreading & comment:	Margaret, Pearce, Barbara and Barry Mitcalfe; Jan and Prue Wilson; Ali Ward and Stu Allan; Marg Clarbrough; Rob Rowlands; Brian Smith; Brigid Pike; Susan, June and Arthur Heighway; Graham Mourie & Shona Fokerd; Victoria Phillips
Guidance throughout:	Ray, Barbara & Nicki Richards
Encouragement & support:	To all our family and friends who have continued to talk to us, visit us, invite us out to dinner or sailing to the South Island, knowing there was no chance of a return invitation from us until we'd shed ourselves of this manuscript — thank you.

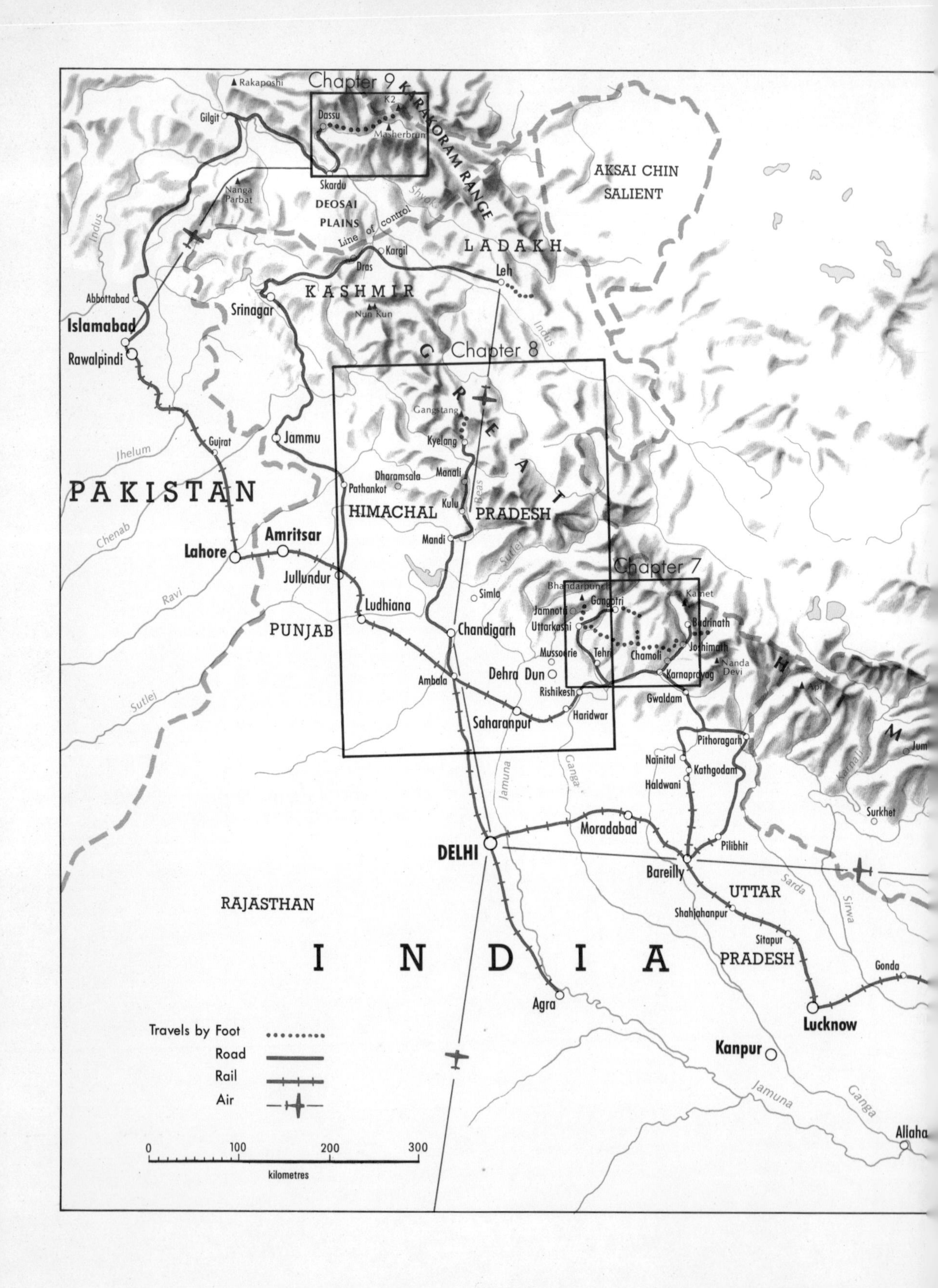
Chapter 9
Chapter 8
Chapter 7
Rakaposhi
Gilgit
Dassu
K2
Masherbrum
KARAKORAM RANGE
Skardu
Nanga Parbat
DEOSAI PLAINS
Shyok
Indus
Line of control
Kargil
Dras
LADAKH
AKSAI CHIN SALIENT
Leh
KASHMIR
Nun Kun
Abbottabad
Islamabad
Rawalpindi
Srinagar
GREAT HIMALAYA
Gangstang
Kyelang
Jammu
Gujrat
Jhelum
PAKISTAN
Dharamsala
Pathankot
Manali
Beas
Kulu
HIMACHAL PRADESH
Chenab
Mandi
Amritsar
Lahore
Jullundur
Sutlej
Ravi
Simla
Bhandarpunch
Gangotri
Kamet
Jamnotri
Uttarkashi
Badrinath
Ludhiana
Chandigarh
PUNJAB
Mussoorie
Tehri
Chamoli
Joshimath
Nanda Devi
Dehra Dun
Ambala
Rishikesh
Karnaprayag
Gwaldam
Api
Haridwar
Saharanpur
Pithoragarh
Jumla
Nainital
Kathgodam
Haldwani
Jamuna
Ganga
Karnali
Surkhet
Moradabad
Pilibhit
DELHI
Bareilly
Sarda
Sirwa
UTTAR PRADESH
RAJASTHAN
Shahjahanpur
Sitapur
INDIA
Gonda
Agra
Lucknow
Travels by Foot
Road
Rail
Air
Kanpur
Allahabad
0
100
200
300
kilometres